A HOUSE in ChinA

Curtis Lim

A House in China

ISBN-10: 0988615118
ISBN-13: 978-0-9886151-1-3

For my mother and father,
family and friends.

ALL ALIENS arriving at a port of continental United States from a foreign port or a port of the insular possessions o

PRINCESS VICTORIA

S. S. _____Empress of Canada_____ . *Passengers sailing*

Given name	Age Yrs.	Age Mos.	Sex	Married or single	Calling or occupation		Able to—	Nationality Country of which citizen or subject	Race or people
Xing	60		M		Countryman	Yes	Chinese	Yes U.S.A.	Chinese
Tin Wing	20		M	M	Student	Yes	Chinese	Yes U.S.A.	Chinese
Quak Leng	16		M	S	Student	Yes	Chinese	Yes U.S.A.	Chinese
Man Kwong	20		M	S	Student	Yes	Chinese	Yes U.S.A.	Chinese
Man Gen	19		M	S	Student	Yes	Chinese	Yes U.S.A.	Chinese
Wing Xing	14		M	S	Student	Yes	Chinese	Yes U.S.A.	Chinese
Ling Fon	18		M	S	Student	Yes	Chinese	Yes U.S.A.	Chinese
Ling Yot	15		M	S	Student	Yes	Chinese	Yes U.S.A.	Chinese
Tee Keng	17		M	S	Student	Yes	Chinese	Yes U.S.A.	Chinese
Man Shoon	60		M	M	Merchant	Yes	Chinese	Yes U.S.A.	Chinese

Author's Note

This is my father's story. Or, mostly his...

I set out to tell his story, but took several side trips. It's something my father used to do too. When we were younger, he liked to drag my brother and sisters and me on all his errands and excursions. He'd take us for a drive and we'd find ourselves in an old green barn buying vegetables. He'd take us to see his parents and we'd end up in downtown Detroit picking out a chicken for dinner.

In the course of writing this book, I've done the same: dragged everyone on this little jaunt of mine. I've invited my mother along for the journey, brought some old friends and family into it, and for good measure, included the China of my father's past... all while pointing out passing glimpses of how much his China has changed throughout the years.

Parts of this story will feel like we're meandering down an old stone road. Other parts will feel like a switchback, where we get to look at the trail from reverse. Some of that was intentional. A little was discovered. For me, it's like walking about, trying to make sense of a map, and when I look back up, suddenly I'm where I should be.

My father was my guide. He started telling me his stories when I was very young, and I've been wanting to retell those stories for most of my life. Some of them are painful. Some are beautiful. Some amaze me simply because he can recall names, places and faces from over seventy years ago, when he was just a child.

I'm not sure when he first started telling me these stories. They just seemed to appear. Often they'd be over breakfast or dinner, or to keep me and my siblings occupied during long family trips. But I remember the day I became aware that his stories meant something to him, and that he was trying to share something very personal with me.

I was about eight years old and we were driving around Detroit, not too far from my grandparents' apartment. It was winter and my father was wearing his dark overcoat and gloves. I was wearing my fuzzy purple coat with the tight hood. I was the only other one in the car that afternoon so I got to ride in the front passenger seat and, sitting there beside him, I must've looked like a small purplish bear. I asked him a question and he started talking about his mother, but this didn't sound like the grandmother I was familiar with. He was talking about an entirely different woman. A woman in China. A woman who lived on a farm. At the time, I wasn't aware that the grandmother I knew was my grandfather's second wife. In Chinese, there's a word for each member of the family and their exact relationship to you, so I asked my father if he meant my grandmother on his side of the family. And he said, "No, I'm talking about my mother!"

He started to choke a little as he told me about her — this woman who raised him. A woman of the old country. I can even still see her now, stepping out of her rustic little house, standing quietly, in peaceful repose.

"It sounds like you loved her."

And his eyes filled with tears as he said, "She was a good woman. She was an angel."

It was the first time I'd seen him cry and he wasn't ashamed of it. I felt as if he'd wanted to tell me about her for quite some time now. And it made me start to wonder who my father truly was, and the effect his mother had had on him.

Half a lifetime later, in 1998, I started to formally record interviews with him. I was filmmaker by then so I shot interviews with both my father and my mother. I noticed that my father's favorite stories revolved around his house in China. We first visited the house as a family in 1973. I asked if we could go again, and in 2006, we did. We followed that with another visit in 2008.

This story relies mostly on the memories of my father, me, and my older sister Leslie. But because they *are* memories, I've tried to confirm names, dates, places, and even relationships wherever possible. Sometimes I called on other family members and friends to corroborate events; other times I relied on journal entries, pictures, and videos. In some cases I turned to my father's documents, and was so very grateful for his habit of photographing and taking notes of everything. That must be where I get my own peculiarities from.

I've included dialogue in this story, but took two routes with this. I put the words in quotation marks only if I believed a person's recollection of a conversation to be consistent and clear, or, after conducting multiple interviews, heard the words echoed by someone else.   In situations where I no longer had access to a subject and had to rely on another person's retelling of a story (for example, my father recounting my grandfather's early years) or when I felt a memory wasn't completely reliable (which sometimes included my own), I paraphrased the dialogue; or put the scene in the context of a remembrance.

I also tried to use real names throughout this story. For the Chinese names, most of which are in Cantonese, I enlisted my father's aid in spelling the names out phonetically in English. Unfortunately there's no way to capture their tonal sounds, which helps give them their proper meaning. But I did change the names of two people in the story. My friend in Beijing, the business instructor I went bicycling with, has been changed to Brian. Brian is my middle name, and I used that name because my friend took on a brotherly quality to me. The name of the farmer in Imlay, Michigan, has been changed to Frederick. I did this to be sensitive to either their situation or their history.

My father is preparing to go back to China again soon. I have to admit, there were times during the research of this story that I regret reawakening some of his memories. Every time he goes to see his house, I can tell he's trying to see his mother again. Every time he talks about his mother, I can tell he's trying to reach out to her, to rescue her. He might not see this in himself, but I do. While I would love to include his further journeys in this book, I felt that this story had arrived at a completeness all its own. One day I'll join him again, but I also know that, despite the feelings of regret his travels back home sometimes bring him, they also offer him a sense of duty and redemption — and a kind of comfort — that only he understands.

1

It started with the seaplanes.

My father Yot was thirteen years old when he first saw them. He and his brother Fon were playing by the edge of the pond outside their house, trying to catch some small fish, when they heard a strange, low hum in the distance. They turned to the northeast, toward the sound, but didn't see anything, not right away. Then they appeared. Two dark spots in the sky. Small, like little floating birds or faraway hawks, and together they sounded like a steady, hollow car engine — *"woa-woa-woa-woa-woa-woa-woa"* — and the humming got louder and more mechanical and the spots grew bigger and bigger until they became two seaplanes skimming through the air.

The boys had heard about the attacks in school; their teachers had told them of the invasion. The newspapers warned everyone about the ships anchored near the mouth of the Pearl River, just outside Hong Kong. The boys had even seen pictures of planes in their general science books, and now here, in the field, Yot clearly recognized the pontoons on the bottom of the aircraft; like large logs, like rowboats; and he knew immediately they were seaplanes and that they'd taken off from one of those ships.

They were flying in so low and so close that Yot and Fon could even see the pilots, and for a moment it seemed as if the pilots were aiming for them, coming to kill them, so the boys ran to a ditch at the end of the pond for cover, trying to hide behind some shrub. But then the pilots turned and the boys knew they'd spotted their target. The seaplanes circled, dropped their bombs and the boys watched them fall like little black dots. The bombs hit a locomotive sitting on its tracks in nearby Taishan and the boys heard the explosion and felt the ground shake.

Then the planes curved around once more, flying over them, and that's when Yot noticed the large red circles, like small suns, painted on the underside of the wings.

One of their neighbors had gotten caught in the blast and his foot had been blown off at the ankle. When his fellow villagers heard the news, they tied a sheet of burlap across two wood poles to make a stretcher, then two of them rushed into town to bring the man back. When they returned, Yot, standing with the others, watched as they carried him to his house, and he could see the man's bloody foot placed crudely beside his leg. For Yot it was a gruesome sight, made more horrifying when he saw that the man was still awake, and in pain. Some doctors tried to help him but two days later he bled to death.

After that, the seaplanes started to appear more frequently. Every other day, then every single day. One day the boys counted fifteen seaplanes in the air. Always looking for a target, always aiming for the locomotives, and always, their propellers making that ominous *"woa-woa-woa-woa-woa-woa-woa"* as they used the railroad tracks to guide them through the air.

The boys had hoped to go back to school that year and everyone wanted their lives to return to normal but their prospects seemed so unlikely that one of their cousins, Yip, wrote to his father, and Yip's father arranged to bring him to America.

Then one day school simply didn't reopen. It was November and the two boys talked with their mother about what they should do next. Their mother, with her long black braided hair tied in a knot behind her head, often sat and discussed family matters with her two boys after dinner, before they all went to bed. It was winter and the days were short. In the evenings, their small brick house would be lit by a single kerosene lamp and they'd talk in the warm amber glow of its light.

"Yip is lucky. His father is getting him to America," Fon said one night. "Maybe we can do that too."

They'd talked on the subject before, but not at any great length. That was when they all thought the war might be over soon. But now they knew where this conversation was headed.

Fon was sixteen and had an eighth grade education. Yot was still in sixth grade. Their mother had gotten only three years of schooling, so she said, "Maybe it's a good idea that Fon should write a letter to your father."

Their father, Quong Lim, was living in Detroit at the time, running a restaurant there, and although he wasn't a rich man, he was in America. That alone put him in better standing than most of his own countrymen, and he regularly sent back whatever money he could to his wife and family.

His family lived in Guangdong Province, in the southern part of China known as Canton. They spoke a dialect called Taishanwa, a kind of hillbilly version of Cantonese. Most of their fellow villagers were farmers, and although Yot and Fon helped tend the fields, the money their father Quong sent home allowed his family to get by without working all day long like their neighbors. The boys' mother used the money to fill her storage pots with rice and on the holidays she could afford to buy chicken and pork from the butchers that passed through the area.

Up until July of that year, the biggest concern the villagers had was the twice-annual harvest. Then the Japanese invaded Beijing in the north. After that, anyone who owned a radio or could read a newspaper shared reports of the impending war with everybody else. Most people believed that warplanes were still double-winged so the newspapers printed pictures of Japan's single-winged planes. They showed photographs of cruisers and destroyers. Yot remembered seeing a picture of a submarine and an aircraft carrier. The government wanted to educate people so they made life-sized models of bombs out of paper and cardboard and displayed them in the towns, in the markets. Yot saw models of hundred-pound bombs and two-hundred-pound bombs, and even what he thought was a ridiculously huge, twenty-foot-tall, five-hundred-pound bomb.

That was in August, when the Japanese invaded Shanghai and Nanjing in the east, and it seemed like they were slowly making their way south, attacking cities along the coast... and the township of Taishan lay less than fifty miles from the southeast coast.

Then soon after Yot's birthday came the seaplanes, and by December the boys didn't see the large pontoons on the planes' undersides any longer — because they'd been replaced with land bombers.

When Fon wrote his letter, he told his father that the war was getting closer, asked his father where could he put them for their safety, and was there any way he could get them to America?

A month later, their father wrote back telling them that he'd been thinking the same thing. In fact, he'd begun making arrangements to bring them over and had contacted a cousin of his to arrange their travel.

By April of the following year, Yot, Fon and their mother were on their way to Hong Kong. From Hong Kong the boys would board an ocean liner and cross the Pacific.

They took a passenger ship up the West River to the city of Guangzhou. Yot had been on vessels like this before, but this was a new ship, painted gold on top, red on the sides, with varnished brown wood surfaces all over. To Yot it looked like a mansion floating on water. It had three decks, and on the top he counted three crewmen using a big beam to steer the rudder.

The ship was large enough to hold a couple hundred people but business was so poor that it held no more than a third of its capacity that day. He could tell the ship was unable to run on its own, and from his place on the deck, saw that it had to be pulled along by a small white steamer. He watched the steamer's crewmen shoveling coal into its engine and could smell the thick, dark smoke billowing from its black-painted stack.

They boarded at three o'clock that afternoon for an overnight trip. They traveled third-class, which meant sleeping in a cramped room on deck level. First-class passengers were given private rooms. Second-class passengers were given a common room with mattresses laid next to each other. Third-class passengers were given a room with a ceiling so low that Yot, whose travel papers listed him as just forty-eight inches tall, couldn't even fully stand up without bumping his head. To enter the compartment they had to bend down, crawl through a small opening, and pull their luggage in after them. Several small, dim lights were spaced across the ceiling but it was still too dark to see very clearly. There were forty other passengers in third-class with them and quickly, upon entering, they all found their own places in that tight room. The floor was simple cardboard placed over straw matting. Some of the passengers rolled up their clothes to make pillows for themselves. One woman brought her own pillow. Everyone slept in their street clothes. There were bed bugs but Yot didn't care. He wanted to tour the ship and kept standing up, forgetting about the ceiling. He hit his head so many times he was sure he was going to get a concussion.

Tempers sometimes flared in compartments like this. Yot remembered two women he'd once seen on another ship quarrelling over a space. One woman called the other, "Whore!" and the other referred to the first woman as a "Dead Body!" It was akin to calling her Something That Stinks.

4

They continued until one man said, "Don't swear like that. There are children in here."

Another time a woman brought chickens with her and the chickens clucked so loudly and insistently that the other passengers told her to take them away. One man mentioned that the feathers might stir up dust. "The feathers could bother a lot of people."

The woman replied, "I'll hold them and keep them quiet."

Finally one of the crew members came down and took the chickens above deck.

When the boys and their mother reached Guangzhou they stayed with Yot's aunt, his mother's oldest sister. He noticed that his aunt had become a city girl who sometimes put on airs. They stayed in her apartment for three nights, then all four took the train to Hong Kong. The line was operated by the British and was safe from attack; the Japanese didn't dare bomb it. For two hours they got to enjoy a train ride with wood bench seats, a wood-walled interior and curtains on the windows.

In Hong Kong they stopped in on a man they called Gui Wei Gung, or Grand Uncle Gui Wei. Their father knew Gui Wei's grandson. Everything was about friends and family. Grand Uncle Gui Wei was a partner in a ginseng shop called Dac On Cheong and the boys' father had arranged for them to stay with him there.

The shop was located on Bonham Road, close to Victoria Harbor. Customers could walk in, request the type of medicine they wanted, and an employee would open one of the many wooden drawers against the store wall and pull their order out for them. There was a row of seats where the customers could sit and relax, and although the shop had electricity, the lights were turned on only at night. During the day, the sole source of illumination came from the front door. The shop only got one or two customers a day. Sometimes a whole day would go by without a single customer. But business was good. The medicine they sold was pricey and they only needed to make a few sales a week. Customers could order anything from dried ginseng to dried deer testicle to slices of deer antler — which was supposed to build up the body and cost hundreds, if not thousands, of Hong Kong dollars.

While the partners slept in an office in the back, there was another room, upstairs where guests and employees slept. The boys shared a bed in that room. Three other young men did too, and they were also preparing to go to America, studying English during their spare time. The boys' mother and aunt stayed with a cousin not too far away, in a room above their cousin's jewelry shop.

They were only planning to stay in Hong Kong for a week or so while Grand Uncle Gui Wei booked the boys' passage but Fon developed a boil on his nose. The boil got infected, and he had to be taken to a doctor, so they stayed a little more than three weeks. During that time they visited their cousin Yip, touring his ship, the one they'd originally hoped to join him on.

Every day the boys' mother and aunt would walk the two blocks and one street level down from the jewelry shop to the ginseng shop and take the boys shopping. In Guangzhou their mother had bought shoes for them. In Hong Kong she paid a tailor to make two western style suits.

In one of the shops they discussed their plans, talked about the future. Their mother would stay behind in China; she had her own mother to look after. And she knew her husband would come back one day. But then she said, "When you get there, when you have time, ask your father if it's possible to get me over there too."

The boys agreed, "That's good, that's a good idea."

Yot thought, That's nice. Then we could all be together.

"What about Grandmother at home?" Fon asked.

Their mother chatted briefly with her older sister. Perhaps Older Sister could take care of Grandmother.

At night they said their goodbyes and the boys ate dinner with the employees of the ginseng shop while their mother and aunt ate with their cousin. Only rarely did they go out for a meal together.

When Fon's nose finally healed, Grand Uncle Gui Wei bought them two tickets on the *Empress of Canada*. They would leave near the end of April.

Grand Uncle Gui Wei made sure each boy was given his own suitcase and canvas traveling bag. The suitcases were tan, made of cowhide, about thirty inches long, with a lock and key and two belt straps to tighten them up. Yot wore a dark gray suit, white shirt, tie, and dress shoes. Fon's suit was the same, but deep blue in color.

The boys' mother and aunt boarded the ship to see them to their steerage. The ship had a wood deck. The walls were steel, painted white. Their compartment was below deck, a triangular-shaped room near the front of the ship. Third-class accommodations. Yot would later laugh that he and his brother traveled all the way from their village to America entirely by third-class.

They would sleep on a bunk bed: a metal frame with thin mattresses placed over wire springs. Fon, being the taller boy, took the top; Yot, the bottom. They noticed immediately that the beds had a little bounce and were so much nicer than the beds they had at home, which were just straw mats placed over hardwood boards.

At last their mother gave them some final words. She tended to speak mostly to Fon, her oldest son. "You two be sure to stay together. Don't get lost. Take care of yourself. Behave yourself on the whole trip."

She tried to put on a good face but then she turned, lowering her head. She was looking away from them and Yot could tell that she was sad.

When it was time for visitors to disembark, a whistle blew and a crew member came by and said, "Time to leave!"

Yot can still remember what his mother looked like that day. She was a simple, pretty, country woman who almost never wore city clothes. Her sister typically wore city clothes and Yot thought his mother would look prettier if she did too. But that day she wore a loose, light pair of trousers and a short shirt jacket, both gray, almost tan, made of linen. They were comfortable for her, like pajamas, and her sister dressed the same.

As they were about to leave the room, his mother paused at the door and gestured to Fon first. She took his palm, licked it, said a few words, and closed his hand. Then she gestured to Yot. He stepped toward her. She took his hand, opened his palm, and licked it.

"Something to remember me by," she said as she closed it back up.

When my father Yot first told me this story he wasn't sure how to explain what his mother did so he told me they hugged. "I was happy that I got to touch her one last time. Hug her." But later he explained that his family didn't really hug. In China, the licking of the palm was called a "saliva fruit." It was a souvenir from his mother. A gesture of affection so he wouldn't forget her.

The two women left the ship and the boys hurried to the top deck where they ran to find a good spot to watch their departure. It was an exciting moment for them. Yot was overwhelmed with the adventure of the trip. He saw other passengers throwing streamers

7

— colored rolls of paper — back at the port. It looked like a fun thing to do, so when a porter walked by carrying a box, Yot stole one and threw it over the side, watching it unravel in the air.

Finally they found a place to stop and wave goodbye. There were several hundred people on the dock below and it had taken their mother and aunt a few minutes to make their way through the crowd, but the boys spotted them standing by the railing beside the bow. As the ship started pulling away, Yot watched his mother wave with a handkerchief in her hand. Then she dipped her head slightly, touching her face with her handkerchief, and Yot could tell she was crying. Slowly they receded into the distance. His aunt continued waving and his mother looked up again and waved to her two sons.

The year was 1938.

2

The year is 2006.

My father Yot is eighty-two years old.

He's slim, and always has been. When I was growing up I'd often hear my mother bemoan his weight. "You're so skinny!" she'd say whenever she'd see him changing into a short-sleeve shirt or standing alone in his baggy slacks. She'd say that of both of us. Of me, she'd say, "I used to worry that a wind would come along and whoop, take you away." And, "Like father like son."

My father is active for his age. He walks three miles a day. Now in his retirement, he's finally put some fat on his belly. Not a lot, just a little, but he likes to show it off as a small achievement. He has curious, inquisitive eyes, will raise his brows involuntarily at the slightest hint of a joke and still has a few dark hairs in his mostly gray scalp. I can only hope to be like him when I'm that age.

We're on an airliner flying to China. My father and my sister Leslie sit in first-class. My friend Nancy and I are in coach.

Nancy is Irish by descent, with long red hair down to her waist and gray-blue eyes. We were a couple once, years ago, but now we're just friends. For a long time people would ask us about our relationship. "What are you and Nancy?" "Are you together?" "Are you boyfriend and girlfriend?" As of this writing I'm forty-four years old, unmarried, and living in a small apartment in San Francisco. Not knowing how to respond to those kinds of questions I would usually half raise my hands, half shrug. We were horrible as a couple, always fighting, never happy, but as friends we're wonderful together, so what can I say?

We're flying from San Francisco to Beijing, and the flight is sixteen hours long with a layover in Narita, Japan. The trip across the Pacific is eleven hours alone. A week before the trip I asked Nancy what we were going to do for all that time. "Sleep," she replied. On every trip she brings a comfortable pair of eyeshades and earplugs and reserves a seat by the window so she can control the light. After takeoff, the shade goes down. When we land, is there anything interesting to see? The shade goes up. She's the

Mistress of the Airways. Born in Massachusetts, with summers in Plymouth, she's a product of her New England upbringing. She knows the proper way of doing everything, and to demonstrate this she brings an extra set of eyeshades and earplugs, knowing that I forgot to buy some for myself.

We're half an hour into the flight, trying to get some shut-eye, but there are two Chinese women behind us chatting loudly. From the little Cantonese I know I can tell they're gossiping about their families but they talk nonstop and some of it seems like nervous chatter just to fill the silence. Every couple of hours Nancy and I will lift our eyeshades to give each other a look that says, "How can two people *talk* for so long?"

My sister Leslie lumbers back to coach to ask us how we're doing, but also enjoys teasing us by showing us her first-class menu. "I'm having tea-smoked duck," she grins.

Great, I think to myself. My revenge will be to see you fall off your diet.

"BaBa is thinking of having steak." *Baba* means father in Chinese. But later, feeling a little guilty, Leslie sneaks us some cheese and chocolates.

An elderly man sitting diagonally in front of me wears a bright headlamp to read a newspaper and the light bouncing off his paper keeps everyone around him awake. Another man glares at him angrily, then tries to cover his face with his own newspaper. Finally he tosses his paper down in exhaustion and turns his whole body away from Headlamp Man. Headlamp Man is oblivious.

The two women behind us talk for nearly the entire way to Narita. Eleven hours of chatter.

When we arrive in Beijing, our tour guide, Tiffany, meets us at the gate outside customs holding up a sign that says, "Lim". She's a thin, petite girl with a short, boyish haircut. I see an intelligence in her eyes right away and within a few short sentences can tell that her English is excellent. We each take a moment to compliment her and she says, "Really?" I can only assume she's being humble. She must hear this all the time.

She takes us straight to our hotel and checks us in. She asks if we need to exchange any money. We're tired but my father says yes. The exchange rate is 7.75 yuan for every one American dollar. My father gives the clerk twelve dollars and the clerk hands him back a little under a hundred yuan.

The lights in our hotel room are dim. It's something we'll notice over and over again in China. There never seems to be enough indoor light. At the airport the lighting was soft and muted, even hidden in some spots, and I thought our customs official would go blind reading all those passports in that barely lit concourse. Later I'll learn that the power provided to our hotel room is generous compared to the amount allotted to the average Chinese household.

Nancy and I share one room; my father and sister share the adjoining one. I unpack a few things, then go to my father and sister's room.

Leslie calls her house. It's two a.m. in Beijing but nine p.m. in Walnut Creek. We're ahead of California by fifteen hours. She chats with her husband Don for a few minutes before speaking to her daughter Jillian. Jillian is five years old. She's never been away from her mother for anything longer than a school day. Jillian tells her mother, "I wish I could hug you over the phone." Leslie's eyes fill with tears. When she's finished, she hands the phone to my father. He talks with my mother and tells her that the flight went well. Leslie sits on her bed crying to herself for the next half hour.

Then my father lies back in his bed and stares up at the ceiling. He wears a charcoal gray sweater and rests a hand on his chest. Like me, he's too tired to sleep.

The first time he'd seen an ocean liner was in a photograph in his house.

It was a black-and-white picture, about two feet long by one foot high, and it showed a ship on the ocean with a wave hitting its bow. His father Quong had sailed American President Lines for one of his trips back to China and brought the photograph back with him, framing and hanging it on his wall. This was before Yot was born so Yot had grown up with the ship always floating in the background. He'd spent more time in the company of that photo than he had with his own father. It hung next to a picture of his father sitting at a banquet, but the banquet picture was so small that

Yot and Fon could barely make out their father's face. But the ship fascinated Yot. A neighbor once told him that the ship was as large as their village and the notion of it made quite an impression on young Yot.

He'd later discover that the ship he and his brother were on now, the *Empress of Canada*, was even larger. The compartment they slept in, filled with bunk beds and tables, held a hundred passengers alone. Thirty of the passengers were Filipinos heading to Hawaii, a few came from other countries, but the majority were Chinese. Some were emigrants, some were on a return trip to America, and some were going back with children, mostly sons. Yot guessed that perhaps eighty percent were emigrating and, like he and Fon, on their way to Seattle. With three compartments like this, Yot surmised that there must've been about three hundred third-class travelers aboard the ship.

He got seasick during the first five days of the trip. "I would throw up all day until there was nothing in there left to throw up." Being sick made him miss his mother and he would lie in his bunk thinking of her. "Oh I wish she was here." He would think of how she used to dote on him when he was ill, carrying him piggyback around the house, up and down the wood steps. He was a slight child, but she was a small woman, and he knew it was no easy chore for his mother to shoulder him around like that.

The bow of the ship was constantly buffeting against the waves and because his compartment was near the front, it rocked the most. Sometimes he would walk over to the stern because it was calmer there. He wasn't allowed to go near first or second-class but there was a compartment at the stern called Special Third-Class that he'd often visit. The only other time his seasickness would subside was when the ship pulled into harbor.

From Hong Kong they sailed to Shanghai where they stayed overnight. Shanghai, he'd heard, was now occupied by the Japanese, but part of the city was still under Chinese rule, and there they picked up more passengers and cargo. His compartment was located next to the cargo hold and the walls narrowed as it approached the prow before ending against a flat wall. Behind the wall was the hold, and he enjoyed seeing dock workers hoist shipments into it.

Two days after Shanghai they stopped in Kobe, Japan, the port of his country's occupier, although Yot didn't give the situation too much thought. There he watched some dock workers board the ship to operate the long white cranes mounted on deck, hefting large sacks of flour and grain onto the ocean liner.

From Kobe they traveled to Yokohama where he saw dock workers lift a curvy, black automobile into the hold. It wasn't the first time he'd seen one. There was a road by his village where he'd often watch them speed by. They were sleek with rounded fenders. Sometimes when he heard them coming he'd run through the field just to get a glimpse of them. The villagers called the cars *bun si kam*, or "shit-digging bugs" because they were shiny and black like the beetles.

After Yokohama his seasickness disappeared. Still, sick or not, he always found something to do. Sometimes he would watch the Chinese men in his compartment play mahjong. They also gambled a lot and he'd watch that too. On three of the evenings the Chinese who worked aboard the ship organized an opera, and Yot loved opera. In Special Third-Class he found children's puzzles, and he'd distract himself putting the puzzles together. He made friends with some of the other kids and they'd go to the bow to watch the small flying fish leaping ahead and to the side of the ship. The fish were silvery and six inches long, but they would leap five to ten feet out of the water. Their fins were large and birdlike, and Yot was hypnotized by the way they reflected the sunlight. Sometimes he and the other kids would steal rice or pieces of bread from the dining tables to throw over the side, hoping to feed the fish, but the fish wouldn't notice.

But his favorite activity was still throwing streamers. After Hong Kong he noticed that the passengers threw streamers at every departure, and he became an expert at spotting a box, stealing a roll, and pitching it over the side.

The journey lasted twenty days.

From Yokohama they sailed to Honolulu where most of the Filipinos got off, and from there it was another five days to Victoria, Canada, where a loudspeaker instructed all passengers heading for Seattle to disembark. An officer guided the passengers to the dock and Yot and Fon found themselves in a crowd of about two hundred men, most of them Chinese, walking slowly across a field.

The men seemed to know where they were going so Yot and Fon followed them, ending up at an immigration building.

Inside they entered a dining hall where a Chinese cook yelled, "Everyone have some coffee or tea!" So the two boys sat down and Yot tried his first coffee. But he didn't like it too much.

After another few hours some officials escorted them to a ferry which took them across Puget Sound. There wasn't much to do aboard the ferry so they paced around, then sat in some seats and took a nap. When they awoke, it was dark, around seven o'clock in the evening. They were in Seattle, and another official escorted them to the American immigration center.

The year is 1997.

It's fifty-nine years later and my father is making his third trip back to China. My mother Elayne and my younger brother Mike are with him, and my father is overjoyed to have Mike on the trip. He calls him "Little Buddy." My brother is the fourth child in our family, the youngest, the baby, and "Little Buddy" is what my father has called him ever since he was a toddler. It's what my father's used to coax him along on all his little trips and errands. But Mike's thirty years old now and my father still says, "Hey, Little Buddy." "How's it going, Little Buddy?"

When they arrive in Beijing they check into their hotel but my father and Mike are so hungry that they have one more errand to perform: search for food. They find a small restaurant in a nearby alley, a hole-in-the-wall that serves noodles, and they return to the hotel to usher my mother along. The floor of the restaurant is tiled white and blue but the place isn't very clean. My brother notices that the waiter wears a dirty shirt, an old sports jacket and white gloves... As if, my brother thinks, the white gloves somehow make him a maître d'. My father orders noodles with shrimp. My brother orders thick, Shanghai-style rice noodles with pork. But even before they finish they wonder if it was such a smart idea to eat there.

During their tour they'll visit the Forbidden City before flying to Guangzhou to see my father's village, and my brother will notice that most of the men in Beijing wear dirty shirts and old sports jackets. Without, of course, the white gloves.

It's cloudy in Beijing. Cloudy and dusty and gray.

The year is 2006.

My father, Leslie, Nancy and I are staring at a breakfast buffet of eggs and bacon, sushi and udon, tamales wrapped in corn husks, and pork fried rice. Our hotel appears to be catering to the tastes of all their most popular tourist groups. Service has come a long way since my father's first visit here. A young cook stands in front of a small frying pan with a portable flame and will make an omelet using any combination of mushrooms, scallions, shrimp or anything else we can find. Leslie loves the idea but I notice that before the cook adds his mixture of eggs, he'll pour a generous helping of oil from a silver teapot into his pan. He'll stir the mixture with a chopstick but he's using so much oil that the egg will swirl around as if floating in its own soup. No thanks. Not for me. We'll be riding around in a van all day and that's the last thing I need.

It's our first morning in Beijing and our tour guide Tiffany is taking us to the Forbidden City, the palace built during the Ming Dynasty to house the imperial government. It sits in the center of Beijing and is known most famously as the home of Puyi, the last emperor of the Middle Kingdom.

It's my father's third visit to the Forbidden City but he doesn't mind. He loves seeing the smile on our faces, loves hearing us talkative and excited. And this giant museum reminds him of how much the China of his youth has changed over his lifetime.

My father and Puyi shared thirteen overlapping years in the same embattled country; my father as a villager in the south, and the Lord of Ten Thousand Years here in the north.

The year Puyi was forced to abandon the Forbidden City, 1924, was the year my father was born. By the time Puyi was thirty-two and installed as the puppet leader of the Japanese territory of Manchukuo, my father had landed in Seattle.

The immigration center was a large red brick building that sat half a mile from the pier.

Yot noticed that most of the men around him were Chinese, and the moment they entered, the officials separated them by age, directing those who were over eighteen to the north side of the facility, and the others, like Yot and Fon, to the south side, to the Eighteen and Under section.

Just as it had been on the ship, their room was filled with rows and rows of bunk beds: metal frames, tan in color, with wire springs. They didn't get mattresses this time; just two dark gray wool blankets laid over the springs and one blanket for their cover. But the beds still had a nice bounce to them and Yot and Fon still thought they were better than their hardwood boards at home. Once again, they were assigned to a bunk together and once more, Fon, being the oldest, got the top; Yot, the bottom.

They explored the room. It was well lit — bright enough to read inside — with windows on three of its sides. From one window they could see a gas station outside with a green dinosaur on its sign. It was the emblem of Sinclair Oil, although they didn't know that at the time. They also didn't know what a dinosaur was and Yot exclaimed, "Oooh, they sell gas with a dragon sign!"

There were forty other boys in the room and once a day they were all allowed an hour in the exercise area. The exercise area was an open-air courtyard on the fifth floor that acted like a bridge between the north side of the building and their side. Yot often felt cooped up in the Eighteen and Under room so he looked forward to his exercise time. Usually he played ping-pong but there was only one table and that meant everyone had to wait their turn. But there was also a basketball court, and he'd learned basketball while away at school. His gym teacher had persuaded his school to get a ball and put up baskets, and Yot and Fon had even gotten quite good at the game. When Fon returned from school he convinced his mother to buy a basketball and they often played in the village or lent the ball to their neighbors.

For the first two weeks, Yot and Fon were allowed to remain together until they were called in for their initial questioning. Then they were separated while the officials mailed their father a questionnaire. It took a week to reach Detroit and when Quong received it, he answered it promptly, sending it back with all the proper paperwork. Two weeks back and forth. But that was hardly any time at all. They knew some people had been in the immigration center for months. Some, years.

16

During the wait, Fon was placed in a room with an older Chinese man who was facing deportation. After the man was deported, Fon got another roommate, a Japanese man, also facing deportation. Despite not being able to speak a single word of each other's language, Fon and the Japanese man became friends and just as the man was leaving, the man stopped to write down his address in Kyoto so he and Fon could stay in touch.

On his own in the Eighteen and Under room, Yot noticed the atmosphere could sometimes get a little tense. He had to watch for theft. He knew none of the boys would steal anything big or obvious like his clothes; there was nowhere to hide it; but they might try to steal whatever little money or food he had. Sometimes the boys were given cookies and Yot had to keep his eye on even those. He thought it was a miracle that he didn't get into a fight while he was there.

And a clique formed among the boys. He heard some of them were over eighteen; some were over twenty and he assumed they'd lied on their applications. The ones who were the oldest, or who'd been there the longest, became the leaders. He remembered one man, around five foot six and chubby, who had been there for two years, was considered the leader of the group. The man was facing deportation and had a lawyer fighting on his behalf in Washington D.C., but Yot and everyone else knew the man wouldn't win. Yot also knew enough not to get involved in the clique. Emotions could run high, and when someone found out their case had been rejected they sometimes fell into a dark depression.

But there were also good times. There was a small recreation area that was partitioned off from the rest of the room with wire, and it had tables where they could play cards or games, and it was there that Yot learned to play mahjong. He also engaged in some youthful antics. One day the younger boys gathered up all the towels and blocked up the door to the shower room, then switched on the showers in an attempt to turn the room into a pool. The floor was concrete and it worked for a while, but the towels didn't hold and all the water flooded out of the room.

On a few occasions, members from a nearby church came to sing to them. Afterward the members tried to convert them but Yot wasn't interested. During those moments, though, the officials would gather everyone into one room and that's when Yot got a better look at the other people in the building. Near the exercise area he'd noticed a room with a small group of Chinese woman. And he'd seen some Caucasian men in another room. Seeing the

17

men up close, he assumed they must be emigrants from their own countries. "Those people were kind of weird when you looked at them," he recalled. Most people would try to talk with the others, but the men kept to themselves, not even so much as attempting eye contact. And a few times, Yot saw them in the courtyard boxing with each other.

But Yot's biggest challenge was keeping himself occupied during his stay.

One window looked down on the exercise area. From another window he saw the gas station, and beyond that were some hills. Beyond the hills, a hospital. The third window looked onto a railroad station, and in the distance he could see what he thought was Puget Sound.

All day long he looked out the windows. He watched ships come and go in the sound. He counted the trains that went by. He loved trains; loved the whistle and loved the roar. He counted the number of cars that stopped at the gas station. About a dozen or so arrived each day. When a car pulled up, an attendant in a gray shirt and cap would step out, fill the tank, wipe the windows and check the fluids, and from what Yot could tell, he was the only one working there. And every three or four days a fuel supply truck came to deliver gasoline. He'd watch the supply man unscrew a cover near the pump, put a stick into the hole and measure the fuel level.

And every morning he watched a little girl, about eight or nine years old, walk to the station, sit, and wait for her bus. She was Asian, and he assumed she was Japanese because he'd heard there were a large number of Japanese citizens in Seattle. She carried a couple books with her every day, probably on her way to school, and he'd watch until she got on the bus and disappear; then thought it was funny that he never saw her getting off the bus later on, so he assumed she must've taken another route home.

Yot and Fon passed their questioning five weeks later. Their father had been so meticulous in his planning that he'd been able to inform them by letter months in advance that a man named Dang Ma would meet them when they were released. As always, everything was about friends and family and using your connections. When an official escorted the boys downstairs, Dang Ma was there waiting for them. He was a Chinese man in his late fifties. Short, stout, with round glasses. He looked so much like the little round merchants Yot had known in China that when he saw

Mr. Ma he thought to his worldly thirteen-year-old self, "How typical."

They rode in a Buick to the hotel Mr. Ma owned, called, appropriately enough, Hotel Ma. It was three stories tall, located on the edge of Chinatown. It had a dining room and a cook and Mr. Ma's daughter ran the front desk. During the day the boys walked around Chinatown; another guest gave them a small tour; and they ate all of their meals with Mr. Ma and his staff, enjoying fish and barbecued chicken, while Mr. Ma arranged the next part of their trip.

A week later Mr. Ma drove them to the railroad station, the one Yot had seen from the immigration center. As they boarded the train, Mr. Ma handed them two brown paper shopping bags and a knife. One bag contained a ham and two roast chickens, each wrapped in tin foil. "You don't need a cutting board because you have a table," Mr. Ma told them. The other bag was half filled with apples, oranges and bananas. He also advised the boys that if they needed anything to drink they could ask for water on board the train.

Then before he left, he said in Chinese, "You guys have enough food for the trip but when you get there, don't forget to tip the porter fifty cents."

Inside the train, across the aisle from them, were two older Chinese gentlemen they'd seen at the hotel. The boys said hello and took their seats. Their seats consisted of two benches facing each other with a table in between. The benches were soft, covered with fabric. The boys sat together on one bench and placed their bags on the other. When they got hungry they put the chicken on the table and carved some meat off with the knife. It was a delicious. A porter wearing a gray uniform gave them a towel and there was a washroom at the end of the car to clean themselves.

A little later the porter came by with a cart full of refreshments. What little money they had was held by Fon, so he ordered for them. He didn't need to say any words. He pointed to the milk, the porter poured him a glass, and Fon paid him. They each took a sip but the milk tasted sour so they put it aside on the table. After a while Fon took the glass to the washroom and threw the milk out.

Later their father would explain that the boys had probably been served buttermilk, which would've tasted sour, almost tangy to their palate, because in China, when they drank milk, they usually added a little sugar to sweeten it.

They rode in a Pullman car, which was designed to be converted from sitting to sleeping compartments. At night the porter would come and wave for them to stand. They didn't need to speak English to know that he wanted them to get out of his way. They'd wait in the aisle or go to the end of the car where there was a small sitting room. As they watched the passing scenery, their porter would lower a berth down from the wall above, then pull a curtain across it to create a private bed. There was an upper berth and lower berth but this time they both took the lower one, which they shared while their bags of food sat at the end of their feet. It made for a somewhat uncomfortable sleep.

By the second day they finished one of the chickens and part of the ham. From their dialect, the boys recognized the two older gentlemen across from them as Cantonese so they said a few words but the gentlemen didn't seem like they wanted to talk. They were, however, getting off at the same station in Chicago so the boys asked if they'd be willing to help them find their transfer point and the gentlemen agreed.

Occasionally Yot and Fon would walk up and down the aisle to break the monotony. They noticed two elderly women who seemed friendly and curious about them. One was in her sixties; a portly, matronly woman. She struck up a conversation and asked them how to say several phrases. Yot recognized a couple words but Fon knew more English so he answered.

"How do you say 'hello' in Chinese?"

"Wei," he replied. It was more of a telephone greeting but Fon knew the word was simple enough for them to understand. *"Wei, wei, wei."*

"How do you say 'dinner'?"

"Sihk tahn."

"How do you say 'How are you?'"

"Neih hou ma?"

"How do you say 'boy'?"

Yot recognized that word but again, Fon answered.

"Hou sang."

By the third day the boys grew bored with their food and wanted to try something different. They asked the Chinese

20

gentlemen where they could buy some food and the gentlemen pointed toward the dinner car.

Through the glass of the door they could see the restaurant inside. The tables were covered with white tablecloths. The waiters wore short-jacketed, navy blue uniforms. One man wore a longer jacket with gold braids on his shoulders.

The two boys entered, were seated, and handed menus. They had arrived off hours so there were no other customers in the car, and they noticed the waiters paying a quiet but courteous attention to them.

None of the words on the menu made any sense but the two boys understood numbers. They made an agreement with each other that they would find the lowest priced item and split it between them, whatever it might be. When their waiter, a black gentleman, came by, Fon ran his finger down the menu until he came to the smallest number and pointed to that item. Then they looked up at their waiter. And the man nodded.

Minutes later the man returned with their order. The two brothers recognized bread. They'd had bread in China. But this bread was warm and sliced into two pieces. It had been grilled. The waiter watched with polite interest as Yot and Fon debated which of them should take the first bite.

"You try it first," said Yot.

"No, you try it," said Fon.

Back and forth they went until finally, cautiously, Fon took the first piece. There was something creamy in the middle, a texture he'd never tasted before. He didn't pass out... he didn't die... so Yot took the next bite. Not bad. Not necessarily good either. But interesting. The waiter smiled, nodded, and moved on.

Years later they would discover that their first taste of American cuisine was a grilled cheese sandwich.

By the fourth morning they arrived in Chicago and got off the train with the two older gentlemen. The gentlemen took them to the gate and told them to wait; they needed to check on something and would be right back.

So the boys waited. And after a while they began to wonder what had happened to the gentlemen. Had something gone wrong?

They saw people walking to and fro. After half an hour they began to worry. Up till now, every step of their trip had been taken care of, and they knew their father would be there waiting for them in Detroit. Should they stay where they were or try to find the transfer themselves? After forty minutes they saw another Asian man. They asked him if he spoke Cantonese and he did. They showed him their tickets and he told them to follow him, quickly, and he got them to their train just in time.

They never found out what happened to the two older gentlemen. Had they misjudged their time? Perhaps they saw the boys as bothersome.

It had been their first moment of panic in the new country.

During the four hour train ride from Chicago another dilemma crept up. Neither of them knew what their father looked like. The only picture they'd seen of him was the banquet photograph in their house, but his face was too small to be recognizable. Their mother had told them that their father was a stocky man, and in a letter to the boys their father had informed them that he'd be waiting at the station, but what if there was more than one Chinese man there? What if there was a crowd?

Sitting across the aisle from them was a young black man, about twenty years old. He was tall and slender and wore a nice suit. He was curious and started asking them questions but they couldn't understand anything he was saying until he asked, "Where you going?"

"De-Troit," Fon managed to say.

The young man indicated that Detroit was his stop too and that he'd tell them when it was time to get off. Then the boys returned to their predicament.

"What do you think he looks like?" they asked each other. "Do you think he looks more like you or more like me?"

Fon had a rounder, more open face, with eyes slightly larger than Yot's. He had a happier demeanor, more carefree. At the age of sixteen he was considered somewhat of a charmer. He always seemed to get out of work, always seemed to slip out of trouble. Yot, with his slimmer, more serious face, seemed shyer, quieter, but was more mischievous. He was always incurring his mother's wrath, always getting spanked; more so than his older brother it seemed.

As the train pulled into their stop, Wabash Station, the young black man stood up, grabbed his bag and said, "Come on, Detroit." He then made his way to the exit.

The two boys remained seated. From their window they could see two men standing together on the platform just outside their car: a short Chinese man and a tall Irish-looking man. The Irish man was about six-foot-two with a mustache. The Chinese man was stocky and had the same nose the boys did, although they didn't notice that at first. The men were a few yards from the boys' window, and the choice should've been obvious, but the boys were excited and confused.

"Now which one do you think is BaBa?" asked Yot. He was mesmerized by how tall and imposing the Irish-looking man was.

They continued to stare until finally the Chinese man waved his arm as if to say, "Come on!" And the two boys quickly grabbed their bags.

"He won by a wave!" my mother likes to laugh whenever my father tells that story. The Irish-looking man was the station attendant. The boys' father couldn't find the platform and had asked the man to help him.

But had the attendant waved, my father and uncle would belong to a different family entirely.

3

We're inside the Forbidden City. And just a short stroll from the entrance gate is the infamous Starbucks coffee shop.

It didn't exist when my father last visited with my brother and mother. Starbucks didn't open the shop until three years later, in 2000, and only at the invitation of the palace managers who were trying to raise money to help maintain the walled grounds. But its placement was controversial from the very beginning, and now, in 2006, opposition to Starbucks' presence has only grown. To some Chinese, it's an eyesore. An offense to their rich cultural history.

Still, I have a friend who would enjoy seeing it. And no, my friend isn't me. He's simply someone I know who tires of having to honor ancient landmarks. He thinks most historical sites are too sanitized, that all the dirt has been swept behind nice clean signs, and that the landmarks don't represent anything about their countries today. He thinks they're the equivalent of putting pleasant picture albums on the glass table of the country's living room. He likes seeing new things, new buildings, even if it's a new shopping mall, and I know he'd smile at the Forbidden City Starbucks. The shop tries hard to blend into the existing architecture. Except for the window displaying its very recognizable corporate green logo, it's almost hidden beneath an orange temple-like rooftop. But for my friend, Starbucks is the real icon. It represents the spread of one economic culture into another.

We walk the half mile of sprawling stone grounds and red-colored buildings. We see the Chinese characters for "Double Happiness" emblazoned onto the emperor's wedding carriage. And within an hour, the grounds quickly fill with other tour groups. Several of the groups are quite large, with about fifty people or more, all wearing colored caps — yellow, orange, white — presumably to help keep them in their separate herds. Their guides direct them using megaphones and matching flags. Yellow flags for the yellow caps, orange for orange. The tourists in these groups are all Asian, and I can only guess that they're citizens from other parts of China seeing their own palace for the first time. I'm sure that all these footsteps, including our own, only add to the further damage, and cost of maintenance, of the site.

Pausing beside one wall, I say to Tiffany, "Nice overcast weather." She politely agrees. I tell her that this is considered perfect lighting for outdoor photography. The light is so evenly diffused that there are no sharp shadows, no glaring surfaces, nothing to make a subject squint unattractively.

But as we reach the Palace of Heavenly Purity I look at the sky again. It's more like a lazy mist, and there's a slight bluish tint to the clouds. I also notice the smell. It's smoky, almost acrid. I turn to Tiffany.

"That's not overcast, is it? Is that…pollution?"

"Yes," she says, and clearly she's used to answering this question. "Beijing is having a problem with pollution. Almost every day is like this."

She tells me that the city government sometimes issues warnings to its people to stay indoors or keep the windows closed. She says part of the problem is the number of cars in Beijing these days. Everyone wants a car. One in every six citizens owns a car, and the number is increasing. In its attempts to curb air pollution, the government has started restricting the number of cars on the roads. Cars with license plates ending with specific numbers are banned from the roads on specific days of the week. The numbers and the days change depending on how many cars Beijing wants to remove at any given time.

From where we stand I can look out onto the city. The mist is gray and sits low in the sky in every direction. It hovers around one of the taller buildings with wispy, ghostlike tendrils. And it has such a strange, burnt, candy-like scent to it.

The year is 2008.

Leslie and I are planning our second trip to China. China is hosting the Olympics this year and Leslie will occasionally send me news articles about Beijing's attempts to clean itself up.

Months before the games, Beijing increases its driving restrictions, allowing cars with odd numbered license plates to drive one day, and cars with even numbered plates to drive the other. They're trying to cut their traffic in half.

And they've been seeding the clouds: using anti-aircraft guns to fire silver iodide pellets into the sky to induce rain, hoping to clear away the smog.

2010.
Beijing becomes home to a daily sixty-mile traffic jam, the longest automotive snare in the world.

June, 1938.
After two months, the boys were finally in Detroit.

The first thing Yot noticed about his father was his smile. He had a very friendly smile on his face. And Yot and Fon were very glad to see him.

He wore a light blue suit and tie. It was the usual attire for someone who ran a restaurant (although Yot didn't know that at that time) and Yot thought he looked quite dignified.

It was late in the evening and as they walked through the parking lot, single file, the boys following their father, no one said anything until they stopped at their father's Pontiac and Yot exclaimed, "Oh, a car!"

It was a two-door silver sedan. Yot, being the youngest, climbed into the backseat. Fon got the front passenger side. Their father started it up and headed out of the lot.

"You came in with a car?" Yot said.

"In my business you have to have a car. I have another one at the restaurant for delivery. A delivery boy is using it."

The boys were impressed. Detroit was the car capital of the world, and here, their father owned two. And this one was comfortable too. Cloth-covered bench seats… a radio… a soft gray interior.

"It's a Pontiac Deluxe."

It was less than a year old, he told them, and he'd bought it for eight hundred dollars.

He asked his sons about their trip, about Hong Kong, about his family.

"How are your mother and grandmother?"

"They're fine," Fon said.

After half an hour they arrived at their father's restaurant and he parked in the street behind it, in a small space beside the kitchen. He lived in the apartment above and took the boys up the back stairs so they could drop off their bags. Inside he showed them where they'd be sleeping. Yot would share his room. Fon was given a rollaway bed and a sheet to put over it.

Then he took them back down to the restaurant. It was ten o'clock and he knew his sons had to be hungry so he cooked them a meal: pan-fried pork chops, two apiece, which they ate with rice.

Four other men lived in the apartment with Quong. They all worked for him downstairs, which was a common arrangement for Chinese immigrants.

The apartment had two windows: one facing the front street and one facing the back. A waiter and two cooks shared the room in front. Another cook slept in the back. There was only one real bedroom, and Quong slept there. Yot would share his father's bed for a while. And there was a hole of sorts, a spot in the middle that was normally used for a dining room. That was Fon's place.

The next morning, Quong took his sons back to the restaurant. It was a red storefront, one of five on the block, all owned by the same landlord. The stores were all the same: rectangular in shape, about twenty feet wide and sixty feet deep. The back of Quong's business extended out another twenty feet. He'd built his kitchen there so he wouldn't have to sacrifice any of his interior space. The kitchen ate into his parking spot so he had to park in his neighbor's. But his neighbor didn't mind; he didn't own a car.

The front of the restaurant had a white sign, almost light blue in hue, standing out perpendicular from the facade, and it read:

Pacific Garden
Chop Suey

The letters were in red, and the words "Chop Suey" were larger than the name "Pacific Garden". Noticeably larger. They had to be. Most people wouldn't know it was a Chinese restaurant if they didn't see the words "Chop Suey".

Quong gave his boys a tour. He introduced them to the dishwasher — a tall, slender Jewish boy about eighteen years old.

"This is Mickey," Quong said.

"Hi," said Mickey. He seemed like a nice, quiet young man.

Then their father brought out a bicycle and showed it to Fon.

"Can you ride a bicycle?"

"Oh, I learned to ride one in Guangzhou."

"I bought this one, just for you. When I show you how to make carryouts, you can ride this."

Two days later Quong went to a nearby bicycle shop and bought one for Yot too. It was a simple bike, green and chrome in color.

Within a week, Yot and Fon were working in the restaurant. Fon learned to cook while Yot helped Mickey wash dishes. In between lunch and dinner, Quong gave Fon some tips on how to ride better and after Fon caught on, he started teaching Yot.

Another boy, a neighbor named Bill, also helped. Bill was about sixteen years old, stocky, Caucasian, and played football in high school. He sometimes came to the Pacific Garden with his family or on his own for ice cream. He often had friendly words for the two boys and when he heard Yot was learning to ride, offered him his assistance.

"At the time, we only knew a few words of English," Yot recalled. "'Yes', 'No' and 'Hello'. I would say 'Hello Bill', and my father also taught me to follow it up with 'How are you?'" Then Bill would usually hold the bicycle so Yot could climb onto it.

And on Mondays and Tuesdays, during his time off, Quong would drive his two sons to Palmer Park near 6 Mile Road so they could practice riding.

When he wasn't washing dishes, Mickey doubled as the restaurant's delivery boy. During the evenings, if an order came in, Yot would do the dishes while Mickey made the delivery. If the delivery was far, Mickey would drive Quong's second car. It was a two-seater Ford with a big trunk in the back. A very fashionable vehicle. If the delivery was close, Mickey would ride his bicycle. After a couple months Yot started riding with him.

At first Yot and Fon weren't paid anything, nor did they expect pay. They ate at the restaurant, and if they needed anything, like clothes, their father bought it for them. Later their father paid them each a dollar a day. Occasionally, while making a delivery, Mickey and Yot would stop at a customer's house and Mickey would let Yot deliver the food. Yot would knock on the door, hand the customer the package, ask for the money and be sure to give back the correct change. A typical delivery was $2.50 and Yot was sometimes tipped a dime, sometimes a quarter. Eventually Mickey left for school and Yot took over, earning an extra fifty cents a day.

A couple months later a cousin of theirs came to live with them. His American name was Robert T. Lim. Another Lim. Yot remembered him from one of the nearby villages. There were now eight people in the apartment. Yot still shared the double bed with his father but after a while his father bought a second, smaller bed. He took the small bed for himself and gave the large one to Yot.

Perhaps the only benefit to living in that crowded apartment was that the men were spared kitchen fumes from below. An exhaust fan kept the smoke from wafting upward by sending it out to the back alley, which meant their neighbors got it instead. During the hot summers the people living behind the restaurant would open their windows and their apartments would fill with smoke. They would complain to Quong but he had no choice but to continue using the fan.

"They complained about everything," Yot said of them. "The smell, the noise. But what can you do?"

By September Yot and Fon started school.

There was a Lim Family Association on Sibley Street that Quong often visited. Every major city had small organizations like this: places where people of the same surname gathered to support and assist one another. Those who arrived in the country first helped guide those who came after, and it was there that Quong asked a cousin of his to enroll his sons in an American school. His cousin, David Lim, had not only arrived at an early age, but made his way through high school, and had recently started college, so he was very familiar with the process. He took Yot and Fon to

Hutchins Intermediate School and enrolled them in a special class for learning English.

Class was held in a large room with about thirty-five students. There was no assigned seating so when they entered on the first day, they took two seats next to one another.

Yot wore a white shirt and navy blue trousers. He and Fon knew what to wear because there was another school a few blocks from their apartment, a school they'd later attend, and their father would sometimes take them by the school, or drive them around town, and show them what the other kids looked like.

"This is how the other kids dress." If there were kids in the yard, he'd say, "In school, you might play sports like these other kids."

He also told them how their names might sound when spoken by an American. Their names were pronounced one way in Cantonese but they'd be pronounced differently when called out loud in school. For instance, he told Yot his name might sound like, "YAWT LIM" — flat, blunt, with a low, downward falling tone. It sounded the way a large, stocky Chinese man might sound trying to imitate an English speaker. Their father was basing his pronunciation off the spelling of his son's name: "Y-o-t"... although neither he nor his sons knew who'd come up with that exact combination of letters.

The teacher who taught their class was Miss Blackrow. She was an attractive woman with a Germanic square jaw. Slender with brown hair. A friendly woman who typically wore a white blouse with a navy blue or dark brown skirt.

She sat behind a desk and started by taking attendance for her returning students first. When she finished, Yot could see that she had a list of new students and she took attendance for those students next, telling them, "When I announce your name, you raise your hand" — demonstrating — "like this."

Fon's name was called before Yot's, so Yot should've known his name would come soon after, but when Miss Blackrow called out his name he was confused for an instant because his father had guessed wrong.

"Yaht Lim," she said, saying it quickly, in a naturally feminine manner, with a slight upward pitch.

When they got to the restaurant, both boys told their father how their teacher had pronounced Yot's name.

Well, obviously, the teacher is right, he replied in Chinese.

His name is Lim Lien Yot.

His brother's name is Lim Lien Fon.

Lim, in Cantonese, means "Forest". The Chinese character for "Lim" looks like two trees standing beside each other.

When Fon was born in 1921, his great-grandfather was so pleased to have a boy in the family that he named him Lien Fon. Lien means "Together" and Fon means "Happy". Combined, the words mean "Altogether Happy".

When Yot was born three years later, his great-grandfather had passed away so the honor of naming him fell to his great-granduncle, the younger brother, who said, For the first one we're all very happy. For the second one, we're also very happy. So he named him Lien Yot. Yot means "Joyful" or "Delightful". Combined, the words also mean "Altogether Happy".

So the two brothers have the same name: "Forest, Altogether Happy".

But it would be altered and shuffled about on the way to America. When their father was arranging passage for them, he asked a friend of his, an insurance agent in China (who supposedly knew a lot of English), to fill out their applications, and the man changed "Lien" to "Ling"...

"...for some reason I'll never understand," my father says.

And when they enrolled in Hutchins, their cousin rearranged the boys' names to fit the American standard.

When they asked Miss Blackrow about it, she agreed; that was the proper way to do it. All the Chinese rearranged their names.

"Altogether Happy, Forest".

Every day Miss Blackrow taught a little English, a little history and a little math.

School started at eight thirty in the morning, ended at three in the afternoon, and in the middle of the day was a half hour lunch. Yot and Fon's class ran all day long. Of the thirty-five students, half were Chinese. The Chinese were all boys; there were no

31

Chinese girls. The other half were a mix of nationalities. Among them were five Italians, a boy from Norway, a Jewish boy from Poland and a Jewish boy from Germany. Yot noticed that the Jewish students knew more English than the others; they'd apparently studied English in their own countries. Yot and Fon also met a boy named Sang Chan, someone they were surprised to discover had traveled on the same ship they had. They didn't remember meeting him earlier but the three became immediate friends.

Miss Blackrow's teaching method was to divide the students into different skill levels, instructing one group of students while the others studied on their own.

Yot already knew a little English before entering class. He knew the alphabet. He'd learned it in China by singing the same song American children sing ("A-B-C-D-E-F-G... H-I-J-K-LMNOP"). And he knew a few other phrases like, "Good Morning." He laughs when he remembers that for the longest time he used to say, "Good Afterloon" until he was finally corrected.

For homework Miss Blackrow would tell Yot, "You go home and try to practice."

Sometimes Bill, the boy who helped him ride his bicycle, would also help him read.

"What did you learn today?" he would ask Yot.

And Yot would tell him about a book they were reading.

"Bring the book."

Bill would read out loud from the book and then ask Yot to read the words the same way he did. And Yot appreciated his help.

His life, as well as Fon's, would soon become a routine of attending school during the day and working at the restaurant on the nights and weekends.

The year is 2006.

It's our second day in China. My father, Leslie, Nancy and I are in the van riding to the Great Wall.

We're heading to Mutianyu, one of the three most visited sections of the wall. There's Badaling, Mutianyu, and Simatai. There are more, but those are the ones that most guides in Beijing recommend.

My father has visited the Great Wall twice now. On his second visit he took my mother and brother to Badaling. It's the most popular of the three destinations because it's so close to Beijing, but for this trip, his third, he steered us away from it.

"Too crowded," he said, shaking his head, scrunching his face in distaste.

There's a marathon held on the Great Wall each year and my parents are aware of my interest in it. I've brought my running clothes on this trip, hoping to squeeze a mile in on the belief that I might never get a chance to run that race.

"Then you don't want to go to Badaling," my mother advised. "It's so crowded you won't be able to walk three steps. There are people all around. Your arms will be like this –" and she held her arms tight at her sides as if packed in a sardine can.

On the way to Mutianyu we drive through a small town in the Huairou District. It's a mix of factories, family restaurants and franchises. There's a McDonald's and a Kentucky Fried Chicken in Huairou, and more than a few mobile phone stores. It's also an area that borders on farmland, and farmers carrying tools or slabs of meat walk casually alongside city dwellers on the streets.

Tiffany, all too familiar with this route, has gotten us on the road early, but still we run into a traffic jam. Our driver, Mr. Guo, notices the cars tightening up in a small roundabout just ahead of us as a white-gloved police officer brings everyone to a halt. Mr. Guo pulls our van out of the jam and quickly tries to slip around the officer but another small car has the same idea and we end up blocking each other. The officer glares at Mr. Guo and explodes. In an instant he turns from friendly officer to fierce tiger, his eyes bulging, fangs bared. Tiffany, sitting in the front seat beside Mr. Guo, translates his yell:

"What are you doing?! I told you to stop and you try to go around?! Get back there!"

He orders us to the end of the line. Mr. Guo and the driver of the smaller car, as well as the other drivers who attempted to follow us, are ordered to loop the roundabout and take a position farther back than where we started.

We see the other cars shutting off their engines and we can tell we're in for a long wait. The van beside ours slides open its door to let an old grandmother sitting inside stretch her feet. We take this as a cue to open our doors too. I step outside to get some air. So does Tiffany.

Tiffany asks the other drivers what's happening. They tell her that some factory workers have scheduled a march up ahead in the street just beyond our sight. They're demanding better wages and working conditions.

We're back on the road but Tiffany tells us that we now have less than two hours to see the Great Wall.

We're entering the countryside. There's a wide green mountain in front of us and as we approach it we can see the Wall snaking along its side.

It's autumn. The streams are low and weak, the trees are losing their yellow leaves and the fields are turning orange brown. The air is clearer in this region and there's none of the acrid smell that comes with urban Beijing. It's beautiful here. I wish we could stay a whole day, but we can't.

Mr. Guo parks the van and I quickly change into my running clothes. As of this visit I've finished one marathon. By the following year I'll finish my second. During the second marathon I'll feel a pain in my legs and hips so excruciating that I'll almost wish for death. At the 22nd mile it'll start to rain and I'll find myself hoping that a bolt of lightning will strike me down and end my torture. The Great Wall Marathon would be much more of a challenge. The organizers of the race warn runners that there are over five thousand steps, many of them going steeply up or steeply down. I belong to a running group and a friend in the group ran the Great Wall for his first marathon. The race takes place in the summer and I asked him about the heat and difficulty of the course and he told me that while both were a problem, the very notion that you're running on ancient stone steps is enough to carry you along. And besides, he added, "How often do you get to run on the Great Wall?"

On the way to the sky lift there's a dry, sandy trail lined with vendors hawking their souvenirs from tent stalls. In a small dusty white clearing is a camel sitting next to a sign that reads:

Do not take pictures!
Pictures $3

Take a picture with Genghis Khan
$15.00

Genghis Khan is a local man standing in a suit of golden armor holding a long sword.

The vendors all have their patter down. They know a few English phrases and as Nancy, with her long red hair, passes by one vendor, the woman says, "Pretty lady, would you like anything?"

Nancy stops to look at the postcards but Tiffany tells her we don't have much time.

"I'll come back," Nancy says to the woman.

"Okay! When you come back! I will remember you!" the woman says.

By the time our sky lift reaches the top, Tiffany tells us we only have forty-five minutes left.

My run will be a lot shorter than I'd hoped. We take a few pictures. My father and Leslie stroll along on their own. I ask Nancy to watch my bag and she's selfless enough to oblige, but I only manage to squeeze in half a mile. There are too many other tourists to dodge, too much to see. There are square watchtowers every quarter mile. The gray stone steps leading up to the towers are hard and uneven, and the tourists tend to congregate there.

But, as my friend says, there's nothing like the feeling of running on ancient stone steps.

The air is cool, the sun is bright and I'm grateful for it all.

4

My grandfather Quong was thirteen years old when he hunted for frogs to feed his family.

Ambition could be found in the fields and pond outside his house.

He'd get up before dawn, when things were still quiet, while most of the other villagers were still asleep, leaving his house with nothing more than a kerosene lantern and bamboo scoop. The scoop was a tool he'd made himself by taking a bamboo pole, splitting one end into four pieces, splaying the pieces out wide, and attaching a small net he'd woven out of string. The string mesh, about six or seven inches in diameter, spread across the pieces and acted like a ladle, turning it into a netting pole. He'd then go into the fields while it was still dark, holding the lantern in one hand and pole in the other, and just before sunrise, he knew, the frogs would climb out of the water to sit at the edge of the rice fields, presumably to feed themselves. When Quong shined his lantern on the frogs they'd momentarily freeze, hypnotized by the sudden light, and he'd scoop them up in his net. A morning's catch would feed his family for a day.

They were small frogs, about half the size of his palm or smaller, and light tan in color with a trace of green. Some were very green. Most were small because the larger ones tended to be caught first. Catching frogs wasn't a routine Quong thought up himself; other villagers had done it before him; but it was something he'd learned quickly, and, like most things, a skill he wanted to excel at. He was always trying to better himself; always outdo the others.

The name Quong means "Light" or "Brightness".

He was born in 1899, just before the turn of the century.

At birth he was named Lim Quon Poy. Quon Poy means "To Grow or Raise", as in "To Grow a Tree" or "To Raise a Child". His grandfather had named him, and it was an indication of the nurturing hopes he'd had for him.

Quong took on several names during his lifetime. Before immigrating to America his uncle reported him as Lim Quong. To match the western convention, Lim Quong rearranged his name to Quong Lim. Upon returning to China, he took on the married name of Dung Yip. Taking on a married name was an indication of his maturity level, his rising status in the family; and Dung Yip means "An Advancing Business" or "Venture", so it was also one more sign of his enterprising nature. In contrast, when he'd first arrived in America, at the age of seventeen, everyone there called him Poy Doy. Doy means "Boy". It's a common way of nicknaming someone, much the same way Americans might call a young man, "Johnny Boy". The name stuck so stubbornly that when his sons followed him to America they would meet friends of his who'd say, "Oh, you're Poy Doy's boy." They even called Yot, "Doy Poy Doy" or "Boy of the Boy named Poy".

He grew up in the village of Tin Sum. This was the village where he was named, renamed, would be wed, and have two sons. There was a pond in front of his house and the pond helped provide for his family.

Before it was a pond, it was simple farmland. About fifty years before Quong was born, the villagers decided to dig up the ground underneath, build a wall around the resulting pit, fill it with water, and stock it with fish. They harvested the fish several times a year and the owners of the original land got a share of the harvest. The leaders of the village kept a list of the owners' names and as the years went on, the owners' descendants were added to the list, so every year the descendants got their lineage's share. Eventually the leaders of the village decided to lease the pond out and they auctioned the lease off every three years. Quong's family once owned part of the land so they got a share of the harvest as well as a share of the lease.

Quong's grandfather once leased the pond himself. His name was Gui Doon Lim and he'd stock the pond with minnow bought from the fish market. He'd buy the minnow young, when they were about an inch in size, and the minnow would feed on the algae and tiny insects in the water and after three or four months the minnow would grow to about a pound in weight and Gui Doon Lim would invite the local fish mongers to fish for a fee. Whatever the fish mongers caught, they sold at the market. Whatever they didn't catch was left for the villagers to harvest. And it was a share of that leftover harvest that went to the descendants. Sometimes Gui Doon Lim and his family would get ten to fifteen pounds of fish, just in time for the New Year. Then Gui Doon Lim would use the money he made from the fish mongers to pay the lease and buy more minnow to restock the pond so that the following year he could let the fish mongers fish again.

Quong lived a short walk from the pond, about a hundred and thirty feet from the edge. The house he grew up in was old, built over a hundred years ago, long before even his parents were born. Back then, to build a house, people would place some wood together to start the walls, put clay between the wood, use a stick to pack the clay down, then lay bricks on the outside of the clay. The walls would be about a foot thick and they'd finish by building a roof over the structure.

Years after Quong moved to America, a long rainstorm hit the area. Southern Guangdong has a tropical climate, and the storms can last for so long a time and be so thick that the rains can come pouring down like black walls of heavy water falling from the sky. Sometimes, during those rainstorms, the clay in the older houses would soak up the water. This happened especially if the roof was leaky or the wood was old. The walls would grow heavy, the foundation would become weak and the house would collapse under its own weight, and this was exactly what happened when Quong's mother was in the house one day. During a particularly bad storm the house crashed in on top of her. Her neighbors rushed over and called out her name but heard nothing. After some furious digging they assumed she had to be dead but were surprised when, minutes later, she crawled out from under the debris on her own, bruised but alive. Quong was already sending money home by then, and he'd long since hired someone to build a new house for his family by the pond; it was the house his wife and sons would live in; so his mother simply moved into the new house.

His mother was a nice woman, but was dependent on Quong's grandfather, her father-in-law, to help her along. Her husband, Yan Jiao Lim, smoked opium, and Quong's grandfather looked down on him for that. This was his own son after all. Quong's grandfather, Gui Doon Lim, was the patriarch; the one who held the family together. He not only managed the pond but often had to do more than his fair share of the farm work. Quong's mother was limited in the amount of work she could perform. At an early age she had had her feet bound, and this not only deformed her feet, it prevented her from working in the rice fields. Later, after the Chinese revolution of 1911, she became what was known as an "Unbound Lady", a woman who was finally able to free herself from the traditions of foot binding, but her deformity still left her relegated to the lighter chores like cooking and raising the chickens and feeding the pigs. And she was considered a meek woman; so meek that the other villagers sometimes picked on her.

Worse yet, her husband Yan Jiao Lim lived away from her. He worked in a brick factory about six miles south of their village. It would take him a little over two hours to walk home so he simply ate, slept and lived at the factory, as workers tended to do. One day a rain came down that lasted for four days, almost a whole week. It caused a flood in the area and Yan Jiao Lim, not knowing how to swim, drowned. He was in his thirties.

Quong was twelve years old at the time. He had a younger sister, and after his father's death, his grandfather stepped in to raise the two of them.

By the age of fourteen Quong was fishing in the pond, further feeding his ambitions.

He used a larger net for this: one his grandfather had woven out of linen string. It was square-shaped, about five feet by five feet, with a weave just tight enough that small fish couldn't get through. Each corner had a stick tied to it to weigh the net down and Quong would lower the whole thing into the water, letting it sink to the bottom. He'd then drop gobs of ground shrimp paste over the center and wait. The surface of the water would calm down, grow still again, and when the fish came nibbling, Quong would see their small movements along the surface. Or spot their tiny bubbles. He'd then pull the net up and haul the fish in… yet again, providing food for his family.

By the time he was fifteen, his grandfather thought it was time to show him a new skill. In addition to all his other roles, his grandfather was also a butcher, and butchers were highly valued in the villages. His grandfather worked in a small shop with four other butchers about a mile from Tin Sum and he invited Quong to travel with him so he could teach him his trade. The butchers were regularly hired by pork vendors to kill a pig, and once killed, the butchers shared the duty of splitting it up for the vendor, who then walked from village to village selling the meat.

Quong learned his new trade quickly and, being a strong, stocky young man, was often tasked by the other butchers to do the killing. The pigs were kept in small bamboo cages and the butcher had to take a long, thin knife, about sixteen inches in length, and stab the pig just under the mouth and through the throat, quickly and stealthily. If the butcher did it right, he pierced the pig's heart and the animal died instantly. If the butcher did it wrong, he had to keep stabbing and stabbing. The pig, in pain, would try to fight or get away and the whole affair could easily turn into an ugly, bloody mess. Quong was known for stabbing quickly and once.

He earned so much money as a butcher that many of the villagers soon offered their daughters to Quong for matrimony. When that occurred, a fortune teller or soothsayer would be asked to read the girls' signs. Quong would later confess to his son Yot that he *did* give these matches some consideration but after a reading, the girls usually turned out to be bad matches.

Unfortunately Quong was also a gambler, and he'd lose money just as quickly as he earned it. But he had an uncle working on the railroads in America at the time, and the railroads offered the Chinese a chance to earn more money than they ever could in their own land (they'd already given California the name, "Gold Mountain") so families often pooled their money together to send one of their men overseas. The man would then work and send money back home. With Quong's gambling problem, his grandfather thought it best to send Quong to his uncle; he'd learn more skills in America anyhow; and since Quong's father was dead, his uncle was willing to claim him as his own.

He arrived in 1916 at the age of seventeen. His uncle had been living in San Francisco but had moved to Detroit by then, so Quong joined him there. The following year, America entered World War I and Quong got his draft notice. Not even a citizen yet, Quong was required to join. He applied for his medical examination but by the time his appointment came, the war was over. It was something he'd always felt lucky about.

He got a job washing dishes at the Far East Restaurant instead. As my father Yot once told me, "Everyone starts out washing dishes. He washed dishes, I washed dishes, and when you started out, you washed dishes too."

40

He worked his way up from dishwasher to cook. Quong had only been there for a year but in between trays of incoming dishes, he would watch the cooks at the restaurant; study how they cut the vegetables and meat and mixed everything together. One day one of the cooks left and Quong asked the manager if he could try the job out to see how it worked. The manager had already noticed that Quong had outlasted all the other dishwashers, could see that Quong was a strong young man, so he gave him the chance.

At first Quong's main duty was to prepare the food for the head chef but the restaurant tended to get so busy that even the head chef had trouble keeping up with the orders, so Quong asked the manager if he could cook some of the dinners too.

Okay, young man, said the manager, you see what you can do!

Eventually Quong took over as head chef as well.

He also learned to become quite thrifty. Like most Chinese workers, he ate at the restaurant and shared an apartment with his fellow workers and the only thing he ever spent money on was clothes. He didn't need a car. If he went anywhere he took the streetcar. By the time he was twenty-one he'd saved about $1500. It was a lot of money at the time, and like most Chinese man of that age, he decided to get married.

The year was 1920. He had been in America four years. There were almost no Chinese women in Detroit. The Chinese Exclusion Act had seen to that. When the country needed its railroads, it gladly welcomed Chinese laborers, but when they were seen as stealing jobs, the country passed laws to limit the number of men coming in and to keep the women out.

So most Chinese men went back home to find a bride. With all that money to his name, Quong would be considered a successful man and the matchmakers would have no difficulty finding him a girl.

Matchmaking was so customary that an unmarried Chinese man could be sure that matchmakers would flock to his door the moment he returned from overseas. Sometimes in their eagerness, the matchmakers even approached the man's family before the man arrived home.

Matchmakers were usually the older men and women in the villages who knew of boys and girls they thought would make good matches. Sometimes the boys and girls themselves paid the matchmakers to find them a match, but because most girls didn't have jobs and couldn't earn a living, their families typically paid their parts. A few matchmakers even tried to practice their pursuits in America. A matchmaker in America could make up to five hundred dollars, but because the potential pairings were better in China, most matchmakers performed the tradition in the villages there, and in the process earned a lot less. For payment, a family usually gave their matchmaker a *lai see bao*, a little red envelope containing cash. It was known as "Lucky Money". Sometimes payment was given in the form of a simple dinner. Occasionally a family would even chase a matchmaker out of their house if they felt the matchmaker had failed them, or if their in-laws weren't as ideal as they'd expected. It was hard for matchmakers to make a living doing what they did.

Part of a matchmaker's job was to find out, down to the hour if possible, the time of birth for both the boy and the girl she was matching up. She would then take the information to a fortune teller to see if there were any conflicts between the two, and if none existed, the matchmaker proceeded to negotiate the size of the dowry. How much would the girl's family be willing to pay? Sometimes, among the wealthier families, the dowry was paid with money, but more often than not it came in the form of furniture. A bride's family traditionally offered the groom's family a large cabinet, usually something over eight feet tall. Inside the cabinet would be a dining table, a square table, another table, a hardwood chest for holding clothes, and a wash basin stand. All told, a proper dowry consisted of eighteen pieces of furniture. It was a gift, not only to the groom's family but to the young couple who were expected to utilize it. Sometimes the dowry even included a maid. Quong had a cousin who had been given a maid as part of his dowry. A maid was really just a poorer girl who had fewer prospects. Usually, though, a dowry amounted to whatever the girl's family could afford.

But it wasn't just a one-way offering. The boy's family was expected to reciprocate in kind. The girl was, after all, leaving her own family to join his. She was expected to move into the boy's household and look after his parents as they entered old age. So the boy's family was obligated to give the girl's family a compensatory gift. Sometimes the gift was in the form of cash; sometimes in the form of land. For Quong's cousin, the one who received the maid, his family had to pay the girl's family half an acre of farmland. Later, when that same cousin's four younger sisters got married, his family had to pay dowries to four other families... and was likewise compensated in kind.

Arrangements of this nature were negotiated by the matchmaker. Because the notion of compensation was such a delicate subject, it was usually spoken of euphemistically, in terms of "cakes". The mother of the bride asked for five thousand cakes or ten thousand cakes or any number of cakes until the families finally settled on a proper figure, and then the mother of the groom quickly converted the number of cakes into the amount of money it would take to buy those cakes. That figure was then given in the form of money or land.

And if they could afford it, the matchmaker sometimes gave the boy and girl pictures of each other. But photographs were a rarity and the matchmaker usually just gave each person the other person's name. The villages were small and everyone knew each other anyhow. The boy's friends or relatives typically already knew of the girl and would arrange for him to get an advance look at her. If she worked in the market they'd arrange for him to take a peek at her from afar, or sometimes he would pretend to approach her as a customer and talk with her for a little while.

Quong got to see his future wife in this manner.

The matchmaker who arranged his marriage was a slender, elderly woman in her late sixties who lived in a nearby village. She was yet another woman with bound feet, and even after the practice was banned she would continue binding her feet for the remainder of her days. When she approached Quong's family she said, I have a girl who might be a good match for your son.

She told Quong about the girl she had in mind and one day, while visiting the market, Quong thought he'd try to get a glimpse of her. He visited his old butcher shop and asked his friends if they knew of the girl, and they pointed her out to him.

The girl, he discovered, was pretty but poor. Attractive, but with no money to her name. She had two older sisters and her mother had spent all the family money on her sisters' weddings, so the matchmaker had to inform Quong that the girl had no dowry to give. That also meant he needn't offer anything back in kind.

Quong told the girl's mother not to worry about it. Just give me your daughter, he said. I don't want anything else.

The match was made, and over the coming weeks Quong began building furniture for the two of them. The only thing left to do was perform the marriage ritual.

The bride was brought to the groom's house in a wedding sedan carried by two footmen. The footmen were wedding specialists: part of a team hired by the bride's family. The sedan was an upright rectangular box made of bamboo, about six feet tall, painted green. The bride sat on a small bench inside facing the front. The front was open, covered by a curtain, and the curtain hid her from view. No one could see in, and she couldn't see out. She saw only the ground moving before her where the curtain didn't meet the floor, or when the curtain swayed. There were brackets on both sides of the sedan for two bamboo poles to hold it aloft, and the footman bore the poles on their shoulders as they marched the two miles from the bride's village to the groom's.

When they arrived, they were met by the groom's family and his groomsmen. The footmen lowered the sedan near the front of his family's house. The bridesmaids waited. The groom had six groomsmen. If the groom's family had been wealthier, they could have hired the traditional Ten Groomsmen: five pairs of men. But they weren't, so they had three pairs: friends of his.

Starting from about twenty feet away, the groomsmen approached the sedan. They took five steps, and bowed. Five steps, and bowed. Altogether, three bows. Had there had been more groomsmen, there would've been more bows. Then the groom stepped forward and did the same. When the groom approached, it was called "Kicking the Sedan". He pulled the curtain aside and welcomed the bride.

She wore a red gown, like a robe, from foot to shoulder... although he still couldn't see her face, not fully. She wore a Phoenix Hat. Most hats were sedge hats, the kind worn in the fields, but adorned with veils. Some were flowery, some wide-brimmed. If the bride's family had been wealthier, they might've decorated hers with a bird's feather. But they weren't, so she wore a hat made of paper and bamboo, red and purple in color. It was a very simple, common Phoenix Hat.

Her feet weren't allowed to touch the ground so a bridesmaid carried her piggyback into his house while the groom's family lit firecrackers to scare away ghosts and evil spirits.

Inside the house the groom performed the "Lifting of the Hat Off of the Bride". As he removed the Phoenix Hat he told her his birth name, Quon Poy. It wasn't necessary to say his surname. Then he asked,

What is your name?

Sun Moon.

She was born the third girl of the Liu family. Her name meant "New Full". Sun means "New" and Moon means "Full". Together the words indicate joy or good fortune. My father says it's akin to "a bucket of fun" or a "full pot of gold" but my mother says it means something more like "plentiful".

Her sisters were similarly named. Her second oldest sister was named Sun Hop, or "New Together." Her oldest sister was named Wun Choy. Wun means "Fate." Choy means "Lucky." Together the words mean "Good Fortune".

She had one older brother and three younger brothers. Altogether, with her parents, she came from a family of nine. They were farmers, and although they didn't have much, they could still afford to have Sun Moon's front teeth capped with gold. This was considered attractive for a young bride.

Then Quon Poy and Sun Moon paid their respects to Quon Poy's ancestors and he introduced her to her new parents. Sun Moon brought out a tray with two small cups and one of Quon Poy's groomsmen poured double brewed rice liquor into them.

Thank you everyone, Quon Poy said. He thanked his friends and family for their patience and then they began the banquet dinner.

It was customary for a bride's belongings to be delivered ahead of her, but Sun Moon didn't have very much. She arrived with only a small chest made of sugar pine, painted red. It contained everything she owned: some clothes, a wash basin, some jewelry and some pots and pans. After she had been carried into the house, the groom's family had performed the "Passing of the House Key to the Bride", where a small boy handed her the key to her new home. Years later, her son Yot would be asked to play this role for a neighbor of his. By then he'd heard his mother's tales of footmen and rituals and of her single piece of property. She often spoke with amusement of how poor and simple her wedding was, and once, when he was five, as he listened to her stories, he asked, "Where's your chest?"

Sitting, she pointed with her feet: "Right there."

And he turned to see a wooden chest small enough for a boy his size to fit inside.

Quong Lim and Sun Moon Liu were married in February of 1921. Nine months later, on November 26, Sun Moon Lim gave birth to her first son, Fon. But Quong wasn't there to witness the event. In addition to his sister, mother and grandparents, he now had his own family to support, so three months before the delivery he was on his way back to America.

Most marriages were based on practical necessities. Sometimes you married to improve your social standing. Or you married to keep your life the way it was: to continue farming, or even just to survive. Or you married to have children. It was disrespectful to your ancestors not to have sons. So it was a rare thing if a couple also happened to love each other. And as my father would later tell me, his father loved his wife.

Still, Sun Moon wasn't without her concerns. She'd once heard some distressing news from a blind fortune teller who lived in the village. The fortune teller was a thin, friendly blind man in his forties who, during the day, would walk to the market where he had a little stall and tell people their fates. Then he'd return to the village and sit by the pond and tell stories to his neighbors. Children loved listening to him. At the end of the year he'd walk around the village and give people warnings, then go house to house and ask for a donation. And he'd say something to the effect of:

"Watch out for fire, and brother and sister should live in harmony, and the elderly should teach the right way to live."

One day Sun Moon heard through one of her cousin-in-laws that the fortune teller had predicted that her husband would have two wives but that he wouldn't marry them at the same time. Her husband, he said, would not last through the marriage and then marry again.

Worried, Sun Moon urged Quong to get a concubine. It was acceptable for a wealthy man like him to have one.

But when he heard the idea, he dismissed it.

Our visit to the Great Wall is far too short.

As we head back to the sky lift we stumble upon a beauty contest being held on a wide, flat stone landing in the afternoon air. There's a large red balloon arch, curved like the top half of a doughnut, with the words:

Best wishes to Huairou.
Best wishes to Beijing.
Best wishes to 2008 Olympic Games!

A crowd of about a hundred has gathered to watch what looks like the crowning of the next Miss Great Wall. Soldiers guard the sides and cordon off the onlookers. A man in a tuxedo introduces the contestants. They're all young and beautiful, wearing shiny, slinky dresses and sashes, and at first I think it's a local contest but not all of the girls are Chinese. I see Caucasian girls, Indian girls, and a Black girl. At least a third of the girls are blonde. They stand on sheets of carpet laid down to look like a big red stage in the bright yellow sun.

The contest is brief enough that by the time I find Tiffany, the winner is announced. But we're so pressed for time I don't get to see which young woman it is.

At the bottom of sky lift we're forced to walk the souvenir gauntlet again. The vendors on the way down are more aggressive and several of them say to Nancy, "Pretty lady, remember me? You promised to buy something." But Nancy is on the lookout for the woman she actually made her promise to... and she spots her. Nancy stops to buy some postcards and T-shirts for her own family back in Florida. I wouldn't have been able to find the woman myself but it's nice to see this small connection made between the two.

At another stand, Nancy stops to look at some baseball caps with the words "The Great Wall" emblazoned across them. The woman at the stand asks for ten U.S. dollars for what looks like a common factory product. I wouldn't pay ten dollars for a cap like that in the U.S. and the woman seems aggressive too so, translating through Tiffany, I haggle with her a little. But the woman is stubborn; she won't go any lower. We say no and start to move on but the woman yells angrily at Tiffany in Mandarin:

You should be helping me, not them! I need the money! You should be helping me!

That's not my duty, Tiffany says. I'm only translating. I can't tell them what to buy.

Nancy buys the caps from a man at another stand. The man willingly negotiates and we talk him down to $2.50, but in the end, Nancy gives him three U.S. dollars. Even with the small half-dollar added in as a tip I can tell she feels guilty about haggling any of these people down.

At a nearby stand I see the little red book called *Quotations from Chairman Mao Tse-Tung*. Another cheap factory product.

According to one estimate, *Quotations from Chairman Mao Tse-Tung* is the bestselling book of all time, surpassing even the Bible. It's impossible to know for sure since no one's ever been able to accurately prove or disprove the claim. The Bible camp says their book is more popular, selling over six billion copies compared to the paltry nine hundred million they claim *Quotations* has sold. As of this writing, six billion copies would mean that almost every living person on the planet earth would've had to have bought one copy of Bible. Perhaps China will surpass that; perhaps it already has; but with China's continued experiments with capitalism — demonstrated even to a small extent by these vendors — the communist leader's *Quotations* probably will not dramatically improve its sales anytime soon.

I buy a copy of *Quotations*. It costs two American dollars, or close to sixteen Chinese yuan.

5

When he returned to Detroit this time, he stayed two years, even after hearing about the birth of Fon.

There was never a shortage of work for someone like Quong. The moment he stepped foot in the city there was already a job waiting for him. In fact, there were several.

Before leaving, he'd earned quite a reputation for himself as a fast, reliable cook. He kept a well-ordered kitchen and, most importantly, made good food. He'd become so well known that when the owners of three different restaurants heard he was coming back, they began asking around for him. But it was his old employer, the manager of the Far East Restaurant, who needed him more. In his absence, the Far East's staff had become disorganized and their kitchen had fallen into disarray.

So Quong returned to his old station, getting it back into shape. He could easily have stayed there too but for the restless quality he had about him. He would often get angry at the "old timers", the cooks who were slow and inefficient. Quong, by comparison, was always trying to learn new things. One day he told his manager he wanted to try waiting on tables, and at first his manager didn't like the idea; Quong's English wasn't very good; but Quong persisted and, as in all things, got his way. He couldn't converse with his customers very well but knew what they were ordering, and that was all he needed to do his job. And privately, he wanted to learn every aspect of the business in the event that he ever opened his own restaurant.

He was there for about half a year when he received a letter from his granduncle informing him that he'd had a son. His granduncle was the one who would send him news from back home, and usually at the behest of Quong's patriarch grandfather. His granduncle never wrote any of the letters himself; he didn't know how. He simply hired a local teacher or scholar to write the letters for him. But this was good news. Anytime a Chinese man had a son, especially a first born son, it was good news all around.

Quong worked for a couple more years but found himself wanting to go back to China. He told his manager, and his manager tried to talk him out of it, even going so far as to offer Quong more money, but they went back and forth on the issue until at last Quong quit.

He had managed to refrain from gambling during his time in America but on the ship back to China, chanced upon some men playing *fan tan* in the cargo holds.

Fan tan was a game that could be played anywhere. All it required was a table, some buttons, and a box. The box was usually a thin square plate: square so that it had four sides with which to gamble upon. Gamblers placed their bets on each side of the plate, each side representing the numbers one, two, three or four. A dealer then put a small heap of buttons in front of him, hid the buttons from view with a pot cover, then used a stick to remove four buttons at a time until only several buttons remained, and the bets that corresponded to the number of buttons remaining won.

The cargo holds were known for their gambling, and a game of *fan tan* could always be found.

At first Quong resisted playing but a fellow passenger invited him to join in.

Are you going to play some? he asked Quong.

No.

But the man persisted, entreating Quong to put some money down. Again Quong refused, and continued to refuse until the man couldn't stand it anymore and handed Quong some money.

Here! he said. That's yours to play with.

So Quong bet the money. And won. And bet again. And won again. And over the next twenty days of the trip found himself on a winning streak. By the time he arrived in China, he was about three thousand dollars richer than when he'd left America. His pockets were full of cash.

But his luck only lasted as long as it took to reach his village.

Over the years he'd been sending money back home to his family through his grandfather, Gui Doon Lim, the man who'd first sent Quong to America to outgrow his original gambling problems. But a couple months after Fon was born, Gui Doon Lim died, so

Quong started sending money to his grandfather's younger brother instead. He usually sent it in the form of American Express checks, which his granduncle would take to the bank, convert to Chinese coins, then give to Quong's mother. But when Quong arrived home he couldn't believe how badly his mother had handled the family's finances. There was nothing left. Not a single coin.

Mystified, he started inquiring around the village. His mother, he discovered, had expected him to send more money than he did, and in her anticipation, not only misspent the money she received but loaned much of it out to her neighbors. And being the timid woman she was, she'd been unable to get it back. Worse yet, she then had to borrow money to make up for what she'd lost, putting her in debt to her other neighbors. So the first thing Quong did was pay off those debts.

Then he called a family meeting. His mother, granduncle, and granduncle's wife were all in attendance around the dinner table with him.

Just after they were wed, Quong's wife was still only nineteen years old; too young and too new to the family to handle any money. But now she was twenty-one, and in his eyes a better choice than his own mother. So he announced that Sun Moon would now be entrusted with the money.

She's too young! said his mother. How can you let a young woman handle that much money?

You must be out of your mind, they told him. You should have more respect for your mother.

But Quong was adamant: This is my decision and this is what it will be.

That settled, he turned his attention elsewhere.

He knew that before his grandfather had died he had started building a small rice paddy at the foot of a hill behind the village. There was still unclaimed land in those days. If a person could clear off some land and make good use of it, he could mark it and claim it as his own. So Quong set out to continue his grandfather's work. The land was still rough. It needed to be cleared and Quong hated farm work. It was one of the reasons he'd become a butcher to begin with. But he had money now, so he hired some young men in the village to clear the land for him. He paid them a small amount for every bag of dirt they moved and eventually he finished his grandfather's rice paddy. Not only would it help feed his family but it'd benefit the village as a whole.

For a while his life took on a carefree nature. He didn't have to work and he'd come back just in time to celebrate the New Year with his family. His younger sister got married. And on October 1st, his second son Yot was born.

Quong would later tell Yot that he was a very cute child. Always smiling. And whenever he woke he had a smile on his face. Quong had been the same kind of child. Always smiling. Altogether happy.

He was enjoying his life but his winnings aboard the ship had reignited the gambler in him. Yot recalled his mother telling him of evenings when his father would load his pockets with coins to go out gambling. After a while he would return, having lost it all, only to load his pockets up with yet more and head right back out the door.

Quong stayed another five months after Yot's birth before returning to America. This time his visit lasted a year and a half.

It's October 2008.

I'm on the Great Wall again. It's my second visit to Mutianyu and I'm walking these stone steps with my friend Brian. Brian is an instructor at a business school in Beijing. He teaches college students how to read American business articles. They read *The Wall Street Journal*, *Time*, *Business Weekly* and any essays he takes the time to clip and copy. Brian is his western nickname, just as Tiffany is the nickname of our tour guide from two years ago. The names are adopted to make communicating easier for Americans... which includes us, the Cantonese Americans who'd stumble over even Mandarin names. I don't know what Brian's Chinese name is and even if he told me, I'm sure I'd forget it, but we were introduced to each other by a mutual friend, a former classmate of his who's living in the United States now.

A month ago I ran my third marathon at Lake Tahoe and I was hoping to run my fourth in Beijing. That's one reason why I'm here again. When I signed up for the Beijing Marathon the bib number they gave me was 445. My sister Leslie said, "Thank god you didn't get 444. Bad luck to whoever got that number." The word for "four" in Chinese sounds similar to the word for "death", so 444 would be like "death-death-death". A friend of mine who's a salesman in Los Angeles says that many of the buildings in his local Chinatown have no fourth floor because the Chinese are as superstitious about that as we are about the thirteenth floor. Every time he visits his customers in Chinatown he gets momentarily confused when he enters the elevators.

Another reason we're here is to visit my mother's village. She grew up in a village close to my father's. But months before flying over, the U.S. economy started to crash. The stock market took one of its worst dives ever, with the Dow Jones dropping 777 points in a single day. Lucky number seven? Hardly. There was a recession coming and everyone knew it. The global economy had been creeping steadily downward for the past nine months but we wouldn't know until after we returned home from China that it would become the worst credit crisis since the Great Depression.

Leslie, who works in financial management, was the most worried of all; she'd lost jobs during downturns like this. Over dinner the night before the Lake Tahoe Marathon, we decided to delay the trip so she could check with her manager to see if it was safe for her to go. She didn't want to leave only to discover she had no job to return to. For me, the delay meant dropping out of the Beijing Marathon. I'd originally planned to meet Brian at the finish line. When I emailed him to tell him of our change in plans, Brian wrote back to say he was sorry to hear that, and asked what I might want to do instead.

Would he mind taking me to see The Great Wall again? I asked. He'd be happy to. We could take a bus, he said. He asked what else I wanted to do, and I mentioned the hutongs, something I'd missed my first time around. I was also hoping to have lunch at the Li Qun Duck Restaurant. I'd be happy to treat. Perhaps we could even visit the food markets.

When my sister finally got the go-ahead from her manager, we booked our flights through our travel agent. Days before writing our checks to him, I saw something I thought I'd never see: a run on the banks. One afternoon I heard a co-worker wondering out loud if he should pull his money out of his bank, and the next day, on the way to work, I noticed people waiting outside my own bank with the same thought. They were shuffling their feet impatiently, waiting for the doors to open, their hands thrust into their coat pockets like the chilly-looking people I'd seen in black and white photos from the 1930s.

The downward tumble also turned a few fortunate people like me into aspiring Warren Buffetts. Just before leaving for China I bought a couple shares in Warren Buffett's company, Berkshire Hathaway; then two days before getting on the plane, placed an order to buy shares in one of his favorite companies, Goldman Sachs. Then we were flying to China.

I met Brian my first morning in Beijing, just after finishing breakfast in the hotel. I didn't know what he looked like but from our email exchanges I was expecting an older, wise-looking man of about my father's age. So I was surprised when I was greeted in the lobby by a young man of about twenty-five wearing a plain beige windbreaker. Slim, with a rosy color to his cheeks, he welcomed me with an almost shy, ironic smile. It was a smile I'd see over and over again during our days together.

I'd also soon discover that we both had a deep fascination with the economy. We shared an outlook that reminded me of something my brother once told me: that there's an experiment; a study being conducted; the results of the study are fed back to the subjects and the study keeps growing and changing. The subjects are human beings and the study is called Economics.

The first thing Brian suggested we do was bicycle around Beijing. There was a vendor around the corner from my hotel and we rented some bicycles for a couple dollars apiece. Brian was the better bicyclist and it took me a few minutes to get reacquainted with something as simple as the brake on the handlebar. At one intersection I nearly rode into oncoming traffic and Brian had to call out to stop me.

While riding through the hutongs, the ancient alleyways of Beijing, I told Brian I couldn't wait to buy more shares of Berkshire Hathaway and in my exuberance asked if he considered doing the same. His reply was a modest, "I don't think I can afford it." I blinked and suddenly felt embarrassed, like a cocky American who was clueless about how much he took for granted. Quickly I changed the subject. I asked him his views on the global economy and he started talking about John Maynard Keynes. Keynes was the economist who advised Roosevelt during the Great Depression. He said that economies falter because people lose confidence and stop spending, and when that happens, the government should step in and do the spending. Historians debate whether or not his beliefs really saved us but Keynes, Brian said, was about to get a second tryout starting now.

The next day we took a bus to the Great Wall. After climbing up through a hole of one the stone towers, he gave me a short history of the wall. We took some photos of each other then looked out at the dark green mountainside.

We started talking about the economy again. I told him how it was finally dawning on most Americans how deep in debt we were to China. Americans were just now starting to view China's massive purchase of treasury bonds with an uneasy insecurity. Brian said it made China uneasy too. The biggest worry the Chinese had, Brian told me, was that to cover our spending we would simply print new money, thereby devaluing our own currency, and China would be joined with us at the hip all the way down.

"Wait, we can't just print more money. That would cause inflation. Everyone would see it."

"Printing money is just a term, but there is a way to do it where we and the rest of the world wouldn't find out until it's too late."

We started walking down the steps, toward the twisty, rocky, mountain path to the souvenir vendors. Brian continued telling me about the wall, why it was built, and how the Chinese had known for decades of the threat their neighbors, the Mongols, posed. The Mongols, with their nomadic lifestyle, needed to invade China periodically. It was their only way to gather food during their lean years.

Then Brian pointed out a section of the wall to me.

"That's new," he said.

"What do you mean?"

"Not all of the wall is the original. This part is new. They rebuilt it. You can tell from the cement. See how it's a different color? There must have been some damage here so they put in some new bricks and tried to make it look the same."

"How about that," I said. "I would never have noticed it."

"Most of the wall is still old but they have to replace some of it. They just don't tell anyone, but I've noticed it."

There were, once again, restaurant owners inquiring about Quong's services.

The year was 1925 and when Quong returned to Detroit this time, he worked at several different places — the Far East

Restaurant, Peking Inn — whoever asked for him and whatever suited his tastes. He was almost never without a job.

Like most other restaurant workers, he typically turned in eleven to twelve hour days, six days a week, sometimes working every day of the week. Whatever spare time he had after that was his own. The family associations were popular and he tended to visit one association or another. They were like clubs where he could relax and chat, and where restaurant owners could ask if anyone, like himself, was willing to help them out.

Friends and relatives also recognized potential business partners in circles like these. The Far East Restaurant itself was owned by thirty such people, each of whom owned a share of the place, but it was managed by one man, a cousin of Quong's. That was the main reason why Quong kept ending up there. So it was only a matter of time before Quong's friends wanted to start their own restaurant, and a year after his return he partnered up with three of those friends to open the Atlantic Garden. It was a two-story restaurant with a big storefront window. The men all worked together on the first floor and shared an apartment on the second.

The restaurant was successful but within a few years, Quong's attention turned to another space that became available just eleven blocks south. It was one of five red brick storefronts built between Rochester and Chicago Blvd., and there were a series of apartment buildings behind it, which translated into ready customers. When Quong's first cousin arrived from China hoping to become a partner in a restaurant, Quong sold him his share of the Atlantic Garden.

Quong then partnered up with another cousin, Sun Lim, and opened the Pacific Garden. It cost only a couple thousand dollars to start the business. They bought some tables, chairs, and built a kitchen out back. Sun Lim became the cook and Quong became the manager, which simply meant he welcomed customers, seated them, and took their order. And they hired an assistant to deliver carryouts.

But the new restaurant soon created a resentment between Quong and his first cousin, the one who'd bought his share of the Atlantic Garden. His cousin accused Quong of selling him the Atlantic Garden and opening the Pacific Garden just to compete with him. Quong maintained that he'd been honest and forthright in all his dealings. He'd let his first cousin know exactly what he was doing. Their disagreement turned into a bitter grudge that carried on for the next several years. It wasn't until his first cousin made plans to bring his son, Yip, to Detroit, and Quong did the same for his two sons, and both at about the same time, that the two men put their differences aside. Their boys all knew each other and last thing the men wanted was for their children to hear of their quarrel.

But that was the least of Quong's worries. Looking back, he and Sun Lim couldn't have had worse timing when they opened the Pacific Garden in 1930. Just one year earlier the stock market suffered a huge crash. Businesses all around them sputtered to a crawl. Slowly, the Pacific Garden saw its customers dwindle away. Slowly, Sun Lim began losing interest in the place. After a while he told Quong he wanted to leave, to go off on his own. Quong offered to buy him out and Sun Lim's response was, I'll give you the whole thing. I don't want any part of it.

Unable to keep even his assistant, Quong soon found himself running the business alone, becoming the waiter, cook and delivery boy.

For about six months he found himself performing a daily juggling act. When a couple came in, he sat them down, took their order and, not wanting his customers to know he was running the place alone, would shout the order to a nonexistent cook behind the kitchen door. Then he'd hurry into the kitchen and quickly cook their meal.

Sometimes the phone would ring for a carryout and Quong would have to fit a delivery in too. Usually the order was from one of the apartment buildings behind the restaurant. Some of the buildings had three to four hundred units, and they were his biggest source of orders. One place directly behind the Pacific Garden, a red and amber brick building, held fifty to sixty apartments alone. After cooking the meal he'd lock up the restaurant so no one could steal anything while he was away, then hurry out the backdoor and deliver the order. If the delivery was further away he rode his bicycle. If there was a young couple in the restaurant he wouldn't have to lock the door; the customers acted as unwitting guards. But he'd still have to juggle the carryout, the delivery, and the couple's orders all before giving the couple their bill. Sometimes he'd have to ask the person placing the order over the phone for some extra time.

Quong had already been known for his frugality but now, occasionally, he'd skip eating for a day just so he could save a few extra dollars. There's a saying for this kind of man, and people used it to describe him:

If he gets knocked to the ground he'll grab a handful
of sand.

It meant that he was so willfully resourceful that if he fell down
he'd grab something, anything, just so he wouldn't come up empty-
handed.

But even sheer determination wouldn't always make ends
meet. Quong started to fall behind on his rent and had to tell his
landlord, a Jewish man, I can't pay you right now.

Oh don't worry, his landlord replied, nobody can pay anyway.

Over a year later, when Quong's business finally started to earn
some decent money, he offered to pay his landlord the back rent he
owed him but his landlord graciously didn't think it worth the
bother.

What's gone is gone, the man said.

Half a world away, Quong's family enjoyed a modest
prosperity mixed with their own form of hardship.

Quong still sent money home in the form of American Express
checks. The money arrived three to four times a year: just before
the New Year, just after the New Year, and once or twice in the
middle of the year. He sent about fifty dollars each time and at a
one-to-four exchange rate his family received a little over two
hundred dollars in Chinese currency.

The checks still went to his granduncle and his granduncle still
converted them to Chinese coins, but now, according to the new
arrangement, the coins were given to Quong's wife Sun Moon. The
coins were called *sung mao*, or "double tens", because they were
worth twenty cents each. The coins were put in a roll, and each roll
contained fifty coins, and his granduncle would show up at her door
with about four rolls.

They had a maid. Or rather, owned one. Poorer families
occasionally had to sell their children as servants — sometimes
because they were a burden or sometimes just to buy supplies to
start a business and make a living. Sun Moon bought their maid
from a poor family for about fifty American dollars. That was the

going cost for a girl at the time. Boys cost a little more. Sometimes a poor family was so overloaded that they sold the child for less, and in some cases, if they couldn't sell the child, the child was forced to beg on the street.

The Lims were one of only three families in Tin Sum to own a maid, but that didn't mean they were wealthy. As Yot recalled, "We weren't rich, and we weren't poor." And Sun Moon had an obligation to the girl. The girl lived with them. They clothed her, they fed her, and she had to do chores, but Sun Moon had to look after the girl as if she were a daughter. Later, when the girl was older, Sun Moon asked her if she wanted to return to her family but the girl disliked her family so much that she declined.

Yot adored her. She had been a part of his family before he was even born. She was a plain girl with a round face and a long pigtail. He would run to her whenever he fell and hurt himself. They played games with each other and she liked to tease him. She would take some red ink, water it down a bit, dab it with a little bamboo stick that they used as a marker, put it on his hand and say, "Oh you're bleeding." Believing himself cut, Yot would start crying and look for his mother.

When she turned nineteen, Sun Moon fulfilled another obligation to the girl by arranging her marriage. Sun Moon found a young man who had gone to work in Indonesia, and upon his brief return, the girl married him, leaving their household. Yot was five years old at the time, and it broke his heart.

"Oh I loved her! I was crying for quite a while after she left. I told my mother, 'Oh I miss her!'"

He would cry to his mother during the evenings and she'd tell him that in a little while the girl would come back for a visit, but two months later the man took his wife back to Indonesia and Yot never saw her again.

Soon after that, Yot started going to school and assumed some of his former maid's chores. With the money Sun Moon got from Quong, she bought meat and extra rice, wood for the fire and clothes to wear, but they still needed to grow rice to get by. There were two harvests a year: the summer harvest in June and the autumn harvest in late October. After the summer harvest they would turn the soil over to start the next crop, and they reaped just enough to keep themselves going but always seemed on the verge of running out.

When Yot was seven he was finally allowed to venture out on his own and was playing in the fields one day after the autumn harvest. The ground was barren and dry and he accidentally kicked up a small dirt cover revealing a nest of baby mice. They didn't even have hair yet and he guessed that they must've been only a day or two old. So he scooped them up and took them home to show his mother thinking that they might make good pets.

"Ohhhh," his mother said when she saw them, "pretty nice. Let me fix you something."

He watched as his mother started boiling a pot of water and he asked, "What are you doing?"

"Oh, I'm going to clean them up, let them swim a little bit."

She put the mice on a ladle and dropped them into the water. As she stirred the water, she told Yot it would help with their milk, help them lactate. At first the mice seemed to be swimming in the swirl, but before he knew it, the water started to boil. And then his mother picked the mice out, put them in a pan and fried them.

When he tells the story, I can always see the moment on my father's face when, as a young boy, he realized the mice were no longer swimming but were being cooked.

"And then after she fried them, it looked so appetizing. So I ate them. We both ate a little of them, but I probably had two of them."

After that came the mischievous years. From the age of ten to the age of twelve, Yot was always getting into trouble with his mother, always testing her patience, always getting spanked.

He went to school. He swam in the pond. On New Year's Day he got to light firecrackers. There was a small mountain behind his village, five or six miles away, and he dreamed of climbing it.

He also had a friend named Bok Yao, a boy who lived next door and was a year younger than him. They went to school together but Bok Yao had to endure a particularly difficult childhood. As a small child he'd developed boils all over his head. The boils caused scaring, which caused patches of his scalp to go bald, and the other children often made fun of him for it. Later, as an adult, after immigrating to America, he'd shave off all of his hair so that he wouldn't have to be bothered by those patches of baldness any longer.

Yot and Bok Yao liked to play together and one day, when Yot was eleven, they were walking in the fields and found a piece of bark with some glue on it. The bark came from trees that grew around the village and, if the bark was stripped from a tree, beat to a pulp, and kneaded with water, it would produce a glue or sticky paste. The glue wasn't strong enough to be used in carpentry or repairs but the older boys in the village liked to catch birds with it. They'd place a piece of bark in the rice fields with some seeds on it, then place several other pieces of sticky bark close by. A bird, poking at the seeds, would catch its wing on the sticky bark and flounder about, unable to fly away. The boys would then take the bird home and cook it with herbs to turn it into a small meal.

Yot and Bok Yao also liked to play with cicadas, those small winged insects known for their loud, whining buzz. The boys were sticking cicadas with glue that day when Bok Yao momentarily turned to look away. And Yot quietly placed a piece of bark on his head.

"Guess where I put it," Yot said.

He thinks now that if Bok Yao had simply lifted the sticky bark gently from his hair the whole joke would've ended just fine. But Bok Yao grabbed it hard, in fear, pressing it deeper into his hair. And then he and Yot struggled to get it out, making it stick even more. Then Bok Yao screamed in panic, which made Yot scream in panic. Then Bok Yao ran, which made Yot run.

When Bok Yao got home, his mother had to cut the bark out with a pair of scissors, taking a big chunk of hair with it. Then she told Yot's mother about it.

"That was exactly what she didn't want me to do," my father said. "That was bad behavior. The reward was that I got a bad spanking."

His brother Fon, by comparison, never seemed to get into trouble. His grandmother loved him. She and his mother considered Fon the good boy while Yot was the little monkey.

Yot's mother would always say, "Why can't you behave like your older brother?"

And Yot would reply, "Well he's three years older than me!"

But his worst punishment came when he snuck away to see an opera.

There was a village about a mile away where a clan of Wongs had built a temple for worshipping Quan Yin, the Goddess of Mercy. Quan Yin bestowed families with health and peace, and every February the villagers hired an opera company to perform in honor of her birthday. One year, when Yot was still eleven, he and several friends from school talked about going to see the show.

He had an aunt who lived in the village, and his mother had taken Yot and Fon to the opera the year before, but this year his mother had had a quarrel with her sister and forbade Yot from visiting her. Yot told his mother he wanted to see the show and his mother replied, "Well you can't go."

But go he did. On the day of the show a parade swept through Tin Sum and Yot and his friends followed the parade to his aunt's village. His friends returned home but Yot stayed. He'd gotten carried away, but was also aware that he was defying his mother's wishes, and for him it felt a little like running away from home. He stopped in to see his aunt who said, "You just stay here and enjoy the show and you can go home later." So he did, sleeping overnight at her house.

The next morning he met a girl about his own age and they went strolling through the market, seeing what the vendors had to offer. There were bamboo stalls all around and he and the girl paused at a stall selling dumplings when suddenly Yot's mother grabbed him by the arm. When he hadn't come home that night she knew exactly where he had gone and went to track him down. She dragged him, pulling him hard by the arm, all the way home.

And there she gave him a whipping so hard and so furious that he cried, and cried out in such pain that his mother realized she'd overdone it, and she fell to her knees and held him, and they both cried together. And now, even when he retells the story, he laughs at how funny and ridiculous and hurtful that moment was.

"That was the last beating she ever gave me."

He also realized how much his mother loved him, and that he might've been her favorite.

But a year later, he started eyeing the mountain behind his village. The mountain has a flat top, as if missing its peak, and they used to call it The Mountain With The Head Cut Off.

I've seen the mountain. It's low and small and sits behind fields of uneven, brushy terrain.

"We tried to climb the mountain," he told me. "Well, I climbed it once. As a little kid, you can't climb very high but once, eventually, after I grew up a little bit, I managed to get up to the top." And thinking back on his achievement, he added, "Once in a lifetime is enough."

He returned home that night to face an angry mother. "Don't do that again," she told him. But he didn't get a spanking or a whipping, and he knew that now that he'd made the climb there was nothing she could do about it. She couldn't take it away from him.

They once ran low on food.

It was the middle of the year, just before the summer harvest in June. They were waiting for money from their father but it hadn't arrived in quite some time. The rice plants hadn't matured enough so they were living as they normally did off the rice stored in their large terra cotta urn.

The urn sat in their grandmother's bedroom. It was short, squat and round, and reminded Yot of a little fat person about twenty inches tall. It had an open top that they covered with a round wooden board and the urn could hold about a hundred pounds of rice. Every family had an urn like this.

Sun Moon would use a piece of bamboo called a *mai sing*, or "rice measurer", to scoop out the rice for their daily meals. Bamboo was used because its hollow, sectioned culms made handy measuring cups. But as the days went on, she noticed their supply of rice slowly dwindling lower.

Yot was eight years old at the time. He didn't see his mother's worry, not at first, but noticed that every day their portions got smaller and smaller.

"How come we got so little rice?"

His mother told them that she was trying to conserve what small amount remained by rationing out less and less.

"We're going to be running out any day now if your father doesn't send money right away."

She took even less rice for herself so that Yot, Fon and her husband's mother could have that much more, but still she tried to prepare them.

"You have to expect that we're not going to have enough."

Until finally the urn was empty and she had to go to her cousin and borrow some.

The next day a check arrived from America and Granduncle took it to the bank, cashed it, converted it, and brought over several rolls of double tens.

Years later, after meeting up with his father in America, Yot would tell him about that moment, when food became scarce and they wondered when the next check was coming.

"How come we weren't getting the money when we needed?"

It was between 1932 and 1933 when it happened, and his father told him that America had been in a depression and that he'd had trouble finding the money. He then told his son that he'd left some gold coins at his grandfather's house for just such an emergency. But somehow Yot's mother never heard about it; never knew the coins existed.

Brian and I are in the parking lot waiting for our bus. It's supposed to arrive every half hour but we've been standing here for a while now and Brian wonders if we missed it.

We're hungry. We both skipped lunch to walk the Wall so we start to wander around the lot. We walk toward the souvenir stands at the base of the sky lift. When I was here two years ago I saw a little restaurant off to one side of the lift and I remember being a little curious about it, so we start heading that way. The restaurant looks decent enough: a hardwood exterior, nice windows; inside the tables are covered with flimsy, disposable, white plastic sheets; but the only people we see when we enter are the staff sitting at a table in the back, and as the door closes they suddenly all turn to look at us.

Brian stops in place and I can tell he's noticed this too. When the host asks if we'd like a seat, Brian asks if we can see a menu first. The man gladly hands us one and we stand at a table turning the pages.

"What do you think?" I ask.

"There's no one here," he says under his breath. He says it in a way I'd normally expect a westerner to say it, and his next words nearly make me laugh out loud.

"It's a dive."

With that single phrase he's not only demonstrated his knowledge of American colloquialisms but his own generation's expectation of quality.

We politely decline a seat and as we walk back to the parking lot a local man approaches us. He's an older man, a little scrawny, and he offers us a ride in his rickety little van for fifteen yuan apiece. That's a little less than two U.S. dollars each. He'll drive us into Huairou, he tells us, where we can catch a connecting bus back to Beijing.

We share the ride with another man and a young couple and I realize the driver probably makes his living off of people like us who have missed the bus, or at least people he can convince have missed the bus. At two U.S. dollars each the margins for his business must be pretty slim, but if he's the only one doing it, and does it several times a day, he's probably making a steady living.

When we reach Huairou we have an hour before the next bus arrives so Brian suggests we get dinner. There's a restaurant right behind the bus stop so we go there. We sit down and the hostess hands us two menus. Brian looks at his, then holds it up and smiles, "It's called the Hillbilly Cafe."

I'm fortunate to have made contact with Brian. The day before, after bicycling around Beijing, we went to the Li Qun Roast Duck Restaurant. It was at my request and Brian had had the forethought to call ahead to make a reservation. The restaurant's specialty is Peking duck roasted in a brick oven over firewood. Each duck takes about forty-five minutes to make. They have about five chefs and the one who cooks your duck brings it to your room on a metal tray and carves it on a small table near your own. While there, I noticed that most of the customers were Caucasian. The explanation soon became obvious. The bill for two people came to about thirty U.S. dollars, higher than most restaurants we visited, and higher than I assume most Beijing residents are willing to spend. Brian later introduced me to the owner, an older, silver-haired man with a modest, happy smile. He wore a simple, loose, dark brown autumn jacket and as we stepped outside, to the front of his charcoal-colored brick restaurant, he told me that when he first opened, he served five ducks a day. Today he serves about forty ducks a day. He said his business became really successful after it was featured on the Discovery Channel and, as a show of his contentedness, he slowly ended his story with t'ai chi movements of his arms and legs.

The restaurant isn't far from my hotel on Wangfujing, the shopping district. After riding around the hutongs we dropped our bicycles off and Brian and I tried to catch a taxi to the Li Qun but none of the drivers would oblige. The restaurant is less than a mile away but it's a modest little place in a narrow, dusty, gray hutong. It's in the middle of nothing really, and the drivers all considered it a waste of their time. But our reservation was coming up so we jogged there. During our jog I found out Brian was also a runner, sometimes running five miles a day.

Once our duck was finally placed in front of us, Brian showed me how to eat it. I didn't mind the demonstration. The Peking duck I've had in the states usually comes with little flat white buns, but this order came with a small plate of paper-thin white rice crepes. Using his chopsticks, Brian peeled one off, put some meat on it, dipped some slivers of green onion into a small dish of sweet brown sauce, then folded the whole thing up before taking a bite. I know it's not exactly rocket science but he was so adept at pulling that sticky crepe off the others, using nothing except his chopsticks, that it was a total joy to watch.

After we finished, we asked the waitress to put the leftovers in a container and I told Brian that he should take it home. He insisted I take it back with me.

"I don't have a refrigerator in my room," I said.

"I don't either."

"You don't? Where do you keep your food?"

"I usually eat at school. We have a cafeteria that serves good food. I don't do much cooking, but if I do I buy only enough vegetables for one night and if I have any leftovers I have to put it in a pot. But I have to eat it the next day or else it'll go bad."

"Where do you put the pot?"

"On a table. I cover it with a lid and I just put it out on a table."

"You don't worry about pests? Ants or mice?"

"Sometimes. But I eat it the next day."

Two years ago, when my sister and I planned our previous trip to China, we'd heard that Beijing wasn't known for its cuisine. As my brother Mike told me, "I think the food in any American Chinatown is better than the food in Beijing. It's just not very special." And the restaurants that our travel agent booked for us seemed to confirm this. The first lunch we had in Beijing was so utterly unappetizing. The tofu sat in a clumpy, not completely congealed, brown sauce, the vegetables were swimming in oil, and the rice was soggy. I'm always astounded when a Chinese chef can't cook rice correctly. The trick is simply to rinse the rice thoroughly so that all the excess starch is cleaned off before you cook it. The cook would almost have to go out of his way to make all his vats of rice that soggy.

But now, on the second day of our second trip, I'm sitting in the Hillbilly Cafe with Brian and we're eating tofu noodles with cilantro. The noodles have such a perfect balance of firmness and ease that they still retain the texture of the cheesecloth that pressed them. We're trying lean and fat beef: strips of meat with dark and fatty beef packed together to make deliciously striped ribbons. And we're enjoying a potato and corn chowder with a smooth but spicy milk sauce.

After dinner we catch our connecting bus back to Beijing. It's so crowded we have to stand for the entire hour-long trip. On the outskirts of Huairou, just before the city turns into a patch of farms and fields and highway, two men enter carrying crates of squawking chickens and a dead pig tied to a long wood pole. They place the crates in the middle of the aisle then hoist the pole up between their shoulders. The pig dangles between the seated passengers, some of them wearing suits and dresses, and no one blinks an eye.

I smile at Brian. There's a rapidly growing class divide in his country. I see it in the two men and wonder if he sees it too.

The year is 2006.

It's five-thirty in the morning. I'm taking one last run around Beijing before we board our plane to Guangzhou. In a little side street beside our hotel I see some small lights behind the trees. I see some people shuffling in the darkness. I get closer and notice they're food vendors setting up for breakfast.

I'm running past them. They wear cheap down jackets, long cotton jackets, scarves and caps. It's chilly outside. I see them only by the dim glow of the street lamps and their own lanterns. They cook on portable steamers and grills that they've set up beside makeshift tables. Some have even set up long conference tables. Most are elderly and I notice them selling food to younger city workers. They serve steamed pork buns, dumplings and thin green onion pancakes. Outside a small brick shelter, one man has set up a tower of bamboo steamers and a barbeque where he grills meat on thin wooden skewers.

They remind me of the vendors I saw when I was nine years old and my parents took us to China for the first time. Some of the men would attach a small cart to the front of their bicycles and ride it around town. Others would push a cart to the middle of a street or park it by an empty corner, unfold a small table and chair, and cook up a tray of beef or pork in a dark sauce that smelled salty and sweet. To the side would be a small tub filled with water for washing dishes. The water in the tub wasn't even soapy. Every now and then I'd see an old man sitting at a rickety metal table, in a rickety metal chair, eating a bowl of food with chopsticks while reading a newspaper. Once I even saw a young couple eating dinner beside a cart. Our parents tended to hold our hands tightly whenever we walked through the city and as I passed by the carts I would lean toward them like a dog tugging on its leash.

"Ma, can we try some?"

"No, it's not clean."

To vindicate that memory I promised myself I would taste some street food on this trip but I realize I've forgotten to bring any money with me so I continue running.

I pass by Beijing West Railway Station. It's the largest train station in Asia. From the back of the hotel it looks like a giant fortress topped with a temple but here, in front of the station, I see people sleeping outside on the sidewalk. A few use flimsy cardboard for their bedding. Some sleep right on the cold concrete using their jackets rolled up as headrests. Most sleep in groups, lying side by side. They look like migrant workers and poor family members traveling together.

I know it's a little dangerous running around a place I'm unfamiliar with; Tiffany even warned us to stay away from this area; but I love exploring a city like this. When I was training for the San Francisco marathon earlier in the year I would get out of bed at four in the morning to hit the streets. I could go as slow or as fast as I wanted, run through the intersections, and just enjoy the open, quiet roads. The only people I saw were the homeless sleeping in the Haight Street doorsteps and the crab fishermen sitting on the pier. I felt like I owned the entire city.

I loop around the block and enter Lianhuachi Lotus Park just as the workers open up the gates. The sun is starting to paint the sky purple and pink. Lianhuachi Lotus Park is behind my hotel, between the hotel and the train station. There's a large pond in the middle. I see some employees cleaning the walkways with leaf brooms. There are elderly people playing ping pong. Outside a small courtyard I hear some music playing from inside a blue tiled building. It's an old tape playing some warbled Beatles music.

It's one o'clock in the afternoon. We're on the plane to Guangzhou. Nancy, Leslie and I are on one side of the aisle. My father is on the other. Beijing hovers at roughly the same latitude as Detroit, and Guangzhou sits where the Florida Keys would be. It's late October and Beijing has cool windbreaker weather, while Guangzhou is hot and sticky. Leslie has been following the weather on the English news stations and tells us to expect 90 degrees Fahrenheit. It'll be a rise of almost thirty degrees.

The flight attendants serve us a lunch of steamed pork and green beans in black bean sauce over rice. It comes in a round metal container and the rice is bouncy and soft. The pork is tender, just a little overcooked. The sauce is rich and oily. Slightly bitter and slightly salty. It's perfect and delicious.

A Chinese movie is playing on the overhead monitors. The story is about a peasant girl on a bus traveling with some farmers and their animals. She meets a young man with glasses, an intellectual of some sort, and they fall in a chaste kind of love as the girl helps her fellow passengers. The girl has long braided pigtails and a dimpled smile. She's the kind of girl I remember seeing in pictures of Maoist opera, only sweeter and less militant. This is a romantic comedy, although the girl does spout some proletariat platitudes. The bus breaks down, the passengers get off, the farm animals run amok, and the girl solves every crisis with plucky resourcefulness.

Her intelligence and determination reminds me of Tiffany. On the way to the airport we got to enjoy one last conversation with her. She's the only child in her family, she told us.

Under the one-child policy, if you give birth to only one child, your child is guaranteed an education. If you give birth to two children, you face fines that can approximate your annual income. The Chinese government frowns on abortions but some parents, so intent on having a boy, will abort if they find out the child is a girl. The result is that the current generation of Chinese is disproportionately male. There are almost twenty percent more males than females in China.

At first, Tiffany told us, her family was a little disappointed that she was a girl but the disappointment didn't last long. Her parents and grandparents are very proud of her now and happy that she's chosen a career as a translator. We asked how she's managed to stay so fluent.

"I belong to a group that practices English. We get together every week to practice. And I also have friends in America that I sometimes talk to."

At the airport, we say our goodbyes and give Tiffany and our driver Mr. Guo a tip of 775 Chinese yuan apiece, or the equivalent of 100 US dollars each, folded into two lucky red envelopes.

I'm finishing up my lunch.

It's two years before I meet Brian. Two years before we visit the Hillbilly Cafe.

The food on this flight is better than anything we've had in Beijing so far. I say this to Leslie and she agrees. We also agree that we're looking forward to the food in Guangzhou.

6

Yot learned to swim at the age of seven, in the same pond his father did.

His father wasn't there to teach him so he had to learn on his own, mostly by watching the other boys, especially the older ones. Sometimes the water was the only relief he got during those hot, humid months. He'd see boys as old as twenty swimming as early as spring, as soon as the heavy rains subsided around May; and they'd continue jumping into the water well into autumn, when the weather started cooling down around October.

There were about a dozen boys in the village and sometimes Yot would see them all in the water with him. He typically wore cotton shorts, a simple pair of pants his mother had sewn for him for everyday use. Swimming wasn't taught in school so whenever Yot and Fon got the chance, they'd both be in the water trying to imitate the others.

They all did something called "beating the water drum". Yot couldn't remember where the phrase came from; it was just something everyone said. They would try floating on their stomachs and, trying not to submerge their heads, lift their feet up and kick, trying to push themselves forward. Sometimes they'd pound with their arms and hands too, but mostly they used their legs and feet. He saw some of the older boys attempting what he'd later learn was the breast stroke, but for Yot, he beat the water drum year after year until one day — surprise! — he could float on his own, then move forward on his own.

The pond was large, rectangular, about five hundred feet long by a hundred fifty feet wide. One side started from the road, so a visitor would be greeted by the pond before even entering the village. The pond then spanned a tree, then a large open field where the villagers dried their rice, then passed four houses intermingled with four alleyways before ending on the other side at another tree.

And it wasn't very deep. There were spots that were five feet deep but Yot wouldn't swim there, not at first. In the beginning he'd enter the shallow areas, places where he could simply walk into the water.

The pond also had a ridge that lay three feet below the surface of the water. The ridge was a strip of solid ground running across the middle part, connecting the two steeper walls just off center, with one end starting just a short stroll from Yot's house. The water would be waist-high for him when he walked across that ridge. Before the villagers built the pond, when it was still just farmland, a feng shui master had told them that the ridge — or the path that existed before it became the ridge — was where a dragon, coming from the mountain in the west, running toward the east, passed through... so the villagers dug up the dirt on either side of the path, leaving its surface just under the water for the feng shui, the harmony between the land and the people. Or as a villager once explained to Yot:

"That's where the dragon is running through."

Yot was under the assumption that Fon had learned to swim at the same time he had but it wasn't until high school, at their first indoor pool in America, that Yot was surprised to discover that his brother had been "beating the drum" but had never truly mastered the march. He asked Fon how much he'd learned and Fon replied, "Well I only swam ten feet or so."

It was at that nice, clean pool Yot realized how dirty the water in his own pond had been. He'd suspected, but hadn't known for sure. For him, the water had smelled just fine. It tasted fine too, like any old water. Some of the other villages had dead ponds where no fish could live but Yot's pond had plenty of small fish. The boys could see the algae and grime but it tended to stay on the surface, and usually floated away to the sides, and mostly to the south side of the pond, whenever they'd kick and thrash about.

And Yot enjoyed swimming so much he often got carried away with it. His mother would try to set a time limit, telling him, "You go in, and when I come out to call you, you have to come out. You can only be there for so long."

Then, after an hour, she'd yell, "Come on out!"

But he'd continue frolicking about until finally she'd grab her laundry pole, a ten-foot-long bamboo stick she used to dry clothes, and step up to the edge of the water, threatening to whack him. He hadn't yet learned to swim to the deep part or the middle, so he knew she could reach out and hit him if she wanted, and just the very sight of her, standing menacingly with that pole, was enough to make him hurry out of the water.

Perhaps it was all for the best because the pond was also the village dumping ground. Yot sometimes saw water buffalos pee in the water. They'd shit in the water too if the farmers didn't consider it so valuable as fertilizer that they'd quickly try to catch every last little clump by holding a bucket behind them. Sometimes the farmers would try to catch the buffalos' urine too but the buffalo were too fast, pissing right into the pond or doing it while wading into the water.

And after a rain, sewage water from the streets would pour right into the pond. Or whenever the villagers dug up an old corpse to relocate the body, they'd throw the coffin into the water. After a while, they'd pull the coffin out, cleaned by its grotesque wash, and use the wood for other purposes. Or sometimes after a swim, Yot and Fon would get bitten by the tiny, tiny red bugs they called water fleas, and if they didn't brush or pull them off, their legs would itch all over.

Most of the boys knew enough to dry and clean out their ears after a swim, and Yot knew this too, but often forgot to. One summer he got an ear infection and he told his mother, "All of a sudden, my ear is hurting."

"That's what happens when you go into the water too much," she replied.

Then both ears got infected and he began to feel a sharp pain. The pain would subside, become a dull, soft, lingering pain, and during those times he would try to sit as comfortably as he could, or lean back, and try not to do anything to disturb it, but the sharp pain would come back and finally the infection got so bad that pus started to run out of his ears. He would cry and his mother said, "If you're like that, we have to go see a doctor."

She took him to the small town of Shui Bu not too far away, where a doctor gave him ear drops, and for the next few months Yot's mother administered them to his ears.

His ears healed, and he continued swimming, each year becoming a better and better swimmer, but each year he'd get another ear infection, some lasting days or weeks, and slowly he noticed his hearing diminishing a little more with each passing year.

One day he was playing outside his house when a friend of his called out to him. His friend was five years older, and bigger too, and often protected Yot from some of the bullies of the neighboring villages. He also helped Yot do things he couldn't do himself. Yot once owned a little pet sparrow and when he accidentally let it go, his older friend climbed the front of his house to retrieve it for him. On the day his friend called out, he asked Yot to do him a quick favor.

"Yot, go to my mother and get me two ropes."

The word for rope, *sin*, sounds like the word for money, *tin*, so Yot walked to his friend's house and asked his mother for two dollars.

"What does he want two dollars for?" the boy's mother asked. Two dollars was a lot of money and people weren't too eager to give it away, so she said, "You tell him to come home and get it."

Yot went back and told his friend and his friend was forced to get it himself. When he came back with two pieces of rope, he said, "This is what I asked you to get."

And that was when Yot realized his hearing was a lot worse than he thought.

Attending a swimming class was part of the curriculum at Hutchins, and it was there that Fon finally learned to swim, mostly by diving into the water and using the momentum to propel himself forward.

After a year, Miss Blackrow promoted both Yot and Fon. She said to Yot:

"You have now completed your English lesson here. Next school year you're going to go to a regular school and start from the seventh grade. Fon is going to the ninth grade."

She filled out a form, signed it, and handed it to him.

Looking back, he wished he could've spent one more year under her tutelage. He recalled a college student who'd returned to Hutchins by his own volition to polish his speaking skills. One more year, Yot thought, would've greatly improved his own English.

But as instructed, the following September he took his form to the administration office at Durfee Middle School, handed it to a girl behind the counter, and began his next semester at the new school.

Fon went to Central High School for a year, then to Cass Technical, where Yot eventually joined him. It was there, in high school, that Yot noticed his hearing had deteriorated even more. Sitting in the back of the classroom, he heard only two thirds of what his teacher was saying. Sometimes his teacher asked Yot a question and Yot had to ask him to repeat it. He mentioned the problem to his teacher but didn't want to ask for any special treatment; seating had already been assigned and Yot was too shy to request being moved up front; so his teacher spoke a little louder and Yot continued as best he could.

By late 1940 he was sixteen years old. It was a busy time for his brother and him. Most of their hours were spent between school and the restaurant, and every two or three months they'd receive a letter from their mother.

Their mother had a very limited education. She hadn't gone to school as a child and it wasn't till after she'd gotten married and took in her maid that she finally had time to go to school to learn to read and write. By the time her two sons said their farewells to her, they'd received better schooling than she had.

She wrote to them using a brush and ink on Chinese paper. The ink came from a black ink stick called a *mak chui*. It was a solid concentration of ink which she'd buy at the market, take home, and put in a dish with some water, just as Yot had done when he was a child. She'd grind the stick into the water, let it dissolve into the proper solution of black ink, then, using a small goat hair brush, write her words in Chinese characters.

Her letters, usually written to both Fon and Yot, said things like:

Be sure you behave and go to school.

Study hard and listen to your father. Do what he tells you to do.

Or simply:

Make sure you study hard.

The brush she used was made of either goat hair or sheep hair, although Yot remembered people referring to them as goat hair brushes. The hair of the brush was thin and soft and some calligraphers were so adept with it that they could write extremely small Chinese characters. The paper she wrote on was typical Chinese stationary: a thin white paper with fine red lines running up and down, printed for guidance. The paper was so thin it could absorb ink in such a way that the solution wouldn't spread too quickly and ruin the calligraphy.

Her words often contained the usual parental advisements:

When you're home and at the restaurant always
make sure you listen to your father.

Always work when you have to and always help
out at the restaurant.

And make sure you keep yourself out of trouble.
And do not cause problems for your father.

But they almost always ended with:

I miss you.

Or:

I miss you two and I'm always thinking about
you.

Sometimes she would say:

You should write back more often.

Keep writing.

Or she'd tell Yot that she would love to hear from him.

And Yot wanted to write back, always intended to, but only managed to write two or three times a year.

When he did, he'd also use a brush and ink. In China, he'd used a brush and a pencil to do his schoolwork, and it wasn't until he arrived in America that he started using a fountain pen. Still, he liked using that goat hair brush to write his personal words. From a Chinese store in Detroit he bought a bottle of ink, and from the bottle he'd pour ink into an ink box that contained a bed of cotton. The cotton absorbed and held the blackness. And the box, with its small pictures on the side, reminded him of the one he'd used in China. When he wrote to his mother, his letters often began with an apology:

I'm sorry I cannot write more often.

He told her about school and how he learned to ride a bicycle and how he delivered food on the bicycle. He didn't think his mother would understand what was involved in working at a restaurant but he told her anyhow, knowing she'd enjoy it.

His letters were usually a page long, and he was more likely to write if he did so immediately after receiving hers, although he still couldn't match Fon's frequency.

When his mother would write, she'd send her correspondence to the address of the restaurant, and if the boys were around when the mailman brought it inside, they'd find it in a glass case at the front of the store. If not, their father would hand it to them when they got home from school.

"Here's a letter from mother."

"Oh good."

Their father received his own letters, and after he was finished, he'd let the boys read them. Once, Yot noticed that his mother told his father:

Yot is too lazy to write.

Another time she wrote words to the effect of:

Maybe you should get me over to the United States. The two boys are growing up and pretty soon they'll be ready to be married.

It was the strongest hint Yot had ever seen her make.

At about the same time, Yot's father started mentioning the possibility of selling his restaurant. Sometimes Yot would hear him say, "If anyone wants to buy it, I'll sell it."

He had grown it from a one-man operation to a business that employed a waiter, three cooks, and now his two sons. For a short time he'd even hired a woman as a hostess, which was a common thing to do, but she didn't stay very long, perhaps a year, which was the typical duration.

At maximum occupancy the restaurant could seat a little under sixty customers. It had seven tables and eight booths, and the booths were like compartments: tiny rooms built against the walls with tables that held anywhere between six to nine people. The compartments were separated by high wood slats and at one point Quong even hung curtains on the door-like frames to give his customers privacy if they so desired. It was the kind of decor that was very much in vogue at the time.

But Quong was ready to part with it. He'd been contemplating a visit back to China to see his wife again and his sons thought that that was a good idea. "We were glad he was going back to China because my mother would like to see him again," Yot recalled. So when one of the young men who'd once lived with them, Robert T. Lim, told his own father that the Pacific Garden was available, Robert and his father found some fellow buyers and all together, comprising a total of four partners, they made Quong an offer, and Quong accepted it.

Quong wasn't terribly worried about what would happen to his sons in his absence. He knew he could put them up with friends and that it would be better for them if they stayed. They were still in school, their English was improving, and they had derivative citizenship: they were the children of an American citizen. So Quong arranged for them to live with a friend of his, Mr. Toy, the owner of a restaurant called La Fong Gardens, just down the street. His sons were familiar with Mr. Toy. When they'd first arrived in the country, Mr. Toy dropped by to visit, and later, when he needed some assistance, Quong asked Yot if he wanted to wash dishes for Mr. Toy, which Yot gladly did for two weeks. Mr. Toy had a business similar to their father's. He employed two cooks, a waiter and a dishwasher. One of the cooks had a young son and they all lived on the second floor of the La Fong Gardens' storefront. With its makeshift living room and bedrooms, the floor served as shared housing, and Mr. Toy occupied the bedroom in the back.

"You go and stay with Mr. Toy," Quong told his two sons, and then in preparation for his trip, he moved himself into a small hotel room in Detroit.

Yot would never truly figure out what "La Fong" meant. He just assumed Mr. Toy was giving his restaurant a little flair by trying to make it sound French. But he still had a great respect for Mr. Toy. Mr. Toy was one of the few Chinese men Yot knew of who'd gotten an American college education. In China, Mr. Toy had even received the equivalent of a high school education, which was an impressive accomplishment itself.

Mr. Toy was only a couple years older than their own father but tended to act older. With his gray hair, always trimmed into a crew cut, he looked a lot older too. He also tended to walk a little funny, and after Yot got to know him well enough he would jokingly ask, "How come you walk like that?"

"The corns are bothering me."

The boys liked Mr. Toy, and they'd expected that during their time in America they'd have to move about, so they did as their father instructed and one afternoon packed up all their belongings. They didn't own much. Some clothes, books, a few personal items. Everything Yot owned could be packed into a single suitcase. They moved from their own apartment to Mr. Toy's in the space of an hour and soon became La Fong Gardens' new dishwasher and kitchen help.

Were they sad to see their father leave? How did it feel to move in with another group of men after only two years?

"We had to accept it. That was the life," Yot remembered. At least his brother was moving with him. They still had each other. "Wherever we go, we go together. Whatever comes up, comes up."

But even before Quong sold his restaurant, while he was still planning his trip, he sensed trouble on the horizon. And it was coming from his uncle.

His uncle, Yan Toy Lim, had originally came to work on the railroads but settled in Detroit, opening a Chinese laundry and taking on the American nickname, Charlie. When Quong emigrated to America he purported to be his uncle's son. He had his uncle's cooperation, and it wasn't too uncommon a thing to do. If a Chinese immigrant like his uncle became an American citizen, he could claim to have children in the old country and then pass along, or even sell, the identities of those children to others. Men who bought those identities were known as paper sons; women were paper daughters.

But Uncle Charlie's story went one step further. He'd arrived in San Francisco just before the turn of the century and was living in the city when the 1906 earthquake struck. The Hall of Records was destroyed in the resulting fire, and with it burned all proof of birth, marriage, and citizenship. Afterward, when government officials asked everyone to reestablish their identities, a number of Chinese saw an opportunity to claim America as their birth country, instantly making themselves American citizens. It didn't matter if they had accents or not; officials had to take their word for it. And Charlie was among them. Or so the story goes.

So Quong was a paper son of a false father, and he arrived accompanied by three similar siblings. One of them, a woman named Rose, was his uncle's real daughter. But the other two, like Quong, only pretended to be his uncle's sons. They weren't related to Charlie like Quong was so they were forced to pay for the privilege. Their identities cost only a couple hundred dollars apiece but wages for Chinese immigrants weren't very high. A cook made only fifty dollars a month. A waiter made fifteen dollars a month. One of the paper sons found a job at a Ford factory, which provided a reliable enough living... but then he fell in love with Rose and married her.

Unfortunately the same paper son also had trouble paying off his identity, and this agitated Charlie to no end. He started complaining to the paper son's real father, demanding payment, but that didn't get very far, so he started making threats, and that was when Quong realized his commotion could hurt them all. His

Uncle Charlie was well connected in Detroit and threatened to go to City Hall if he didn't get his money, and he didn't care if he risked exposing his own nephew, his own daughter, or his now delinquent paper son-in-law. And one day, making good on his threat, he did exactly that, going to the police station on Beaubien Street.

There, a customer of his, a city prosecutor, noticed him.

Charlie, the prosecutor said, what are you doing here?

Charlie told him that his son and daughter had married and were living in illegal matrimony.

Charlie, don't you worry about it, we'll take care of it for you.

The prosecutor then issued an arrest warrant for Rose and the paper son, and the two turned themselves in. The next day Charlie went to the prosecutor to recant his story, but it was too late. The prosecutor told him that overnight, while they were locked up, the two had revealed everything. They weren't a brother and sister engaged in an incestuous relationship so the prosecutor dropped those charges...but now he had another issue to investigate.

Quong's worries were about to be confirmed. When he went to the immigration bureau to apply for a passport he was told by an official that there was a case pending against him and the official confiscated his citizenship papers.

It had been fifteen years since Quong last visited his village. Fifteen years since he'd last seen his young wife. Without a passport he wouldn't be able to leave the country. His citizenship was now in question and, by extension, so were his sons'. At least the boys still had their papers, those little slips three inches wide by eight inches long that said Yot and Fon were the children of an American. It allowed them some privileges, but not many.

So Quong busied himself by traveling instead to New York and Washington D.C. He had friends in both cities and when he returned to Michigan, he joined his two sons at La Fong Gardens. The only thing he could do now was work, and wait.

A year later, on December 7, 1941, the Japanese attacked Pearl Harbor.

It was Sunday evening when they heard about Pearl Harbor. Seven o'clock, dinner time, and La Fong Gardens was filled with customers.

Yot was washing dishes. Fon had become a waiter by then. He wasn't on his shift that night, but was in the restaurant. Their father had returned as a cook and was working in the kitchen. The radio was playing in the back of the dining room. It sat high up on a silverware shelf against a wall by the kitchen. Mr. Toy always left the radio on for music, but that evening the music was interrupted by a special broadcast.

Yot remembered that everyone started wondering what the news was all about, "so they all stopped talking to listen to the radio to comprehend what was going on. Right away we heard Hawaii had been bombed, Pearl Harbor had been bombed, and we didn't know how many ships were destroyed but gradually we heard more facts. They said they identified a Japanese plane that attacked Pearl Harbor."

The customers remained seated but Yot, Fon, their father and Mr. Toy gathered under the radio to hear more.

"Our reaction was a little surprised. We didn't expect Japan to start a war like that. At the time they sent a special envoy to Washington to talk about a peace treaty. That surprised everyone.

"We thought, 'Oh no, they're going to start a war.' We thought it was going to be inevitable that the United States would join the war. If the United States joined the war it would help China because they would draw most of the firing power from China. It would divert Japan away from China.

"We thought the war wasn't going to last too long, maybe a year or two because the big navy in Hawaii will just pound the Japanese, but then we heard the talk on the radio and heard they destroyed all those ships."

Yot's father also expressed doubts about how fast the war would go. He said that if Japan attacked the United States it might last longer than they thought because if they were bold enough to attack, they might have enough armed forced to last a few years.

"The next day president FDR went to congress to call a special session of both houses to ask congress to pass an act to declare war on Japan, Germany and Italy."

About a week later, one of the cooks told everyone else in the restaurant, "You should all get a pin." He told them about some small chest pins that were being distributed in Chinatown.

Detroit's Chinatown was small; little more than a block long. It was located on Third Street near Porter, just south of Michigan Avenue, and there the On Leong Merchants Association was handing out the pins for free. The pins were made by a group Yot remembers as the Chinese Overseas Patriotic Organization. "Some Chinese people had already gotten beat up in certain areas so we were in a hurry to get a pin so we could be recognized, so we wouldn't be confused." The pins were small, about an inch wide and squarishly rectangular in shape. "It had a Chinese flag on it and underneath it said, 'China' so it was easy to recognize." The pins were supposed to be worn by the Chinese whenever they went out or were going to be seen in public. Most shirts back then had pockets on the left side so a person simply attached the pin to his shirt pocket. If he wore a coat, he attached it to the same area on the outside of his coat.

"The shock vibrated across the whole country. Then we heard a Japanese submarine surfaced on the west coast and attacked the United States. After that, they wondered what they were going to do about the Japanese on the west coast."

In the newspaper, Yot read about the rounding up of Japanese American citizens for internment camps. "People were angry." Japanese Americans on the west coast were forced to sell their homes, their land, their businesses and most of their personal possessions. "At the time we were all agreed that might be the best way, to round them up and move them inland." Later, "We saw newsreels about the camps. We saw them at the theater." He remembered that "everyone wanted to see the news."

America's involvement in the war elevated it to the status of a World War, but it wouldn't be called World War II until the following year. Even so, it would serve only as a backdrop to the problems Yot, Fon and Quong were already facing.

There was a reason why Fon wasn't working the night they'd heard about Pearl Harbor. Earlier that year, around October, he'd been working as a part time waiter at La Fong Gardens and occasionally assisting at another restaurant, King Fong Gardens. He was nineteen at the time, still attending Cass Technical High School, and was such a dedicated student that if he didn't finish his studies early enough in the day he'd be sure to study after the dinner shift and before the next morning. His father had left the restaurant one evening, returning to his hotel room in Detroit, and the two boys were studying in the apartment above La Fong Gardens, in separate rooms, when Fon started coughing. He coughed so hard he took himself to the bathroom.

Then, immediately after, he came and fetched Yot.

"I just spit some blood up."

He asked Yot to come take a look, and there, in the bathroom, Fon showed Yot the deep red blood against the bright white porcelain toilet.

"Oh my," said Yot. "We should tell dad about it."

If Fon had been feeling ill before that moment, Yot knew his brother would never have said a thing. But they both knew what the coughing up of blood meant.

The next day Fon informed his father when he arrived at work and his father said, "We'll think this over and find out the best way to handle this." His father then arranged for Fon to see a doctor. They knew of a Dr. Sliken who had an office upstairs from the Pacific Garden Restaurant. He was the son-in-law of the landlord who owned the building and they shared the front staircase with him. Dr. Sliken examined Fon, took some X-rays, and the X-rays revealed a shadow on Fon's left lung.

They had known people who had contracted tuberculosis. Their mother's brother had died from it. It could be treated, and sometimes people recovered, but there was no definitive cure. The doctor suggested that Fon go to Wayne County Hospital and told him to think about what he wanted to do for treatment...but told him that he *had* to get treatment.

"At the time we heard the Arizona area, the Phoenix area, might be good because the air is warm and dry and we'd heard that dry weather was good for tuberculosis treatment," Yot recalled. Their father considered that as one of his options. "Another thing he considered was going to a private hospital. At the time private hospitals weren't that much but we knew after five or six months it could really be expensive."

Fon informed Mr. Toy, then stopped working. He also stopped going to school as his father contemplated what to do next. But after giving the matter some thought, Fon decided it would be better to go to the county hospital, so the doctor recommended Maybury Sanatorium, the facility known for admitting tuberculosis patients.

In February, Fon packed his suitcase and went to the outpatient clinic of Herman Kiefer Hospital. There, an ambulance, which arrived twice a week to deliver patients to Maybury, picked him up.

One of the first people to visit him at Maybury was a man named Harry Nelson. Harry Nelson was an older man in his fifties who worked as a sign painter in Plymouth, not too far from Northville where the sanatorium was located. Harry was a friend of Miss Blackrow and, while in Detroit one day, decided to drop by the restaurant. From the moment they met, he and Fon became great friends and before heading off for Maybury, Fon even stayed with Harry for a few days.

The first time Yot visited his brother, Harry Nelson gave him a ride in his black Ford. They drove through the sanatorium's tree-lined road to the south parking lot where Harry led Yot a few yards to the dark, two-story brick building that Fon was housed in. There he saw his brother lying in bed wearing his pajamas, looking as normal as ever, but "it was not a happy occasion, that's for sure," Yot recalled. Still, his brother didn't seem depressed. The depression had come when he'd first gotten confirmation of the disease but he now had a better idea of what his options were and besides, it was important not to get too depressed.

Afterward Harry Nelson showed Yot which bus routes would get him to the sanatorium and Yot found himself visiting his brother every two weeks, sometimes once a week. He would go on Sunday afternoon, his one day off from work. Miss Blackrow even accompanied him once.

To get there, Yot had to take a streetcar for three miles, get off, catch a bus and ride another five miles to the facility. The trip would take an hour each way. He became such a regular rider that once, when he was running late from the streetcar, the bus driver of his connecting bus, anticipating his arrival, even held the bus for him. When Yot arrived at Maybury, he would give his brother the latest news and deliver letters from his mother. For a while Yot's routine consisted entirely of school, the restaurant, homework, and seeing his brother.

Then one day Yot noticed that the letters from his mother stopped coming.

He knew something was wrong. He usually heard from his mother every two to three months but he was becoming aware that he hadn't received a letter from her in almost a whole year.

There could've been any number of reasons. Travel across the Pacific had become severely restricted. The Japanese now occupied Guangzhou and Hong Kong and this sometimes stopped all news and communication.

In the dining room of La Fong Gardens, in the back, was a booth where employees usually took their breaks and ate their meals. The booth was made of wood and was a deep mahogany in color; the chairs were covered with brown cushions; the table was an unvarnished wood and, like all the other tables in the restaurant, covered with a table cloth. Yot read most of his correspondence there. The mailman usually arrived mid-afternoon and would place the mail on a desk at the front. During a free moment, Mr. Toy would pick it up, go around the restaurant and hand each employee his due. It was just after the lunch shift one day and everyone was moving about, doing odds and ends, when Mr. Toy handed Yot his share, then ambled on. Yot looked forward to each delivery and if he received a letter from his mother, he'd open it right away. But that afternoon he noticed a letter from his grandmother, his father's mother.

His grandmother never wrote — so Yot knew immediately that it was bad news.

It was short. A single page. His grandmother didn't know how to read or write so Yot knew she had to have asked someone else, a neighbor or a more educated villager, to write it for her.

The letter doesn't exist any longer but Yot remembered it saying:

> Your mother was helping a great aunt who was sick and after the funeral a few days later she developed the same disease and died. She was sick for a few days.

There wasn't much more than that. Her words were sparse, but he understood their full meaning. Sitting at the table, he couldn't help himself, and he began to cry.

Mr. Toy, standing nearby, saw him and asked what happened.

"I got a letter from my grandmother telling me that my mother just passed away."

Softly Mr. Toy said, "I'm sad that you have to receive news like that."

Yot nodded his head, accepting his kindness. It was all he could muster.

He sat quietly with the letter for half an hour. The last thing he wanted to do was talk to anyone but then he realized he'd have to be the one to tell his father and brother. They were all living in separate places now; his father in his small hotel apartment and his brother at the sanatorium. Yot had gotten the letter because his relatives knew only of his address. And suddenly he felt so lonely.

His life had become so busy with school and work that the only time he saw his father was on the weekends, usually at night. His father's hotel apartment was on Clifford Street in downtown Detroit. Typically Yot would call, tell him when he expected to arrive, and his father would walk down to the front door to let him in. That day, his father suggested Yot meet him at a restaurant on Woodward.

Yot took the streetcar as he always did, and it was long ride. It was a cold evening and he wore his suede jacket. The restaurant where they met was a self-service diner. It was open twenty-four hours as most restaurants were now that there was a war on, and Yot arrived at eight o'clock.

When he walked in, his father was already seated, wearing a suit and tie, just as he always did. Wherever he went, he always wore a white shirt, suit and tie.

Yot didn't have to say a word. His father saw it on his young son's face.

"You look really sad," his father said. "The only thing that could make you sad like that is that your mother must've died."

And there in front of his father, Yot started to cry. But his father shed no tears.

He hadn't seen his wife in seventeen years but even so, he'd never been one for sentiment. He'd led a hard life and had become a hardened man. Yot could see that in his father.

After a while, Yot asked him how he knew.

"I felt something strange."

He couldn't explain what, his father said, but he felt that something unusual had happened.

He had to wait until the following week to see his brother, and on the next available Sunday, Yot took the long ride out to Maybury Sanatorium.

He wasn't looking forward to telling him the news. On the bus he kept thinking of all the possible things he could say.

"There were lots of thoughts going through my mind... trying to prepare how to tell him, to think of what to tell him."

But he had the letter with him; he could show him that.

Fon had been in the sanatorium for seven months now and whenever Yot walked in he'd enter with a pleasant demeanor. He would ask, "Hey, how are you doing?" or "How are you feeling?" or "Any improvement?"

One of the things Yot tried to do was help his brother pass the time. He brought whatever books or magazines Fon requested. There was a library on the grounds where patients could check out books and a small shop where they could buy magazines but Fon typically requested Chinese books and magazines. His favorite magazine was "The Great China Weekly," published in New York, which Yot would pick up from a little store in Chinatown. His brother also had a radio he listened to, and he shared his room with another patient. And the male patients often corresponded with the female patients in the sanatorium. Sometimes Yot would ask his brother about some young lady Fon was writing to. Anything to keep his brother cheerful and optimistic.

Usually when Yot stopped by, Fon's roommate would leave the room to let them talk. The two brothers spoke in Chinese anyhow but Fon's roommate would take the time to visit other patients.

On this arrival, Fon's roommate was already out of the room. When Yot walked in, Fon could tell right away that something was wrong.

"Sad news," Yot said.

Fon's first thought was that their grandmother had died but then Yot said, "I just got a letter from home, from grandma." He continued. "Ma just passed away. Possibly from a disease."

He didn't have much more information to offer so he handed Fon the letter. "Maybe you should read this."

There was a long silence. Tears started running down Fon's face. Neither brother knew how to console the other so they just started weeping together.

"Funny thing," Fon said, "I was dreaming about her the last couple weeks."

"That must be some kind of message."

They started to reminisce. They recalled a time when they were both sick with malaria and their mother took care of them. They were just children at the time. Yot was the sicker one but Fon could walk a little so she took Fon to see a doctor in Taishan. The doctor prescribed quinine and she made sure to get enough for both of them.

It made Yot think of how, whenever he was ill, he wanted to be with his mother, holding her. During that bout with malaria, while she was away with Fon, Yot lay in bed, tired and in pain. He kept asking for his mother and his grandmother had to calm him down.

Fon thought about the time his mother accompanied him when he left for the first time to go to school in Guangzhou.

The last time they'd seen her was four years ago on the ship in Hong Kong. They knew there was an epidemic in China but didn't know much more than that. Mostly they regretted leaving her so early and wished they could've seen her again.

Yot stayed an hour and a half until the nurse came by to tell him that visiting time was over. He asked for another ten minutes, and the nurse always gave it to him. When she came by again, Yot told his brother, as he always did, that he would see him again in two weeks. They both agreed that they needed to take care of themselves, and to keep themselves healthy, because that's how their mother wished they would be.

Yot would later discover that, according to the Chinese calendar, his mother died on July 3, 1942.

8

Yot Lim turned eighteen on October 1st, 1942.

There was no birthday celebration for him that year. No cake, no candles. Even when his brother and father had been living under the same roof, they didn't celebrate each other's birthdays. Their father had set the tone early during the boys' first year in the country. It just wasn't important to him. Besides, Yot had his own life to look after now. He was busy working, going to school, and didn't have much money to spend. He liked to joke that if he wanted a cake he would've had to have gone down to the store and bought one for himself.

It was a stark contrast to the happier but frugal life he'd had in China. His father's birthday was September 27th, just four days before Yot's, and his mother always made a small feast in her husband's name. It was a tradition to honor the head of the household and she always made *Saam Sang* or "Three Life Items". *Saam Sang* was three types of meat: fish, chicken and pork.

The night before the feast she would go down to the market, about a mile away, and buy a fish. Fish were brought in by the boat people, the families who lived on the small wooden vessels and sold what they caught. Sometimes they even sold items they'd traded others for, like pine for firewood. His mother would then fry the fish the next morning. And Yot's family already owned half a dozen chickens so his mother Sun Moon didn't need to buy those. She would simply kill one of the chickens, pluck it, clean it, and poach the meat. And she would buy pork from one of the local vendors. These were the same kind of vendors who used to hire her husband to butcher a pig. Almost every day one of the vendors would walk through the village carrying two baskets of pork that hung from a pole balanced across his shoulders. The baskets were covered with cutting boards and together they held ten to fifteen pounds of meat. When the villagers asked the man to cut some meat he'd put the meat on one of the boards and slice it according to what they needed.

She'd then cook some rice and vegetables to go with it. The family owned two stoves, and if it was a small meal, like rice and vegetables, she'd use rice straw to make the fire. For vegetables, like bok choy, she usually stir-fried that in a wok. Sometimes the rice was also cooked in a wok. If it was a larger meal, requiring a pot, she would use their other stove and make a fire using pine wood. Yot didn't know if his mother ever wrote to his father telling him they were cooking a feast in his honor; she probably just assumed he knew.

Once the chicken was done, she'd use it to make a prayer to their ancestors — not a complete prayer, but a small one to ask them to protect their father — and then they'd begin eating.

And because Yot's birthday came so close after his father's, his mother always saved him a drumstick. They didn't have a refrigerator; his family couldn't afford so much as even an icebox; so to save leftover food she'd put the remainders in several baskets that hung from the ceiling. Their meals were served on terra cotta plates and the baskets were made of bamboo. Almost everything that didn't need to hold water was made of bamboo. She would simply put the plates of food in the baskets and cover them with their basket lids. The baskets hung from the ceiling to keep them away from mice.

She kept lots of meals that way. The baskets always held four or five dishes because she was continually recooking the food. Salted fish. Pan fried fish. Pork with shrimp sauce. Eggplant with shrimp sauce. Yot even remembered seeing how the shrimp sauce was made: small shrimp was ground up and then water was added, along with wine and salt to preserve it.

Every night his mother would recook the leftover meat when she made new rice. She'd cook the rice in the pot, put vegetables like green beans on top of the rice, place the meat on top of that, then steam it all together. If she was careful she could make a drumstick last the four days until Yot's birthday. Chicken was a rare treat for children and Yot liked to gloat that he got a drumstick and that his brother, whose birthday came two months later, didn't.

But Yot was poor at remembering his mother's birthday. His mother knew that and liked to tease him about it every year.

"Today's BaBa's birthday, so what are you going to buy me on my birthday?"

Yot would say, "Well, I'll save up my money and buy you something."

And being a child, he'd forget, and when her birthday arrived in November, she would say, "You were supposed to buy me something for my birthday. Where is it?"

"Well I'm going to buy it."

"But that was two days ago."

And he'd realize he had forgotten again. So once more, he'd promise to buy her something. He'd make the promise to himself, promise even just to remember. And just as quickly he'd forget again.

But Sun Moon didn't even celebrate her own birthday. That was one reason why it was so hard for him to remember. Was it on November 18th or the 28th? It was also why his brother was always so jealous of Yot, because Fon's birthday either came a few days before his mother's or a few days after, but there was no celebration, therefore no feast, therefore no drumstick. Back then, Chinese culture simply didn't honor women's birthdays.

If the two boys had stayed in China they would've been considered men at the age of eighteen, just as they were in America, except that they would've *become* eighteen on New Year's Day. And, as men, they would've been offered a share of the traditional pork meat.

On the first day of the Chinese New Year, each family clan would gather together at their temple to honor their common ancestor by killing a pig. Depending on how many descendants that ancestor had, sometimes they killed more than one pig. The Lim clan, for instance, honored a common ancestor going back about ten generations, and altogether there were over a hundred descendants in the area. One or more pigs would be butchered, the meat boiled, chopped and divided among the men — and only the men. Women weren't allowed to partake. Each man would get about a pound of boiled pork and offered some of the broth, although most men didn't bother with the broth. A butcher would slice up the meat and the men would all gather around for their share, with the children looking on... and the children would all try to maneuver close enough to steal some of the pork.

"You'd see a whole pile of meat," Yot recalled, "and your mouth would start watering and you've just got to have a piece."

Some of the adults would say to the children, "Hey, don't you get so close!" — but the children always managed to steal some anyhow. Yot remembered stealing some at the age of ten. The butcher always managed to steal some too. As he was slicing up the pork he'd take some of the best pieces, eating a little here and a little there and the adults would say to him too, "Hey, stop taking pieces!"

But the boys wouldn't truly be considered men until they married. Upon marriage they would take on new names, just as their father had taken on his new name, and they would become the heads of their own households. A married man was referred to as a *for doh*, a cooking stove, because when he set up the house for his family to live in, the first thing he set up was the cooking stove. The stove was the most important fixture in his home.

Yot and Fon carried those beliefs with them even after arriving in America. During their first year in the new country they tried to honor their father's birthday, just as they had before, but they tried to do it the American way.

They were living above the Pacific Garden at the time and there was a bakery next door. The bakery was so small that the bakers had to set up their stove in the shared alleyway behind their shop. Every morning after Yot and Fon washed up, they would walk down the back steps of their apartment to have breakfast in their restaurant and they'd smell the doughnuts the bakers were frying up for the day. The doughnuts smelled so good that Yot and Fon were hankering to try them out.

So when their father's birthday arrived, Yot and Fon, together with their Uncle Don and cousin Robert T. Lim, bought the cake and candles from the bakery next door. They threw a small party for their father but he didn't care for it.

"You kids just waste your time," he said. "I'm not really enjoying this celebration. We're all getting older and don't have time to do all this kind of stuff."

He wasn't angry. He told them to go ahead and enjoy themselves but that he didn't want to do that anymore. So the boys finished the cake; they weren't going to throw it out; but it was the last time they celebrated his, or any of their birthdays. Yot always thought of his father as a good man — just not a close or affectionate man.

Perhaps that was why my father Yot made sure to give me a hug when I turned eighteen.

I'm the second child in my family, but the first born son. That status, and the resulting attention I received, often made my older sister Leslie jealous of me when we were little. My mother used to tell me that when I was born, my father celebrated all night long, visiting friends and passing out cigars. My parents continued that favoritism even as I was growing up, making my sister protect me in elementary school, walk me home, and do laundry for my younger siblings and me. Even into adulthood, my parents asked her to help me fill out my college application and help me do my taxes.

On the morning of my eighteenth birthday I was in the kitchen talking to my older sister. My father had just woken up and every day he had a routine that took forty minutes to complete. He would shower, shave, get dressed, then stroll into the kitchen and make two eggs and a slice of toast. Sometimes the eggs were soft-boiled, sometimes fried, but it was always the same breakfast. On that particular morning he wore a clip-on bow tie, short-sleeve shirt and polyester pants. He dressed like that often, with clothes bought from a Sears catalogue, and his sense of style often left my mother aghast. Sometimes, just before he left for work, she would give him the once-over and tell him to change his jacket. On the Fourth of July he would wear an American flag bow tie with a light blue sports coat and that alone would make my mother's face sour. One afternoon he stepped out of the house wearing dark green polyester pants and a purple polyester jacket and as he walked toward the car where we were all waiting, she stopped him and said, "No! You can't wear that! Go back and change!"

"What's wrong?"

"Change!"

"To what?"

"Anything! Anything but that!"

And, not fully comprehending, he walked slowly back into the house.

The morning of my birthday, I had just finished eating my own breakfast and my father and I switched places at the stove so he could start his. He saw me talking to Leslie and suddenly realized what day it was.

"You're eighteen years old!" A wide boyish grin sprung across his face. "You're a man now!"

He walked over and hugged me. And it took me by complete surprise. It was so rare to receive a hug from him that it felt like winning a medal I didn't deserve.

I smiled back. I told him I'd been holding off my first shave for just this day and asked him if I could use his razor.

"Oh sure!" he said. "Do you know how?"

"Yeah."

I'd been practicing a little here and there but the one thing I didn't understand was the purpose of shaving cream, so that morning I also gave myself my first stinging razor burn.

94

For my father, the only official mark of his ascension to manhood was that he was legally required to register for the draft. His derivative citizenship didn't allow him to vote but it did ask him to fight. The country was in its first year of war and soon after registering he received a notice informing him that he had to get a blood test. He did as instructed, reporting to a doctor's office around Christmas of that year, then went to the draft board to request a deferment until he was finished with his current year in school. He was a junior at Cass Technical High School, in the eleventh grade, one year short of graduation, and the board granted his request.

His mother's death devastated him. In the months that followed, Yot found himself thinking of her all the time.

"I never stopped thinking about her really. Sometimes I dreamt about her." He thought about his days in China... the life he'd had with her... how much he missed her.

He remembered that she told him about her brothers and sisters. There were seven children in her family. Three girls and four boys. The three girls were born first, with Sun Moon being the youngest, but after Sun Moon's birth her parents worried that they might never produce a boy. A boy was considered the natural heir of a family. A boy carried on the family name. It was so important to have a boy that her parents adopted one.

Adopted children generally didn't come from the immediate neighborhood. They came from clans outside the village. If a family wanted to adopt, they simply asked around and often someone knew of a poor family offering up their child. The boy that her parents found was older than Sun Moon and her sisters; he was in his teens; so when he became part of their family, he entered not only as the first son but as the oldest child as well.

Then after his arrival, her mother gave birth to three more children — all boys.

That might've seemed like a large enough family but one by one, Sun Moon watched as they all slowly disappeared.

Her oldest brother, the adopted son, moved to Peru when Yot was still very young. Her brother had gotten married and had children before leaving but, like so many other men, left to seek better opportunities abroad. He died when Yot was in America. Sun Moon informed Yot of his passing by letter.

Her first oldest sister died while Yot was also in America. This was the aunt who'd said farewell to Yot and Fon at the docks with their mother. Sun Moon informed Yot of her demise by letter too. Her sister had married a man who would subsequently immigrate to Chicago. Yot met his uncle-in-law once but decades later he'd hear that the man died of stomach cancer.

Sun Moon's second oldest sister lived in the nearby village of Quan Tin, about two miles away. This was the aunt that Yot had stayed with when he snuck away to see the opera. Every village had a clan and hers was the clan of the Wongs. When the villagers built a new part to their village, the two parts became known as the old village and the new village. Sun Moon's sister lived in the old village and sometime after Yot moved to America, she moved to a new house in the new village. But when she found out she was dying she asked her son to take her back to her old house. She didn't want to die in the new one. So her son, Yot's cousin, carried her piggyback to her old home where she died two days later. It was a journey of a couple hundred yards and years later, when Yot invited his cousin to stay with him in America, his cousin told him that he'd stayed with his mother until the very end.

None of Sun Moon's three youngest brothers had ever been in good health. Yot remembered them all as slim and fragile men.

Sun Moon's first youngest brother didn't want to be a farmer so he found work in Taishan as a drug store clerk. He was always taking cod liver oil. Like his oldest brother, he eventually left to find his fortunes abroad and ended up dying in Singapore in 1937. Again, Sun Moon informed Yot by letter.

Sun Moon's second youngest brother was kidnapped while he was away at school. Bandits were common in those days and were always robbing or abducting people. One day some bandits kidnapped her second youngest brother along with his classmates in Guangzhou. The bandits assumed that if a family was rich enough to send their child to school, they were rich enough to pay a ransom. They didn't take all the children in his class; they were very selective and took only the thirty students that they believed came from the wealthiest families. When Sun Moon's family found out, her oldest sister took it upon herself to raise the ransom money. Sun Moon pitched in, and her oldest aunt contributed some money too. For 500 Chinese dollars, or the equivalent of 125 American dollars at the time, the bandits released Sun Moon's brother. But he died soon after his return and the family always assumed the bandits had poisoned him.

Sun Moon's third youngest brother found work in a factory in Guangzhou. Yot and his aunt went to stay with him once, and Yot got to see his youngest uncle get married. After the wedding, as Yot and his aunt were departing, Yot tried to say goodbye to his uncle's new wife but she was a shy woman. During his stay, Yot only managed to see her a couple times. Soon after Yot returned home, his uncle caught tuberculosis and died. That was how Yot found out how fatal the disease was. His uncle was in his twenties and Yot never saw his uncle's wife again.

Sun Moon was the last to go. Thinking back on it, Yot thought there was more tragedy on his mother's side of his family than in most Chinese families. Only Sun Moon's mother survived, and she had to watch as every one of her seven children died before her.

Years later, Yot would hear through some friends that when Sun Moon became seriously ill, her own mother, who was living with her at the time, went away.

Her mother leaving is best explained by the old Chinese saying:

> A white-haired person does not wish to send away a
> black-haired person.

An older person does not attend a younger person's funeral. It's a custom that's still practiced in parts of China today. It's based on the belief that a parent expects to die before her own child. She shouldn't have to live to see her own child die. It's not the natural order of things. The custom exists to protect the older person's feelings.

So when Sun Moon's mother realized her daughter was dying, she returned to her own village. It was a way to respect herself and her daughter.

In July of 1943, ten months after his eighteenth birthday, Yot received a form letter from the government that began with the word, "Greetings" and ended with the signature of the President of the United States.

It was a notice telling him to report for his physical examination at a local induction center. It told him where to go and when, and instructed him to pack a suitcase with some clothes and other personal items. If he passed the exam he would be put on a bus and taken straight to training camp.

He informed his brother, father and Mr. Toy, but he also knew that, if admitted into the army, he would be granted a couple furloughs: one for a weekend, another for a week, and he'd get a chance to say his final goodbyes then before being shipped off to war.

The induction center was a five-story building on Jefferson Avenue in downtown Detroit. From the outside it looked like an old, brown brick warehouse but inside it was air conditioned and divided into different departments. The physical was set up systematically so that Yot and all the other men entered a line and slowly wound their way up through several floors.

"You go in and step by step you had to take a test. You hand in your paper on the first floor and you register. They ask you to carry some clothes with you in case you have to put it on. You deposit your suitcase right there and they start with the urine test. They give you a container for the urine test. The next step is the X-ray. I guess they're developing it as you take your other tests. Then comes the nose and throat, eye, and hearing tests. Each one is performed by a different specialist. In between they serve you a free lunch because there were a lot of men. It took a long time, half a day, because there could be thousands of young men. And by the time you reached the last floor there was an officer there who gave you your results."

There were several pages with forms to complete and with each test, a doctor signed a form and each form was passed along with each man. Yot's hearing had deteriorated even more since his first days in high school and he had trouble hearing the doctor's instructions so the doctor tagged his paper and told him to come back to his office so he could check him again. But Yot never got the chance. At the last step of the exam the attending officer called him into his office, looked at his results and said:

"Bad news. They found a spot on your lung."

On Yot's paper he stamped:

and told him to go see a doctor.

But Yot knew what the spot was. In an instant, his worst fears were realized.

I asked him once how he felt upon hearing the pronouncement and he said, "You felt the whole world was at an end."

"But you didn't have to go to war. Weren't you relieved?"

"No", he told me. "Everything went dark."

The next day Yot stopped in on his father and told him the news. His father said that if Yot went away like Fon did he wouldn't have time to visit him. His father was a cook, working up to seven days a week at more than one restaurant. He suggested they try to keep Yot in the area and the day after that, they went to Shurly Hospital.

Today, the building that once housed Shurly Hospital no longer stands. My father pointed out its former location while we were walking around old, gray Detroit one autumn afternoon. It's just an empty alley now sitting between two brick buildings opposite a small park. But at its height, it was run by the man it was named after, Dr. Burt R. Shurly, a roundish man in his seventies with gray hair and a mustache.

Dr. Shurly examined Yot and found a dime-sized spot on his left lung, confirming it as tuberculosis. He then recommended that Yot be checked into his hospital, so the following day Yot returned and was assigned to a room. Everything, from his army physical to his hospital admittance, occurred in the space of four days.

The only treatment he received was bed rest. Being confined to a bed quarantined him from the public and, the doctor assumed, helped slow down, and possibly even stop, the spread of the tuberculosis.

Shurly Hospital was a private hospital and Yot's stay was billed on a weekly basis. Every month Quong had to pay a few hundred dollars and after three months his son's bill came to about a thousand dollars. Quong's savings would take care of the cost for a little while but a cook only made fifty dollars a month and he was far from the entrepreneur he'd once been.

But once a month Yot was given an X-ray and after three X-rays, Dr. Shurly noticed there was no change in the size of his spot so he informed Yot he could be discharged. He'd be allowed to recover on his own.

Yot returned to the restaurant and when Mr. Toy saw him, Yot said, "Oh, I just got out of the hospital today."

"Good, you'll be all right."

Yot also told him that the doctor said he could go back to school, so he went back to the large room upstairs, the one he shared with four other men. His clothes, books, and even the springy twin bed he slept in, were all still there. Mr. Toy hadn't moved a thing.

The following year, in February of 1944, he returned to Cass Technical High School to start the first semester of his senior year.

He was required to have an X-ray taken every three months so later that year, in October, he made a visit to Herman Kiefer Hospital. There, the X-ray revealed that the spot had grown a little. The doctor recommended that he return to hospitalization as soon as possible. He gave Yot a choice: he could go to Herman Kiefer Hospital or go to Maybury Sanatorium. At Herman Keifer, he'd have better facilities and, because it was in Detroit, he'd be closer to his father. But it turned out that there were no beds available so Maybury was his only option.

With the distance to Maybury, he knew his father wouldn't be able to see him, but at least he'd be with his brother again.

The next day Yot packed a suitcase with some clothes and belongings, returned to Herman Kiefer Hospital, and signed a consent form. The staff then sent him to a room where he waited for the county ambulance to pick him up, just as it had done for his brother up a year and a half earlier.

He was two and a half months short of graduating from high school.

9

It was more like a large, tall car than the ambulances he'd later see on the streets. It didn't have a blaring siren or flashing lights. It wasn't noisy or brightly colored. Inside it was grayish and felt, to Yot, like a quiet cab ride along an old, familiar road.

There were four other patients with him that day: all men, all a little older than he was, all going to Maybury Sanatorium. They sat on upholstered bench seats that faced each other and ran the length of the back. From the windows on either side, Yot noticed that they took the same route his bus did: 7 Mile Road, passing along the town of Northville. After close to an hour, they turned onto the two-lane private road he'd taken so many times before and passed a quarter mile of grassy fields.

The grounds that the sanatorium resided on had originally been farmland; eight properties that altogether made up nine hundred acres of rolling meadow. When the city of Detroit purchased the land, it was for the sole purpose of housing tuberculosis patients, and the city enlisted the aid of William H. Maybury, a real estate developer who oversaw construction of the facilities.

The reception room was located in the first building near the bottom of the hill. When the ambulance arrived, it parked in the same lot the bus did, in a small area for visitors. Several of the buildings were made of brick and were a reddish brown in color. Some, like the ones that held the patients, were three stories tall and sat on a hill, and Yot could always see the highest building from the outside road.

Building A was located near the front gate and it housed administration. Then, across the parking lot, was a home where the doctors and nurses stayed. Next, going up the hill, came the P.O. store where visitors could buy gifts and fruits for the patients. Then came Building B, which housed the ward for men, followed by an auditorium, and on the other side of the auditorium was Building C, the ward for women. The facilities were just twenty-five years old; only six years older than Yot.

The patients stepped out of the ambulance and the driver handed their medical papers to a nurse who then led them to a waiting room. One by one they were called into an examination room where a doctor listened to their breathing and heartbeat. The check-in process was short, only five minutes long. Their medical papers had been filled out at Herman Kiefer Hospital so all the nurse had to do was record their names, write down the time of arrival, and rate the severity of their disease before assigning them to a ward.

Each patient's severity rating was marked down on their medical chart. Severity was indicated by a number of Xs, ranging from one to five. One X was the lowest rating. Five Xs was the highest rating and meant the patient's health was in danger or that the patient was very contagious and had to be transferred to the infirmary.

Yot was given a rating of one X and assigned to a ward in Building B. An orderly came by with a gurney for Yot to lie upon, then took him to his wing on the third floor. They rode the elevator up and when the doors opened, Yot was wheeled down a long hallway. On either side of the hall were four rooms, for a total of eight, and each were semi-private rooms with double beds for long-term residents. At the end of the hall was the large ward where new patients of Yot's rating were placed. The room could hold five patients and Yot was the fifth.

Fon's room was right next to Yot's. After the orderly wheeled him in, Yot asked the man to wait a moment, quickly went over to his brother's room and said:

"Here I am."

"Oh, I was expecting you today," Fon said.

Yot often wrote his brother letters and when he found out he was going to Maybury, the first thing he did was inform Fon.

But they didn't have long to chat. Yot had to return to his bed so that the orderly could report his delivery. The bed he was assigned to was soft, covered with a dark greenish-brown wool blanket, and he could raise or lower the head of his bed if he wanted. Beside it was a closet with a wood door built into the wall, and he hung his suede jacket inside. He'd brought some Chinese books with him and put those in the metal dresser he was given. Then he had to change into his pajamas. For the vast majority of his stay, he was told, he'd have to lie or sit in bed wearing those pajamas. After a moment, a nurse came by to take his temperature and pulse. He'd soon learn that a nurse made the rounds every day taking everyone's temperature and pulse. The nurse who came by that day wasn't wearing a mask. Some did, at first, but eventually most decided it wasn't worth the bother.

As he was unpacking, Fon walked over to Yot's room to offer his younger brother a little advice. Newly admitted patients were restricted in their activities but when a patient's health showed signs of improvement he was allowed to get out of bed and walk around several times a day. Fon could visit Yot but Yot couldn't visit Fon. There wasn't much Fon could say to his younger brother except to be patient and get good rest.

It was 1944 and Maybury Sanatorium was still a segregated hospital. Whites were placed in one ward, blacks in another. Asians were considered white so Yot was put in a ward with white patients. At twenty years old, he was the youngest man in the room. Fon helped Yot unpack, then took a moment to introduce Yot to the other men, several of whom Fon had roomed with himself. The patient next oldest from Yot was a man in his thirties, followed by a man in his forties and another in his fifties. The oldest was a man in his seventies and Yot thought the man looked very old. The man would say to all the others, "I'm just waiting here for my time. I have one foot in the grave."

They were allowed to get out of bed once a day to go to the bathroom but otherwise a regular schedule of bed rest was enforced. Orderlies would arrive every morning at six a.m. to bring each patient a wash basin and water so they could wash themselves and brush their teeth, and every bed came with a chamber pot. At first Yot had trouble using his. He wasn't accustomed to urinating while lying in bed so he had to climb out of bed, place the pot on the edge of bed and urinate while standing. He did this day and night and, being in a room full of men, Yot didn't mind, but the other men would tease him about it. They'd say, "Well, you have to get used to it. You have to do it the way it is." And eventually he did.

Then once a week the orderlies would bring in another cart with basins and water for the patients to take sponge baths. The orderlies would wash the men's backs but the men had to wash their own private areas. Again the men would tease Yot. "Now don't be bashful," they'd say. And again, he became accustomed to that procedure too.

For the most part the men were friendly and polite to each other. Yot would ask them questions, seeing it as an opportunity to improve his English, and the men would explain things and help him get used to life in the ward.

He asked, "How many patients are in the sanatorium?"

"Approximately three to five hundred."

"Can I get a cookie or candy or something?"

"Yes, someone will come once or twice a week so you can buy something."

And once or twice a week someone from the P.O. store would push a cart through the room so the men could buy any number of items, including snacks, toothpaste, or a tablet to write on.

At seven a.m. the orderlies brought breakfast, which usually consisted of cereal, toast, scrambled eggs, milk and coffee. And after breakfast the men would take a nap or read a book or do a little writing. They didn't have a television in the room so Yot usually read a book or listened to the radio. The hospital supplied each man with headphones — black, plastic and round, almost like ear muffs — and each headphone connected to each man's radio (if he was smart enough to bring one) so that they could listen to their own programs without disturbing anyone else.

During the day Yot listened to soap operas. He tuned in regularly to one show called "Linda's First Love", about a girl (Linda), her boyfriend, and their everyday lives. Or sometimes he'd listen to music. There was one disc jockey he occasionally had to put up with named Eddie Chase. Yot imagined that women must've loved Eddie Chase because he had such a smooth voice but Yot couldn't stand him. The man would talk for ten minutes straight then only play a three-minute song. He talked too much, Yot thought, and to this day he can still recall how annoyed he was with Eddie Chase.

Lunch would arrive between eleven o'clock and noon, and the men usually ate cold cuts, baloney, potatoes, and more milk and coffee. When he was living with his father, and later with Mr. Toy, working and going to school, Yot had started reading some Chinese classics like *All Men Are Brothers* and *The Three Kingdoms* and a series of books about the Spring and Autumn Periods and the Warring States. He loved those books but in the sanatorium he started reading *The Good Earth* and *The Promise*. He caught up on Chinese history by reading *Moment in Peking* by Dr. Lin Yutang, as well as *My Country and My People*. He read a book called *The Pit*, a novel about grain speculation in Chicago, and *Hungry Hill*, a novel about a young girl's struggle in her Irish Catholic working-class neighborhood.

Dinner would arrive between five p.m. and six p.m. and the men would have lamb stew or spaghetti or macaroni and cheese or sometimes cold cuts again. Afterward, in the evening, he would listen to radio shows starring Bob Hope, Jack Benny and Fred Allen, or comedy shows like Fibber McGee and Molly or Edgar Bergen and Charlie McCarthy. He remembered Hollywood Radio Theater and evenings when actors would read dialogue from films like *Tale of Manhattan* and plays like *Arsenic and Old Lace*.

At nine p.m. the lights went out. If he wanted to stay up and continue listening to the radio he could put his headphones on but he usually didn't do that. The men generally tried not to bother one another.

He lived like that for three months until December when his brother was released.

The spot on Fon's lung was still there, and would be for the rest of his life, just as the spot on Yot's left lung would remain with him for the rest of his. It was the badge they wore for losing several valuable years of their young lives. But the growth of Fon's spot had been halted, and the doctors deemed him no longer contagious, and that was the most any patient could ask for. It gave Yot a ray of hope. He thought that he might be able to make it out in a year or two as well, and told himself to keep a positive outlook.

After Fon's departure, Yot moved into the semi-private room his brother shared with his roommate Harris. Harris was a young Caucasian man in his twenties, about the same age as Yot, and the two found they had similar backgrounds. Harris had an older brother too, and he not only endured the loss of his mother but his father as well. After several months Harris moved out and was replaced by William, a man in his thirties. William was married and had a young boy. William stayed until just after 1945 when he developed some problems and had to be transferred to Herman Kiefer Hospital. And so it went. A third roommate came in; more changes; another person to get acquainted with.

Years later when Yot would think back on the day he was first diagnosed with tuberculosis, he would consider it the darkest period of his life. His brother had contracted it just two years earlier; his mother died soon afterwards. When he arrived at Maybury, it occurred to him that he might never leave. He had more than enough time to think about it now and he wondered how he'd caught the disease to begin with. He'd heard of a nurse at the sanatorium who had contracted tuberculosis, presumably from one the patients, and had to be hospitalized in the female ward. The doctors wore masks and gloves when dealing with patients but the nurses and orderlies typically went without. Perhaps, like the nurse, he'd caught it from his own brother during one of his visits. It was an airborne disease; it could be spread by a cough or a sneeze or even a laugh, or just prolonged contact with a carrier. But it was more likely, he reasoned, that the two of them caught it in Mr. Toy's apartment, in that room they shared with the four other men. But speculate as Yot did, he would never really know.

Fon's release turned out to be a little premature. Four months later he suffered a relapse and had to return to the sanatorium. In the process the two brothers had switched places. As a new patient, Fon was put in the large ward Yot started in, and Yot kept Fon's former bed. Fon's second stay would last two more years.

The treatment for most patients was the same: get as much bed rest as possible, take an X-ray every three months, and, for cases like Yot's, go through a procedure called a pneumothorax.

A pneumothorax is a condition when a lung collapses, sometimes on its own, spontaneously or due to an injury. At Maybury, and the vast majority of hospitals treating tuberculosis at the time, a pneumothorax was performed on a patient to intentionally collapse a lung, or part of the lung. The belief was that if the lung could be folded over, the tissue around the damaged area had a chance to surround the spot, seal it, and prevent it from growing or spreading. At Maybury this was done by inserting a needle into the patient's side and pumping air into his chest cavity. The needles were long and thick to allow air to travel freely through, so the patients were given a shot of Novocain before the insertion. Yot had even started his pneumothorax treatment earlier, during his stay at Shurly Hospital, but his left lung wouldn't fold over as much as the doctors had hoped. It was resistant — held in place by connective tendons — so the doctors gave Yot his first and only operation at Maybury. They cut the tendons to allow it to fold.

The procedure didn't make his situation worse but didn't seem to help it either. His condition remained relatively unchanged. Months went by. The hardest part for Yot was finding ways to fill his days. The county offered to pay for correspondence courses with the University of Michigan, so Yot signed up for a class in English.

He also subscribed to *Time* magazine as a way of staying informed about the world. Decades later he would boast that he managed to keep his subscription continuous since 1944. "I have not broken that subscription once," he said, although he hasn't been very happy with the magazine in its subsequent years. "Now it's not as good because they mostly put their stories on the internet so they don't report as thoroughly anymore."

I inherited my father's love for news and information. As a child, I wasn't sure what the articles in *Time* were saying exactly but I loved looking at the photographs. My father later bought the hardbound Life Science Library, and I became fascinated with the books on *Man and Space*, *Planets*, *The Insects*, *Mathematics*, and *The Cell*. Once, when I was riding in the backseat of our station wagon, I tried to explain to my little brother, who was seven at the time, how the galaxy was created. I'd seen a diagram in the book, *Planets*, showing a dark, gray gas swirling and condensing into a revolving disc of particles and I told him that every night the clouds in the sky slowly spun around and turned into stars. My mother, sitting in the front passenger seat, half listening, said, "That's right!"

My father and I have more than a few characteristics in common. My mother was the first to notice this. She liked to point out that we both had the same walk and the same nose (the Lim nose as my father likes to calls it; the same straight, modest nose he shared with his father); and as an adult I noticed that we both had the same way of talking, of raising our voices in a singsong pitch when talking about a subject we're excited about. And we have the same gestures; sometimes cocking our heads or holding up our hands to make a point.

Still, I wasn't very athletic when I was growing up. My father was always playing outside when he was little but I was more of an indoor child, very shy. My favorite activity was lying on my stomach on the living room floor, drawing on whatever pieces of paper I could find. I would draw all day until my mother would shout, "It's time to go out! Go outside! You need to get some sun!" And she'd wait by the front door until I put my shoes on, then hold the door open as I marched out resentfully. The door would close and I'd stand on the porch for a few moments not knowing what to do before sitting down and drawing again. Or if I didn't have any paper, watching insects.

She was always urging me to eat too. Eating meat was such a rare treat when she was growing up that whenever we'd go to a restaurant she'd order a chicken drumstick for me because she knew how much I liked them. What I really liked was looking like a caveman. Fred Flintstone ate huge dinosaur drumsticks and the cavemen in *One Million Years B.C.* chewed meat right off the bone, and I just wanted to look like one of those caveman. But when I was finished I'd drop the drumstick back on my plate, and my mother, outraged, would pick it up, grab a knife, and scrape the remaining meat, tendons, and cartilage off the bone, saying, "Look how much meat there is! Look how much is left!"… and I'd have to gnaw through the rest of it. Feeding her children was just another way for her to force her love on them.

Then when I was nine I caught a cold that wouldn't go away. It was a chest cold that came in the form of a deep, persistent cough, and it went on for weeks without end. Just when the cold seemed to disappear, it would resurface with a vengeance. It got so bad that the depth and loudness of the cough would echo throughout my entire chest. My body would shake and I'd be surprised that my lungs could hold that much explosive energy.

One day it got so bad that it hurt to cough. It came in the form of a piercing pain in my side, just under my armpit. It felt as if my lung, expanding so convulsively, kept getting caught on some sharp sliver of bone that had somehow splintered out from one of my ribs. It hurt so bad I would grab the sides of my chest in an attempt to hold my rib cage in, sometimes trying to squeeze both sides of my chest in like an accordion, trying hard not to cough, trying so hard I'd shake a little. And that's when my mother became truly alarmed.

She took me to a doctor; a small, friendly, white-haired man named Dr. Hogikian. During the examination I noticed something different about the conversation my mother had with Dr. Hogikian. My mother asked very pointed questions, and the doctor was trying to calm her down, trying to ease her worries. This wasn't a typical checkup and he wasn't talking to her in a typical manner. In fact, his office looked very specialized with its wood-paneled walls and the absence of any other patients. Whenever we visited our regular doctor, his waiting room was always filled with sick patients. I became aware that my mother was trying to ask Dr. Hogikian detailed questions about something without referring to it by name. He prescribed some medicine and I took it, but the cough still wouldn't disappear.

By that time my parents both worked at the restaurant they owned. They regularly came home late, around midnight. One night I experienced a series of coughing fits. I would sleep, wake up coughing, fall back to sleep, and then the coughing would start all over again. I could tell I was keeping my brother Mikey up, who slept in the same room with me. My mother and father arrived home, I could hear the garage door opening, and I had another coughing fit. It hurt this time. It hurt so bad I grabbed my chest, hugging myself to keep from coughing. I clenched my teeth. The pain was paralyzing. I was afraid to move an inch in any direction for fear that that my lung had gotten caught on that imaginary sliver again and that the sharp toothpick of fractured bone would tear it open.

My mother rushed to the bedroom and said, "That's it!" She scooped me up in her arms, took me to the car, and rushed me to the emergency room.

I felt so guilty that night, sitting there in the hospital in my flimsy T-shirt and underwear beside my worried mother, already exhausted from a full night's shift. My cough had subsided. I couldn't reproduce it even if I wanted, and I kept apologizing to her. "I'm sorry," I said. "Maybe it's nothing. I think it's gone away."

The doctors took X-rays but couldn't determine the cause, and less than a week later the cold slowly disappeared.

To this day I sometimes wonder if I'd somehow caused the cold; if it was just a manifestation of a fear that a skinny boy sensed in his mother. When I was little I used to love playing with worms, picking them up on rainy days and putting them in my pocket for later scrutiny until my mother would empty out my pants on laundry night and scream as her fingers pulled those little dried noodles out. And because of that, I learned to fear worms. I used to love splashing around in the water when I was a child until my little brother, little sister and I discovered how frightened my mother was of swimming. And my little brother, little sister and I all began to fear the water.

I love the outdoors now. It's something I share with my mother. She's learned to swim in her old age and will occasionally tell me how many laps she did in her pool. Likewise, I also learned to swim late in my adult life. I can't do one full lap yet but, like my mother, one day I will.

I was talking to her recently and she compared me to my father, just as she always has. She said, "You're like your father. You're both fast healers."

For my father Yot, life at Maybury passed slowly. He saw a series of doctors, most of whom came to the sanatorium to gain experience.

His first doctor was Dr. Fong, a Chinese man in his early forties, medium height, a little chubby. He was from New York and stayed at Maybury a couple years. He'd been Fon's doctor too, and Fon got along with him so well that later, after his release, he took a vacation to New York and visited Dr. Fong.

Yot's second doctor... he couldn't remember the doctor's name but he didn't have a high regard for him. The man was in his fifties and liked alcohol too much. "He hit the bottle pretty good," Yot recalled, and the nurses and staff knew it too. "He was with us for a year then got struck down with tuberculosis and was put in the same sanatorium."

His third doctor was a tall, slender man, named, oddly enough, Dr. Stout. Dr. Stout was in his late thirties and Yot didn't think he was a very knowledgeable man. "One day in the winter I got a cold," Yot remembered. His nose got sniffly and runny so the doctor "prescribed a nose drop but nose drops aren't very good because once you use them you have to keep using them. But after I used it I couldn't clear my nose any more so I told one of the nurses and she said 'You shouldn't be using this,' and threw it out. Some of the patients down the hall had even worse opinions of him. He just seemed to be one of these doctors who wanted to get things out of the way."

His fourth doctor was Dr. Beck, a man from the south who'd come to get some experience. At about the same time, the hospital also had a visiting doctor from China who'd come as an observer. The Chinese doctor was named Dr. Sun. He'd served in the army as a medical doctor and was Cantonese, so he and Yot would chat whenever they saw each other. Yot would ask Dr. Sun about the political situation in China and Dr. Sun would ask Yot about conditions in the American hospital.

His fifth doctor was Dr. Klupenstein, a nice man, slim, about forty years old. Dr. Klupenstein was himself a recovered tuberculosis patient. Most of the other doctors came and went, but Dr. Klupenstein remained there for years, and Yot remembered hearing that he might've stayed till the very end when Maybury finally closed down. As a patient, Dr. Klupenstein had to have part of his ribs removed from one side of his body so that his lung could be collapsed as part of his own pneumothorax treatment. Having part of one's ribs removed was what the patients at Maybury thought of as a "worst case" situation. But it worked; the collapse allowed Klupenstein's lung to heal and it arrested the disease. "His body leaned to one side," Yot recalled, and he assumed it was the side where the doctor was missing the parts of his ribs.

Three years passed. In 1947 Yot read an article in the *Detroit Free Press* about a new drug called streptomycin. The drug was discovered in the lab of Selman Waksman, and Waksman thought it might work well against tuberculosis. He classified it an antibiotic, a substance that could cure bacterial infections, and journalists were already comparing it to penicillin.

The other patients read about it too, and at first they didn't get very excited about the news, but developed a mild interest in it. They didn't know if it would do them any good, or even if they would be getting the medicine, but it gave them a little hope. Then they heard that the drug was being distributed to tuberculosis hospitals across the nation and the next thing they knew, the doctors at Maybury announced that they'd received it for testing.

The first experiment would take six weeks and the doctors needed volunteers. "They asked if you wanted to sign up for it and you had to sign a consent form." So Yot signed up and was soon put on a regimen where he was given a shot of streptomycin four times a day, three times a week. The first shot was injected into one side of his hip, the second shot injected into the other side, the third shot went into one arm, and the fourth into the other. And the shots hurt.

"It felt sore! It didn't hurt when you first took the shot but you felt sore in that area for the rest of the day."

But the results weren't immediate. "It takes time for the streptomycin to have an effect and take control of the tuberculosis. It takes time. We didn't know until the doctors took an X-ray on each patient and evaluated each one."

Dr. Klupenstein was the one who oversaw Yot's tests. Yot recalled that "when the doctor came to your bed, you expected something, and you wanted to hear what he had to say." Some of the patients showed better improvement, faster improvement, but for Yot, the doctor told him, "Not much changed. There was some progress but not much of a change."

But he held out hope.

Then came another round of testing. Six months after the first round, the biochemists had improved the drug. Once injected, it stayed in the body longer, so a patient only needed one shot a day for six weeks. And Yot volunteered for those tests too.

Dr. Klupenstein would check on his patients three times a week and when he entered their room he'd usually say, "How is everyone?" But one day he asked Yot, "How do you feel?"

"I feel good."

"The treatment seemed to work on you a little better. The X-ray showed you had some improvement."

And slowly his prognosis began to look more stable, more favorable. The doctors allowed him walking privileges. After three long years of bed rest they wanted him to get up now, walk around the facilities, exercise his legs. And that's how he knew he was going to be released soon. There was never any sudden notice that a patient was cured. The news came gradually.

"I'll give you some extra privileges," Dr. Klupenstein would tell him.

He could explore the ward now. He could freely stroll the halls. His bathroom privileges were increased to twice a day and he could wash up there instead of in bed.

Once a week he was allowed to sit in a tub of hot water. The tub was ceramic, connected to the wall with a faucet so he could adjust the temperature to his liking. The baths were nice enough although he never stayed for very long.

After a while Dr. Klupenstein told him, "You improved a lot. You can walk around every day for half an hour."

He could go outside, walk on the lawn, stand in the warm sun, even stroll among the trees if he wanted. He could go to the P.O. store just down the hill where he could buy magazines; visit the library and check out books. The duration of his breaks were extended past half an hour. Then he was given two breaks a day, and each increase brought him a little closer to the man he was before.

He enjoyed all these privileges on his own. His brother had left the sanatorium by then — released permanently — before streptomycin had come to Maybury. When Fon's health had stabilized and he looked ready for release, the staff asked him if he had a place to stay. He couldn't stay with his father because his father's hotel apartment was too small; so the county welfare department arranged for Fon to stay in a room at the YMCA, and Fon's friend Harry Nelson drove by to pick him up.

And just as Yot had done for him, Fon came to visit his younger brother every couple weeks. Fon told Yot that the county welfare department asked him what he wanted to do for a job. Was there a trade he was interested in? Fon told them he was interested in photography so they found him work with a photographer named Eva Briggs who owned a portrait studio in Detroit. She had two other women working for her and they'd also been patients at Maybury. And Fon would tell Yot about the people they knew; how their friends were doing on the outside.

One day Fon told Yot about a girl he'd met. Her name was Helen. Fon had started going to church and met her through his church group. A little while later he told Yot, "Well, I finally proposed to Helen. And now we're engaged."

"Oh, that's nice. Congratulations!"

He told Yot he'd proposed to her at a restaurant. "And pretty soon we'll set a wedding date."

Yot was happy for his brother. Happy he'd made it out and happy he'd resumed his life. In fact, Yot could tell his own release was drawing nearer because he was going through the same steps his brother had. And one day Yot's doctor said, "In a way, you're ready to leave the hospital pretty soon. After a while, you get your feet into shape and we'll be ready to send you home."

The world had changed during his stay. World War II was over. Japan had been defeated. The atom bomb had been dropped on Hiroshima and Nagasaki. China was locked in a civil war. Roosevelt died in office and Truman was now president.

In September of 1949, Yot was released from Maybury Sanatorium. He had been there for five years.

10

The Wall of Heat.

That's what I told Leslie it felt like we were walking into when we arrived at the Guangzhou Airport. I know there are hotter places in the world but when you leave a cool, dry city like Beijing and enter a subtropical climate like Guangzhou, it feels like stepping right into the land of humid, heated air. The wall exists where the plane connects to the airport. It's at the border between the walkway and the terminal. First it hits your face, then your chest, and then you're enveloped in it.

A glance out any hallway window will confirm this. There's tropical foliage everywhere: past the runways, past the roads. And the colors of the airport echo the environment. Everything is painted turquoise and white to match the leaves and the bright sun outside.

Our tour guide here goes by the name of Gloria. She's a petite girl with wide set eyes, a friendly smile and tiny dimples. She has a modest, helpful demeanor but within moments of meeting her, my father and sister, both fluent in Cantonese, can tell she's not from this region. That shouldn't be a problem since my father knows the area well enough, but as the days go on, Leslie will start to wonder why we're paying for her services. But Gloria's talents will emerge later; we just don't know it yet.

For now, as Gloria leads us to our van, she tells us she's from the Fujian Province on the east coast. At the van she introduces us to our driver, Mr. Tong. He's young, in his early twenties, close to the same age as Gloria, but tall, about six foot five, and lanky. He wears a white short-sleeve shirt, black jeans and black shoes with thick rubber soles. We'll see him dressed the exact same way every day and I'll start to wonder if he's wearing the same set of clothes or if this is somehow his "uniform". In this heat, those black jeans look incredibly stifling.

It's a two hour drive from the airport to Taishan. The expressway we're on was officially finished a year ago but it's in a constant state of construction. Two years from now, when we return, they'll still be working on it. It doesn't help that Guangzhou is now the largest city in southern China. With its growing manufacturing industry, the city can barely keep pace with all the new cars conspiring to fill up its streets and highways. In fact, when booking our arrival, my father was careful to avoid the annual trade fair that ended one week ago. Had we arrived then, we wouldn't have been able to find a single room in any hotel or a spare seat in any restaurant.

Tall apartment buildings stand over each side of the expressway. Clothes hang from random windows and long, dark stains streak the walls. As the freeway tries to escape Guangzhou, the high-rises dwindle down to wide, flat factories, followed by a bridge over a tributary of the Pearl River. When my father first brought us here over thirty years ago, the highway was just a series of two-lane asphalt roads surrounded by fields and farms. We had to cross three tributaries and at each one, wait for a ferry to carry our car over. It took us four hours to get to Taishan. But the land was beautiful. We saw more red clay hills and dark green trees along the way than we do today.

As we turn off the highway we see our first moped. The driver is coming opposite us on a parallel road. Then at the merge we come upon two more. Then five, passing us by as we head into Taishan. Then we're surrounded by mopeds, all buzzing loudly and darting around us. It's like entering a giant mechanized beehive of long, curving streets, neon lights, and little gadget stores.

Most of the moped drivers are men. Or they're young men with young women sitting behind them, both wearing helmets with visors, short-sleeve shirts and jeans. The timing of the intersections packs them into groups of a dozen or more. And there are the pedestrians. So many pedestrians. Strolling the sidewalks or casually crossing the street or walking without worry against oncoming traffic. And there's the honking. The drivers of the cars seem to be honking reflexively, with no aggression in their eyes, not even as a warning. Just honking. Honking at mopeds and passerby and other honkers. And then our own driver Mr. Tong starts honking and we become part of that noise.

At last our van pulls up outside our hotel. The New Lakeside Hotel. It's a modest hotel, concrete gray on the outside. The lobby is small, with three young women sitting behind the counter. Behind them is a wood wall adorned with clocks showing different cities: Beijing... New York... London. Gloria helps us check in. There are two elevators. They feel small and claustrophobic. They allow smoking in this hotel; they allow smoking everywhere; the elevators even smell like cigarettes.

The hotel restaurant is on the fourth floor. The front half is a banquet hall. It's bright and noisy and filled with large families sitting at big round tables. There's a small wedding reception in one corner and a videographer jockeys about for a shot of the bride and groom. Skinny men in short-sleeve shirts sit in their seats like lazy lizards smoking cigarettes. A gray haze hangs in the air.

It's so loud here that our hostess shouts something to us, but we can't hear her, so she simply leads us to the back. The room in the back is much nicer. It's quieter, and in its dimness almost looks like the inside of a little chalet.

After we've had a chance to sit and relax, my father does something he likes to do in every Cantonese restaurant. He glances at the menu (we don't even bother), he makes sure it has some traditional dishes, then he starts to chat with the waitress. He asks her if they have fish. They do: a bass. He orders steamed bass. Do they have duck? Some squab? They have both. I ask my father if the restaurant has family style tofu. It's the one dish I love. They do. He orders one. But for my father, the steamed bass is all that matters.

And maybe it's because we're hungry or because we're biased, but when the food finally arrives it's the tastiest meal we've had so far. The bass is fresh, covered with ginger and curled slivers of green onions. It sits in soy sauce and oil, but not swimming in oil, and it's steamed perfectly, flakey to the touch. The tofu comes braised in a small clay pot. It's a little mound of golden fried tofu, orange carrots and soft round shrimp, all topped with a light green bok choy. The vegetables still have a bite and the brown sauce is subdued; not too salty, not too thick.

Then my father does something else he likes to do whenever he's back in town. He takes out his Polaroid camera and shows it to our waitress. He asks her if she wants her picture taken. There's something so genuine about my father's face, something so friendly and childlike, that she gladly agrees to a quick shot. The bulb flashes, the camera whirs, a photo slides out the front, and my father tells her to wait a moment. He turns the photo over to shield it from the light, allows it to develop... thirty seconds go by... then he flips it back over to reveal her image. She smiles, and he offers her the picture. Two more waitresses come by. They pose, he takes their photo... and thirty seconds later he hands it to them as a small gift. He loves seeing the instant joy on their faces. Word gets around and soon the waitresses from the front banquet hall start coming to our table. They pose in pairs. In trios. They wear white blouses and dark provincial skirts. They're young and pretty and lively. They smile giddily. My father takes their photos, offers it to them. One of the girls isn't happy with her picture. She didn't smile right. Her friend laughs at her. My father offers to take another. There's a flash, a whir, a short wait. He hands it to her. She looks at it. A quick shake of her fist, Oohh! That's not my best smile! More laughter from her friends. He takes another. A flash, a whir, a wait. Better this time.

They all start to quiet down once more. He'll be back tomorrow, he tells them. There'll be more opportunities. They can tell their friends, the ones that weren't here today.

On my father's second trip to Taishan, he came with my brother Mike. Mike was still single at the time. There was no girlfriend in the picture. So my father joked that this was a good chance to find him a wife, although my brother knew he was only half joking. At one restaurant, one of my father's cousins half-jokingly offered his own daughter for marriage. My brother saw the girl while sitting on a bus. She was too young, he thought. Half his age. She didn't even look seventeen. So my brother ended the discussions right there while everyone was still only half joking and before they became more than half serious. But everywhere my father went he continued to take photos of waitresses and receptionists, with their permission of course. Half of the photos he took, he put in a photo album, and when he came home he showed their photos to me, asking if I was interested in any of them. If I was, he said, he could contact her. This one was a very nice girl, she worked at the hotel we stayed at, do you like her?

Are you serious? I asked.

I'm half serious, he said.

But Nancy is on this trip with us, and he wouldn't do anything to offend her. Every Polaroid he takes he gives to the girl, or the family, or the people posing.

We leave the restaurant and head to our rooms but at the elevator he turns to my sister and says, "Let's go for a walk."

My sister looks at me. Up till now my father's been fairly passive, letting us dictate the trip, but she notices something different in him. Something restless.

Behind our hotel is a man-made lake called Workers Lake. The residents of Taishan created it decades ago by digging up the earth beside the nearby river and surrounding the excavation with a sidewalk and concrete balustrade. We walk over to the edge of the lake. In the darkness we see a distant bridge outlined by brightly colored lanterns that adorn its sides.

Just over our shoulders, diners chat loudly at an outdoor restaurant. Men roast skewers of meat on their portable grills several yards away. Jewelers sell their merchandise nearby. And the constant buzz of the mopeds is just a block away.

A mild breeze blows across the surface of the water. My father stands looking into the distance, arms resting on the thick balustrade. He was ten years old when he first came to this lake. He was with his brother Fon.

"We were going to an old cemetery. Our family has tombs scattered all over the place. One of my ancestors' tombs was a couple miles away from the lake. In those days there was a train. Once a year people would go pay their respects to their ancestors."

The two boys took the train with a group of other villagers. Their mother didn't go with them. Women weren't allowed to visit the tombs. Only men and boys.

"We got off at the train station and walked to the burial ground. The road leading to the burial ground was around the lake. We had to cross the bridge to get there. The bridge was made of granite stone. The lake didn't have that much water. It was kind of dry. The bridge was twenty feet up from the river and when you're a kid it looks pretty high up. I think the bridge was no more than fifty or sixty feet long but in the eyes of a kid, fifty feet is a long way.

"The river was also dry. The lake was wide and there was just a little bit of water trickling in at the bottom. There were weeds and bushes at the shore, and weeds and bushes and sand at the bottom of the lake. Around the edge of the lake was a little walkway. It was made of dirt. Just dirt surrounding the shore. There were stores too. Food stores and utensil stores and repair shops. Dressmakers and fabric stores and herbal stores."

Thirty-nine years later he returned with his wife and children. We had lunch at the same hotel we're staying at today. We walked around the same lake we're standing at now. The trees had white blossoms, finger-length, about an inch around. They were in full bloom and very fragrant. He remembered these flowers from his childhood. Usually a child had to climb the tree to get them, but there was a branch hanging low so my father picked some and gave them to each of his four children.

"Here. It smells good. Have some."

We smelled them, we played with them, and we carried them back to the hotel with us. He also gave one to his wife and she put it in her hair like she used to do when she was little.

It's the next morning and we're sitting in a small private room in our hotel restaurant. The room's about eight feet by eight feet, just large enough to hold a table, four chairs, and a small bench to rest a food tray on. The room is decorated in a soft, dingy yellow. I think it's supposed to be gold but the tightness of the room makes it feel like a honeycomb.

We're here because the dining room we were in last night is filled. Just outside our door we can hear the cacophony of other customers. The door is closed, which allows us to enjoy a leisurely breakfast, but my father is afraid the waitresses will forget about us. He wants to open the door but knows that cigarette smoke will waft in. Both the banquet hall and dining room are filled with smoke. Taishan seems to have more smokers than Beijing did. We haven't been here a full day yet and I'm struck by the gray haze that constantly seems to hover about this place.

It's going to be hot and humid today. It was cooler when I woke up. Chilly, actually. Shortly after dawn I could hear the wind whistling and bumping up against our hotel window so I climbed out of bed, cranked the window open, and a big gust of cold air blew in, filling the room. It was really quite relieving given the exhausting heat yesterday, so I stood by the window to watch the city wake up.

I spied a thin man in a white short-sleeve shirt walking quickly down the street. He looked a little like me: a fast walker; always in a hurry to get nowhere in particular. Then I heard morning exercise music starting up at a nearby school. It was like Communist Party music for children. Very cute, but old, with a warped quality to it, as if it's still being played from an old cassette that was taped from an even older record album.

Nancy and I share one room. My father and sister share the room next door. When I heard the television murmuring from behind my father's wall I knew he was up and getting dressed, which meant he'd woken my sister in the process and she was probably in the shower. He tends to make a lot of noise without knowing it. His hearing might've been impaired during his childhood but one of the side effects of streptomycin is that it can cause deafness, and I sometimes wonder if that worsened his condition even more.

Now we're in this small yellow room waiting for a waitress to knock on our door. A breakfast of ham and eggs isn't served in this restaurant. Here they serve dim sum. It's *har gow*: steamed shrimp wrapped in rice noodles; or ribs in black bean sauce; or *jook*: rice porridge with chicken. Through the wood slats of our door, my father can see the flickering shadows of the waitresses as they push their dim sum carts past us, so he gets up, opens the door, and motions to one of the women. He tells her not to forget about us, then asks what she has in her cart. It's almond jelly. Too sweet for a main course. He asks her what the other women have and she tells him they've run out of the more popular items. This happens at most dim sum restaurants; if you arrive too late all the good stuff is gone. But the kitchen makes some more and soon the waitresses wheel the new dishes to our door.

"Hey Curty," my sister says after the food has arrived. I'm forty-two years old and she still calls me Curty. "Try this." She points toward a small dish of dark brown rectangular-shaped blobs. "It's chocolate tofu."

"Really?"

She nods, but I know better than to trust my sister's unexpectedly kind intentions so I look over at my father. He nods too. He has a very open face. He looks very matter-of-fact, so I cut one of the blobs in half with my chopsticks. It certainly has the consistency of tofu: firm, like hardened pudding.

I eat a cube. And it tastes nothing like chocolate.

"It tastes like liver or something."

Leslie tells me I must not have gotten the full taste yet.

"It still tastes like liver," I say, grimacing. "It tastes like... what MaMa used to give us when we were little. It's got a strange aftertaste."

When I was nine years old my mother put a plate of meat in front of me and told me it was my favorite food: steak. It looked strangely dull and just lay there, limp in a way that no self-respecting steak should. My fork sliced through it as if it was an animal who'd surrendered long before its very unnatural death. I took a bite and I'll always remember how horrible that first taste was.

"Eat it," my mother said. "It's your father's favorite." She knew how much I tried to like everything my father liked. His favorite color was brown so my favorite color was brown. He liked soft-boiled eggs with soy sauce so I liked soft-boiled eggs with soy sauce. No, I didn't really, and never would, but when I was nine years old I could at least tolerate it. So I took a few more bites of this "steak" but it was so hideous I refused to eat any more and I'm not exactly sure when I stopped believing in Santa Claus but at that moment I realized not everything my mother told me was the truth.

Later that night Leslie told me what that steak was. Liver. My mother had tricked me into eating liver.

And now here I was, eating chocolate tofu at my sister's urging.

"You want to know what it is?" she says, smiling.

"What."

"Promise you won't get mad?"

"What is it."

"Promise?"

"I promise."

"It's blood! You just ate boiled blood!"

She starts laughing. And my father grins.

"You just ate pig's blood! They drain the blood from a pig, put it in this pot and boil it down so it's like this cake! How does it taste?!"

"Great."

And now, this late into my adult life, I've just learned that my father, too, can put on a good face. But now he's got the same mischievous grin that he has whenever he tells the story of sticking glue in Bok Yao's hair.

My sister asks me if I'm angry and I say no, but only on the condition that we can play the same trick on Nancy when she joins us.

"Okay," Leslie says. And my father nods quickly in agreement.

Nancy arrives half an hour later, her hair still damp from a shower. My sister asks the waitress in Cantonese for another dish of boiled blood. We keep our faces straight but a little while later the waitress returns and tells us that the restaurant has just run out.

Leslie and I give each other a look. Tomorrow. Tomorrow then.

After breakfast we head to the bank across the street to exchange some money. The thoroughfare outside our hotel is Y-shaped, with a small island of shops rising up in the middle, splitting the road in two. It takes a little nerve to cross the street here. The mopeds don't stop for anyone. At their most courteous, they might slow down, but most times they skirt around the passerby, and sometimes just by inches.

I don't know how the locals tolerate this but Leslie's the first to notice that they don't seem to care. They simply step into the street without so much as glancing in either direction.

"Looks like we just... cross," she says.

But my father has already started, so we shrug and follow after him. It's a little scary, ignoring these giant darts shooting past you, but the locals seem to have developed a harmony about the whole thing. They don't care about being hit and in return the drivers agree not to hit them.

The bank resides on a corner beneath a big red sign. Inside, the tellers sit behind a bulletproof window. Customers take a number and seat themselves in two long lines of chairs facing the window.

There are two ATMs in the lobby but only the customers my age or younger will use them. My father once told me that the older generation fears ATMs. They say the machines swallow their money. Part of the fear comes from not knowing how to use the machines, but the older Chinese simply distrust banks in general. A lot of them grew up in a time when it was easy to be swindled by a bank.

It reminds me of the way the Chinese regarded the lion's head that once sat over the entrance to the MGM Grand Casino in Las Vegas. When the emerald casino first opened, the front doors were built under the mouth of a giant lion. It was Leo the Lion, the Metro-Goldwyn-Mayer mascot, but it was an ugly piece of architecture. All hard edges; a squarish face with empty, glassy eyes, and a mane shaped with triangular shards. Gamblers are already a superstitious lot but Chinese gamblers, being an even more superstitious breed, either entered through the side doors or avoided the casino altogether. They said the same thing that they say of the ATMs in Taishan: the lion swallowed your money. When the MGM Grand realized how many Chinese dollars they were losing, they replaced the head with a smaller, sculpted statue of a golden lion and hired a Feng Shui expert to position it off to the side. They then asked a Chinese priest to bless the lion and light some incense at his feet. It made the news, which is what the casino wanted, and my father followed the story in the newspaper with great amusement.

Here, at the Bank of China, it takes me only a few minutes to get my money, but my father prefers to wait with all the other customers his age. When he finally gets to the window, the bank makes him fill out a form and show several pieces of identification. It costs him forty-five minutes of his time but this is the price he pays for the formality that brings him comfort.

Afterward, Gloria and Mr. Tong pull up in their white van outside our hotel. Mr. Tong already has the air conditioner blowing when we step in. Today we're visiting my father's village.

We stop at a nearby supermarket to buy water and fruit for the trip. I ask Nancy if she wants any coffee. She says yes, so I walk over to a diner across the lot. I've memorized one important word for this task: *gafeh*. It's a cognate of sorts for coffee.

When I enter and say this to the hostess she grabs a menu and offers me a seat.

"Oh, um, no. To go. Take-out." I point toward our van. But she's insistent. Perhaps she needs to brew the coffee. But I want something quick.

"Une gafeh, s'il vous plait."

The moment I utter the words I realize I've mixed up my Cantonese with my high school French. But she gets the point. She gestures for me to wait.

Once I get my coffee I walk back to the van and Nancy is waiting, smiling. She always has a smile for me.

Leslie and my father step into the van and then we're onto a long asphalt road.

We're making a brief stop to pick up my father's cousin Yu Chung.

June, 1949.

Four months before his release from Maybury, Yot attended his brother's wedding.

His brother had proposed to a woman named Helen King. She was Chinese, about five foot three, and was the oldest daughter in a family with four younger sons. She was also Christian, born into the faith, and the wedding was to be held at the Central United Methodist Church in downtown Detroit.

When his brother told him of the wedding date, Yot asked a nurse if he could talk to Dr. Klupenstein.

"My brother is getting married," Yot told him.

"Oh, I heard."

"Is it possible for me to go to the wedding?"

"Oh, that's no problem. You can go anytime when someone picks you up."

The doctor wanted to make sure Yot had a way to get there and back so Yot arranged for Fon's friend, Harry Nelson, to give him a ride.

It was a Sunday morning in June. A beautiful, warm, bright day. Harry Nelson drove to the sanatorium and from there they went to Plymouth where Harry picked up another friend. Together they drove to the church on the corner of Woodward and Adams, an area Yot knew well. It was a block away from Shurly Hospital where Yot had first been diagnosed with tuberculosis. It had been five years since his stay there but even if he'd had time to walk over, he had no interest in seeing the place again.

They arrived a little before eleven o'clock, when the wedding was scheduled to start. Harry parked behind the church and they entered through the back. Almost immediately upon walking in, Yot saw his brother inside a dressing room putting on a black tuxedo.

"Gung hei neih! Gung hei neih!" Yot said. Congratulations to you. Congratulations to you.

The two brothers laughed but Fon was trying to get ready so he asked Yot to follow his usher out.

From there Yot went to the front of the church where he saw his father waiting outside. His father wasn't familiar with these kinds of ceremonies so he'd asked Fon what to do and Fon told him to stand outside by the door and somebody would come seat him.

But his father misinterpreted his words and assumed he had some official duties to perform there.

"Dad, why don't you come inside?" Yot asked him.

"I can't. I'm supposed to stand outside to greet guests until someone comes to get me."

Yot didn't understand but went inside where the usher seated him. He wasn't part of the ceremony, nor did he feel the need to be; he was grateful just to be healthy enough to attend. He sat in the second row with all the other family members and by the middle of the ceremony it occurred to him that he still hadn't seen his father come in, and before he knew it his father had missed his first son's wedding.

Afterward Yot went to get him. He brought his father in and took him upstairs to the fifth floor where a modest reception was starting. Fon and Helen stood in the reception line greeting guests and as Yot approached, he explained to Fon what had happened. But his father wasn't angry. He didn't show any unpleasantness at all.

"He kept it inside himself," Yot said of him. "He never expressed his feelings."

Still, Fon apologized. And Helen expressed her disappointment.

125

"Oh it's just one of those things," his father replied. He said he didn't miss much anyhow because he didn't understand the American style of marriage to begin with.

They moved on to the reception. It was a simple affair. On a long table sat a wedding cake with some small sandwiches, tea and fruit punch. A couple hundred guests were in attendance and they picked up paper plates and placed sandwiches on them. Helen's mother was a dressmaker and she'd made her own dress for the occasion. She received lots of compliments on it and was like the star of the party. Yot assumed she had also made Helen's wedding dress.

Again, during the reception, Fon apologized to his father.

"Oh don't worry about it." He offered Fon and Helen his wedding gift. A small envelope. He handed it to Helen. To Yot it was obvious that his father was preparing to leave.

"I've got to go back and open the store." And with that, he made his departure.

The envelope contained about a thousand dollars in cash. Yot knew this about his father: that he didn't enjoy these kinds of customs but was always very generous about them. His father had even paid for the reception.

After the wedding, Fon and Helen went to the home of Helen's mother to look at the wedding gifts. Yot and some other friends joined them, then drove to Chinatown. They went to Ho Toy Restaurant on Third Street, and on the second floor enjoyed a dinner with fourteen of their guests. They sat at a long table and ate chicken, fish with vegetables, sautéed shrimp, and the celebratory favorite, Bird's Nest Soup.

Fon and Helen left early for Fon's apartment flat. Yot got a separate ride from the best man and arrived at midnight. He could've stayed anywhere: at a hotel, with a friend, but his brother and bride wanted him to stay with them. They didn't mind. The next morning Yot even had breakfast with them. He'd had a brief conversation with Helen at the reception but it was over breakfast that he got to know her in a more relaxed setting. They chatted over fried eggs, toast and coffee. She was a nice woman and he could see himself getting along with his new sister-in-law.

My own memory of her was of a kind, pragmatic woman with short wavy black hair. I remember her wearing a thick black sweater and pants when we went to visit their home one night. In one old photograph she's wearing a simple orange dress. It looks

126

like she and my uncle are dressed for Sunday church. I didn't know her very well. She died when I was just a boy.

I asked my father once if my uncle was also Christian.

"If he became a Christian he didn't tell me about it."

But how did he end up at the Central United Methodist Church?

"He just went to church for the heck of it. It was the thing to do. It was a good way to meet people."

Were you ever Christian?

"No, I wasn't."

"What is your religion? Do you have one?"

"Oh, I just... generally believe whatever the area around me believes."

But I already knew what he was going to say. It's a question I've asked him before. It's a question I ask myself, constantly. I'm always looking for the answer, always trying to find meaning in my life, always wondering. These days I assume Wondering has become my religion because if I believed in anything else I'd still be left wandering.

The first time I asked my father about his beliefs was when I was fifteen, sitting next to him at the dinner table. What did he think happened after a person died? Did he believe in an afterlife? He told my brother and sisters and me that he thought of himself as a leaf on the branch of a tree. One day the leaf will fall, float to the ground, become part of the soil, and eventually become part of the tree again. It will give strength to all the other leaves, and he saw his children as some of the leaves on that tree.

When she heard this, Leslie asked, "Is that Daoism? That sounds like Daoism."

"Daoism," he replied. "That's it. You could say I'm Daoist."

There was a Daoist temple near his village. It sat in a rice field less than a quarter mile away, maybe a thousand feet from his house. It was about forty feet wide by fifty feet long, one story tall, made of charcoal gray brick and covered with a dark rooftop. The temple was shared by seven villages and each village had its own guardian figure, a small statue that they placed inside, each on its own wooden pedestal for worship. Some of the figures wore a warrior's armor. Some wore the long embroidered robes of a high court official.

"Ours looked very pleasant, sitting there like a wise official," Yot recalled. It was about two feet tall, carved in wood, and seated in a small armchair. "He was a gentle figure."

His name was Duc Dae, and he was the Fifth Dragon King. He was adorned with robes painted red, blue and gold, and he had three sets of whiskers, as most officials do, to show age and wisdom; two on either corner of his mouth and one resting under his chin.

Once a year each village would send some of its people to the temple to retrieve its guardian figure for the New Year celebration. Each figure protected its village and was used to bless its people. There were thirteen Dragon Kings, and six remained in the temple for visitors to worship while the others were used for the celebrations. All the rice would be harvested from the fields by that time of year so the temple would be surrounded by nothing except dry clay and earthy topsoil. Yot usually joined his people for the jaunt and there'd be eight, ten, sometimes as many as fifteen men and boys along for the walk. One year Yot took turns carrying the figure with the other boys. He thought the figure was probably made of pine; not a very hard or heavy wood at all, and light enough for a ten-year-old boy to carry.

Most New Year celebrations lasted anywhere from ten to fifteen days, whatever the elders of each village decided was appropriate. For Tin Sum, it lasted thirteen days.

When the figure was brought to the village it was placed in the community center. The community center was an old, gray brick building and the villagers used it for worshipping and holding meetings. They met several times a year, mostly to discuss how things should be maintained and to decide how much each person in the village should contribute. They even had an accountant: someone who would collect money from around the village and keep track of the funds.

Each morning of the celebration, my father's family would light a pack of firecrackers in front of their house. The firecrackers were wrapped in red paper and the quick *pop-pop-pop!* of the explosions helped ward off the evil spirits. The popping also sprinkled tiny pieces of shredded red paper all over the ground near their front door, and red was a symbol of good luck.

Yot or Fon usually lit the firecrackers; their mother didn't. Adults usually let the children have fun with the smaller firecrackers.   Each pack was supposed to have a hundred firecrackers but Yot once opened a pack and counted only forty or so and exclaimed, "That's not a hundred!"

His mother would make some pastries and they'd go visit relatives.   Starting on the third day of the celebrations they'd visit his grandmother's house, then the next day visit his aunt in Guangzhou, then the next day go to his uncle's house.

On the thirteenth day, the final day of the celebrations, the villages would fire off the larger fireworks. These were the ones the adults got to light, and they enjoyed lighting them. They were like small rockets tied to bamboo sticks to help guide them into the air. The rockets were hung on a rack and lit so that they could be shot one by one or in groups, and they exploded thirty to fifty feet above the village.

I once asked my father if anyone ever got hurt.

No, not that he ever saw.

Who got to light the fireworks?

"Whoever wanted to pay for the privilege of firing it off." The village would auction off the rights. Only the men in the village could bid for it. The privilege usually cost about ten to fifteen, sometimes up to twenty Chinese dollars, paid with little red pieces of paper a mix of coins.

The villagers would also hire a priest to bless the village. In addition to their own Daoist temple, there was another temple nearby, a Buddhist temple, and the Buddhist priests would travel from village to village. Some of the villagers were Buddhist. One of my father's cousins was Buddhist and he used to pray to the Goddess of Mercy. Sometimes the villagers would hire Buddhist priests to perform the Daoist rituals but that never made sense to my father.   It seemed confusing to him.   His own father's godbrother was a Daoist priest so he could easily have performed the ritual. But even though he was Daoist he usually stayed at the Buddhist temple and worshippers there would ask him to say a Buddhist prayer for them.

Our van pulls up outside a white apartment building. My father's cousin, Yu Chung, lives inside. He's a little less than thirty years younger than my father but his stark white hair and weathered features make him look older. He's a slim, boney-looking man but the first thing you notice about him is his kind, patient, welcoming smile.

He greets us in the alley in front of his building, then we walk two flights of stairs up to his apartment. My Mandarin teacher once told me that I'd never guess how well-off some of the Chinese are. They're not as ostentatious about their newfound wealth as some Americans, but they're getting there. China's rapid economic growth is making everything more affordable. The cost of most household items is lowering while the average take-home pay is rising. Their buildings might look old and crumbly from the outside but my teacher told me that some Chinese apartments have newer technology than most American houses: bigger television sets, higher quality audio equipment, and all the latest gadgets. The Chinese, she says, are becoming fond of their gadgets. I get my first glimpse of this when we walk into Yu Chung's apartment. I see a television screen larger than any I've seen in an American home up to now. Then one of his sons puts a DVD into the player and cues the menu up to a home movie.

We meet Yu Chung's wife, three sons and daughter. His wife is a friendly woman with short black hair and a happy, beaming smile. She's small and, like Yu Chung, boney with a weathered face. She offers us tea and over the next hour she'll talk to me constantly even though she knows I barely speak a word of Cantonese.

Yu Chung's oldest son is Dak Lung; in Cantonese his name means "Dragon". His second son is Dak Ming; "Bright" as in a bright light. His youngest son is Dak Cheung; "Prosper". Prosper has lived up to his name. He started as an electrician for a construction company but manages teams of electricians now, and with the rapid rise in construction throughout Guangzhou he's had no shortage of work. He's very good looking, dresses well, likes to wear black, and could easily come off as intimidating; but when he walks up to me, he approaches from the side in a friendly, disarming way. It's the same way a perceptive adult might approach a child. He smiles, gestures to me and himself and says a few words. I smile, but shrug, *"Dui m'ji. Ngoh m'sik teng."* I'm sorry, I don't understand.

Leslie laughs. "He's saying you and he are the same. You're both cousins, except you're older!"

He also seems to be saying we're similar in other ways but all I can do is smile and nod.

There are three small children in the room: two little boys wearing green and white school uniforms and a skinny, adorable girl with tanned skin and large, curious eyes. The boys look like they're four and six years old. The girl is about seven. Not hearing any discernible words from our lips, they stay on their side of the room, in their mothers' laps and arms, but then my father starts passing out red envelopes — lucky money — and they step out of their shyness.

Prosper points to his wife. Then points to Nancy. He says something... a friendly way of saying, "Look, we have our counterparts as well."

I look over at Nancy videotaping the gathering. She's just learned how to use the camcorder. Later we'll discover that in her excitement she's pressed pause when she meant to press record, and vice versa. The hour we spend here with my father's cousin will be reduced to a few random shots of their hardwood floor.

Soon after he returned from his brother's wedding, a social worker came to see Yot. She was a little on the heavy side, taller than most other women, and in her late forties with brown hair turning slightly gray. She'd seen him once before to tell him that the county had a budget for helping patients improve their lives and that was when Yot signed up for English courses. But now that his health was on the mend she wanted to know if he had a place to stay after his release.

He told her he would be staying with his brother.

Did he know how he might make a living?

He said he would ask his father for a small stipend.

She then stopped in to see his brother's apartment to make sure it was clean and comfortable. When she was sure it presented no problems for either Yot or the newlywed couple, she approved Yot's release.

Fon had gone through a similar process three years earlier. The county didn't want to put a patient out on the street. If he had no place to go, the county would put him in a temporary residence. They also didn't want a patient to begin working until they were sure he wouldn't suffer a relapse so they required him to get an X-ray every three months. The soonest a patient could start a job was after the first three months.

On the Saturday of Yot's release, Fon and Helen drove to Maybury in Helen's gray Pontiac. The two of them were living in Detroit, in a small residence on Gladstone near Hamilton. It was on the second floor of a two-story house with a side entrance that led to their two-bedroom flat. Fon and Helen slept in one room and Fon used the other for his darkroom. They strung a curtain up in the living room and brought in a fold-out bed for Yot, turning that into his bedroom. Yot was aware that Fon and Helen were still effectively on their honeymoon but they'd made it clear they didn't mind him moving in.

For the first few days he didn't do much. He rested, unpacked and got used to the flat. After a week, on the following Sunday, he accompanied his brother and sister-in-law to a church service. He didn't have a car so he'd also join them whenever they went grocery shopping.

"We didn't have a TV then. It wasn't popular." They couldn't afford one either so Yot continued his correspondence classes with the University of Michigan and "did hobby things, like sewing wallets and ladies' purses. I made quite a few of those."

He even made a leather purse for Helen. It was a skill he'd learned at Maybury. "When somebody ordered one I made one for them." People acquainted with Fon would tell him that they wanted to buy a wallet or a purse and Fon would pass the orders onto Yot. "I must've made a dozen, maybe more."

His X-rays confirmed that his tuberculosis had indeed been halted. The spot on his lung, where the bacteria had destroyed his tissue, posed no further danger.

He visited the social worker a couple times at her office.

She asked how he was doing with his English course.

He told her he hadn't kept up with it.

Did he want to continue?

He said no. He knew the courses cost the county money and he didn't want them to keep paying for it.

We'll just write that off then, she replied. He could tell from their conversation that they both agreed he didn't need the county's help any longer.

That December he went to a Christmas party at Fon and Helen's church. People exchanged words of good cheer and gave presents to children. Yot remembers he was quiet that night. Perhaps too quiet. He didn't make an effort to meet anyone, although people did try to talk to him. They said, "Merry Christmas!" and, "How are you?" and Yot replied politely and in kind, but felt he didn't want to say anything to offend anyone. He mostly sat by himself.

Fon had always been the more outgoing one. He turned twenty-eight that year. He was five foot six and had medium-length black hair. His hair wasn't very long, but later in life, when he started sporting a crew cut, it would seem long to Yot in comparison. He was known for smiling a lot, known for his good personality, and he always seemed at ease striking up conversations with strangers.

Yot, on the other hand, saw himself as shy, more conservative, and not very outgoing. "There's a saying. 'Still waters run deep'. That saying best describes me."

That's my favorite saying too, and I'm surprised when I hear him say that, wondering how far our genetic similarity goes. The first time I read those words, "Still waters run deep", was in a high school textbook, and now I wonder if the phrase resonates with me because I take after my father so much or because I've heard him say it before.

He turned twenty-five that year, the year of his release. I've seen photos of him from that time. He weighed a hundred thirty-five pounds, though he didn't think of himself as skinny. When I was twenty-five I weighed ten pounds more and I considered myself very skinny. My father was an inch taller than his brother and his hair was, as he describes it, "pretty good then." In one photo he's leaning up against a car with a friend. He had a full head of rich, black hair, thick on top and in front, parted on the side, and combed back in a 1950s style. It's a style I've tried to imitate most of my life. It's the look of youth and potential.

He dressed in a simple manner, usually in a white cotton shirt and trousers. He didn't wear a T-shirt. White shirts were typical for the time. "I might've had one suit back then but I didn't wear it very often. I couldn't afford silk shirts." His trousers were usually made of wool, sometimes rayon. "I used to wear corduroy for a while but I didn't like to make that noise so I gave it up."

To occupy his time he also did soap carvings. It was another skill he'd learned at the hospital. "I used a bar of soap, usually Ivory soap, and usually carved little things, like a dog." He carved a small bust of his brother's head at the hospital once and the hospital asked if they could keep it. The soap carvings made him popular there. "When I did that there, the kids wanted to see it so they could learn how to do for themselves.

"One time I had some soap and a kid next to me asked how I would start to carve a dog. He was in his twenties or so, so I made a few carvings and he leaned forward and said, 'That's interesting. What would you do next?' So I did a little more and he said, 'Carve a little more.' I did and he said, 'Keep going,' and pretty soon I caught on to what he was trying to get me to do and I told him, 'You go and carve it yourself!'"

While Yot was in the hospital, his father had opened a small import/export store called the Tung Hing Company. It was located on Sibley Street, a neighborhood in downtown Detroit that was always on the cusp of becoming part of Chinatown but never quite turned the corner. After decades of working in Chinese restaurants, his father now owned a grocery store that sold food to them. And just as he had done before entering Maybury, Yot resumed his weekly bus rides into Detroit.

"At first I wasn't used to the area." Nor was he used to his father's new business. "So I just sat around and watched, learned a little, picked up a thing or two. Every month he would order some canned stuff and dried stuff but the vegetables came every week. After about six months I started working there."

He was paid 150 dollars a month. By comparison, a cook in a Chinese restaurant earned 300 dollars a month. But Yot didn't have many expenses. He paid his brother whatever he could for rent, sometimes 50 dollars a month, and "all I needed was a haircut every now and then. I didn't need to buy a lot of clothes. I only needed to buy what I wore out. You only needed a jacket in the winter. And I would go see a movie occasionally."

He saw *Roman Holiday, They Died with Their Boots On,* and *Blood and Sand* ("That was great!"). He saw Veronica Lake and fell under her spell of her seductive blonde locks. He saw the *Mark of Zorro* ("That was very good.") and was entranced by the lightning-fast sword fight in the end. He caught a lot of Tyrone Powers and Gary Cooper movies. *Sergeant York. The Westerner.* He'd also seen a lot of Errol Flynn movies before going to Maybury. *Dodge City. Robin Hood.* He saw *Shane* and can still remember the little boy calling after the gunslinger in the end. "Shane! Come back!"

He usually waited until the movies came to his neighborhood. "I didn't want to go downtown because it was too expensive, but if you waited until the movie came to your neighborhood it was cheaper. It only cost a quarter or thirty-five cents. Later, when I started working for my father I would watch a movie during the day, then go in and work for him."

At first he helped his customers and rung up their sales. When vegetables came in, he would open the crates and put the vegetables in the refrigerator. The front of the store, where the customers shopped, was about thirty feet by sixty feet. Not too large, not too small. The back of the store, where they kept the produce, was larger, about sixty feet by sixty feet, and on one side was a kitchen where Yot made tofu.

The tofu was made from soybeans that the Tung Hing Company imported. He would soak five pounds of beans in some water and let the beans sit overnight. They needed to be soft enough to be ground into a paste.

"You use a big pot — like a vat — big enough to hold all those beans with water, then you put half a gallon of water in for each pound of bean, and then you boil it. Half a gallon or one gallon, something like that... keep stirring it so it wouldn't get burned on the bottom, bring it to a boil, heat it until it became a liquid, and then you separate it. We used a cheesecloth to separate the bean malt. After separating it, it would become like soy milk.

"Then we used — what's the name of it? — we used a calcium sulfate. You used the powder and poured it into the soy milk while it was still hot, and you evenly mixed it and then let it stand until it became a jelly. Then you made a rectangular form, then put a cover over it and added some weights to force the water out of it.

"But what I did was, when I boiled everything, it was too hot to handle, so once I boiled the water, I poured it over the mixture, then while it was still cool, not too hot, I squeezed the water out of it. Then I let it cool down. That must've been the right way to do it because a lot of people liked it when I made tofu."

Fon was the first to formalize his citizenship. There was a photography job he wanted at Chrysler, and because Chrysler had contracts with the U.S. government, they only hired American citizens, so Fon thought it was time to finally become naturalized. His father knew of another family of Lims; they lived in Saginaw, a couple hours north of Detroit, and were good friends with a federal judge. The judge used to frequent their restaurant when he was in

135

school and had become godfather of their child; so Fon asked them for their help.

Once again, everything was about friends and family and using your connections. Fon went to meet the judge, the judge took a liking to him, and offered to put in a good word for him at the immigration office in Detroit. He made a call on Fon's behalf and shortly afterward, Fon went to the immigration office and became a U.S. citizen. The officer who naturalized him then said, So you bring your brother and your father and we'll get it all straightened out for you.

On February 20, 1952, Yot and his father Quong also became U.S. citizens.

Yot turned twenty-eight by October of that year. He was still living with his brother but had saved up some money and thought it was time to explore life a little. He wanted to travel and see the country. During his final months at Maybury, when he realized his health was improving, he had begun formulating a plan for himself. He considered it his five-year plan. Each year he would set some goals to see how far he could stretch himself. He wanted to challenge himself.

So for the second time in his life he boarded a train, this time on his own, and took a trip out west — in the reverse direction from when he'd first arrived.

The first leg of the journey, from Detroit to Chicago, was five hours. It stopped at the Illinois Central Station and he had to get to the Great Western Station, but this time he wasn't going to take a chance and get caught running for his connection like the last time he was in Chicago, so he took a cab. The train he boarded would take him to Oakland, California, and from there he planned to travel across the bay to see San Francisco.

The second leg, from Chicago to Oakland, was thirty-nine hours, so he rode for forty-four hours. He boarded *The City of San Francisco* in the evening and spent two nights on it, traveling across tracks owned by three different companies: the Chicago and Northwest, the Union Pacific, and the Southern Pacific. At each transfer point the train would stop and a new locomotive would be attached to the car — or superliner as they called it — and the new locomotive would pull the superliner to its next transfer point.

When he was thirteen years old he'd sat on a bench seat and slept in a converted foldout berth. Now he was riding coach, where he sat in a comfortable seat throughout the entire ride. "The chairs were nice. You could swing it around and move it so you could recline, and you could sleep in it."

He also spoke more English and had more money this time. He didn't have to ration out a foil-wrapped roast chicken with anyone. He could visit the dining car for all his meals. He didn't have to wait for a porter to push a cart by just so he could sip sour milk again. If he got bored, he could stroll down to the club car and mingle with other passengers. For breakfast he had ham and eggs; for lunch, a sandwich or "some kind of hamburger"; for dinner he enjoyed "pork chops a couple times."

The first part of the ride, led by the Chicago and Northwest Company, took him from Chicago to Omaha, Nebraska. He sat alone for that ride. The next part, led by the Union Pacific, took him from Omaha to Ogden, Utah.

"From Omaha to Ogden, Utah, there was a lady sitting next to me." She was thirty, a little older than he was, and very friendly. She'd boarded at Council Bluffs, Iowa, but had ridden the train several times before. She told him there would be some nice scenery coming up and when they passed some peaks she pointed out the mountain goats and rams.

There was also a room at the end of the train where the passengers could sit and chat. It was like a club. "When I had time I went to the club where they played cards. I met this couple from Nebraska, so we talked for a while and I found out they were wheat farmers. They would grow wheat and sell the harvest, then feed livestock on the farm. I learned all about wheat farming from them.

"At one point I said, 'Well how many acres do you have?' and the man said, 'Oh I'm a small farmer. I only have two thousand acres.'

"I said, 'What?! When you said you were a small farmer I thought you'd only have fifty acres! How many acres does a larger farmer have?'

"And he said, 'Oh some of them have about ten thousand to fifty thousand acres.'

"And that put things more in perspective for me. In Nebraska with all that land you can have that. But in Michigan it's harder for a farmer to have that."

When he arrived in San Francisco he visited a man named Jung Pon. Jung Pon once owned a Chinese laundry in Detroit, a block from Cass Technical High School. Yot and a high school friend often saw the laundry and thought that the owner was probably Chinese, and someone they'd like to get to know, so one day, after school, Yot and his friend walked over and introduced themselves. Mr. Pon, as it turned out, was a very nice man; tall, fit, and in his forties; and Yot and his friend ended up visiting the shop regularly, doing laundry as they sat and chatted with him.

After the war, Mr. Pon and his family left Detroit. Mr. Pon's father was getting older and wanted to retire so they moved to San Francisco and opened a grocery store on Commercial Street and Grant in what is now the east side of Chinatown bordering on the Financial District. It was an import/export store, much like the one Yot's father owned, a store that sold Chinese produce. Mr. Pon's sister married a man in the area and the Pon family bought a three-story apartment building with thirteen units. The building cost 35,000 dollars and even at that time, they considered it a very good deal. Today the building would likely sell in the millions of dollars.

Part of Yot's Five-Year Plan was to work outdoors, be active and challenge himself again. Meeting the rancher on the train had sparked his interest but he'd already been considering the idea of returning to farming for a while now. It was something he was well familiar with from his childhood. He was especially interested in truck farming: growing vegetables like lettuce, tomatoes, celery, spinach — items that needed to be delivered on a daily basis. So he asked Mr. Pon where he got his produce from and Mr. Pon introduced him to the truck farmer who brought his vegetables in. The man's name was Lo Wong. He was in his fifties, a little smaller than Yot, with dark skin, tanned from the sun. Yot asked the man about his farm and Mr. Wong offered to show it to him.

The property was located in Half Moon Bay, about forty-five minutes south of San Francisco. Mr. Wong was one of ten partners in the farm and his job was to drive the truck, delivering the produce. There, in the field, he pointed out how close the Pacific Ocean was. The only thing separating the ocean from his farm was Highway One, the Pacific Coast Highway. In just a few months, he told Yot, he was planning to relocate east, across the bay to Hayward because of the difficulties he was having with the farm. During high tide the salt water from the ocean tended to wash over the highway and flood the field, killing the crops. Farming could sometimes be a tenuous livelihood.

Yot ran into another friend too, a man named Lim Joe. Lim Joe had lived in a village on the other side of the Daoist temple from Yot's. He wasn't directly related to Yot, but because of his familiarity with him, Yot called him Uncle Joe. He referred to every Cantonese man he was close to as "uncle". By the time he'd boarded the train to San Francisco, Yot was aware that Uncle Joe was already there visiting, and a day after arriving, Yot ran into him on Grant Street.

"Hey! Surprised to see you here!" Yot said.

"You're here!" Joe replied.

The two started talking and Uncle Joe mentioned that he wanted to visit some friends in Sacramento and Stockton, and Yot thought it would be a good chance to see some farms in those places too, so they borrowed a car and took an overnight trip.

Five years later Yot would make a second trip to San Francisco with Uncle Joe. The year was 1957 and they brought another cousin along with them. The three were having dim sum one afternoon in a Chinese restaurant called Oong Ah Cha on Sacramento Street when Yot heard a rumbling sound. It was "like a truck was going down Sacramento and the whole building started shaking. The wall moved one way, then the next. My chair started sliding across the room and then everybody in the restaurant started to run outside. And then somebody yelled, 'Earthquake!' and we all ran outside. There must've been twenty or thirty people at the time. It wasn't such a good idea because we were on the street and if the buildings started to fall we would've been in trouble with all the pieces coming down."

The shaking lasted about a minute, and after it subsided, "we went back inside to eat and pay. The proprietor was worried that everyone was just going to leave."

He had experienced his first San Francisco earthquake but the notion of it wouldn't sink in until a couple hours later.

After his first trip to California, Yot returned to his father's store. His father Quong would later send him on other trips, one to Boston, another to Buffalo. His father had hoped to set Yot up with the daughter of one of his friends in Boston but nothing came of it. On his second trip to San Francisco, Yot's friends set him up with a girl and he took her to Playland at the Beach, an amusement park near the ocean. They rode the bumper cars and visited the arcade, but she had a boyfriend and nothing came of that either.

Quong also began traveling and while he was away, Yot would run the store. The tone of the Tung Hing Company would change when Quong was gone. "Young kids would come around sometimes and buy things and talk. Older people wouldn't come by if I was working."

One of those kids was Chuck Fong, who used to come by to chat. Chuck was younger than Yot, in his early twenties, about the same height, and had just come over from Hong Kong. "We got to talking and getting to know each other and we said a grocery store isn't the kind of place for a young man to work. And we decided we wanted to do something more adventurous so I said 'I've been thinking of farming since about 1952.'

"And he said 'I'd like to try that.'

"And I said, 'Maybe we can both go into it.'"

One of Quong's customers was a Japanese American farmer from Imlay, a city an hour north of Detroit. On his first visit to the store the farmer tried to sell Quong some Chinese vegetables but, as Yot recalled, "They were too expensive." But the farmer wasn't deterred and continued to shop there. So shortly after his conversation with Chuck, Yot approached the farmer and asked if he could see his farm, and the farmer agreed.

The man owned a hundred and fifty acres of land. Yot asked him if he could lease part of the land to try his hand at farming and the man said yes. By October of that year, Yot and Chuck were farming in Imlay together, growing Chinese vegetables — bok choy, mustard greens and radishes — and Yot was seeing the first of his goals come to fruition.

11

We're heading to my father's village. My father sits in the second row of our van, behind our driver. His cousin Yu Chung sits beside him in the center seat. They're very talkative, still catching up. My father will notice something outside his window — a factory or a makeshift restaurant — and Yu Chung will tell him about all the changes that have taken place since his last visit here.

The first time I was on this road was in 1973. I was nine years old. It was a bumpy dirt road lined with tropical green trees that seemed to stretch on forever. We had a driver back then as well, and there were six of us cramped into his rental car: my father and mother, my sisters and brother and me. It was hot and humid, and as I stared out the window all I saw were flashes of trees and leaves and the sun beating down on the dusty road ahead of us. Occasionally the trees would clear and I'd glimpse a field, or a water buffalo, or an old farm house.

My sister tells me I threw up in the car and by doing so, made everyone else sick too. I thought it was my little brother who did that. I don't know how we ever found the collective patience to make that trip but now, thirty-three years later, I was hoping we'd ride that bumpy dirt road again. As an adult, it would be an adventure. But when I asked my father if we'd be taking that path, he told me it was gone. It had been paved over. We're driving on its smoother incarnation now.

It was a day trip that we took from Guangzhou. We'd made it to Guangzhou from Hong Kong. The United States had just reestablished diplomatic ties with China and my father was eager to see his old friends and relatives again. My parents had just sold their first restaurant. We owned our own house. My father would be returning to his village as a success story.

We stayed at the Overseas Chinese Hotel in Guangzhou. It was a six-story building owned by the government. It didn't have any of the modern conveniences that we were used to like air conditioning. We had to leave our windows open in the hopes that a wind would blow past our flimsy curtains and cool down our room... which never happened. We had a simple wash basin and our toilet was old and wooden. We had to use a pull chain to flush it and the seat was so worn that we were afraid to get splinters.

"It was considered a four star hotel," recalled Leslie.

"Yeah, in those days it was considered a four star hotel," confirmed my father.

"If your father said it was a four star, it was like a one-and-a-half star to me," replied my mother.

The elevator regularly broke down so we often had to take the stairs. In fact, the day we checked in, the elevator was out of service and we had to walk the six flights up to our room. The hotel didn't have bellhops.

"You kids were really, really good," my mother recalls. "You carried your own suitcase and didn't complain as we walked up all those stairs."

The hotel gave us what they called the Luxury Suite: two adjoining rooms connected by a middle door. Compared to the other rooms, it truly was luxurious. When the elevator wasn't working, on our way up or way down we'd stop on the other floors to see what the regular rooms looked like. On the fourth floor we saw the lower-priced rooms that travelers from Indonesia, Malaysia and Thailand took. Each room had two beds and they were hardwood boards with straw mats placed over them; the kind my father used to sleep on as a child.

Once, when our own bathroom wasn't working, we had to use the shared bathroom down the hall. The toilet was a hole in the floor with two footprints etched into either side of it. You placed your feet on the footprints and they told you where to squat. I was so scared of that thing that on our last day, when my mother ordered me to use it before we left the hotel, I went to the room, stood there for a few minutes, and only pretended I did.

Our Luxury Suite was composed of a bedroom and what the hotel called a sitting room. There was a connecting door in the middle and we left it open at all times. The sitting room contained a large chair and a gray sofa. The bedroom had a single large bed and a dresser made of maple. On top of the dresser sat a red-and-silver thermos with pictures of flowers on it, and every day the staff would fill it with hot water and give us some tea leaves, which my mother used to make tea. She would also fold clothes and prepare food on that dresser.

There wasn't enough space on that bed for all of us so my parents asked for an extra cot. It was a folding cot with a beige canvas surface and Leslie got to sleep on it. She later said it reminded her of a military cot.

My mother, Christine, Mikey and I took the large bed. The chair in the sitting room had a high, stiff back; too high and stiff to lie against, so my father took the cushion and laid it on the floor. The cushion was three feet by eight feet; large enough to act like a thin mattress. Then he took some cushions from the sofa and used them as pillows. That's where he would sleep, he decided.

At first no one wanted to join him, but my little sister Christine, feeling a little sorry for him, volunteered to share his little island on the floor. She was seven years old at the time; two years younger than me but much more sensitive to other people's feelings.

When we woke the next morning my brother and I complained that our backs hurt. Our mother lifted our shirts and noticed little red scabs on our skin. We'd been bitten by bed bugs. Our bed had a mattress but underneath it was a straw mat; the same kind used in the other rooms. The bed bugs must have come from there, my mother assumed.

She then picked up a bag of oranges she'd bought earlier in Hong Kong. She was always buying fruits and snacks in the event that her children got hungry. She used to pack cookies in her pockets just in case there was no other food around. There were six oranges in the bag, the bag was netting made of string, and she noticed that parts of the string were gnawed and broken.

"Hoo!" she said. "It was bitten by a rat!"

"No, that's not a rat," my father said. He said it must've been a cockroach. He'd seen them last night. In fact, he noticed the hotel had some big ones.

"No, look," my mother said. She pointed to some bite marks on the skin of the oranges.

But my father was sure there was no rat, and even if there was, it hadn't chewed the oranges last night.

Still, it was enough to scare Christine, and she decided she wasn't going to sleep on the floor any more. There was no way she was going to sleep on that floor! She wanted a place on the bed, with the rest of us, so that night she said she saw a rat run past her. Again my father dismissed it.

There wasn't a rat, he said.

So we went back to sleep, and a little while later, Christine started screaming. "A rat!" she whined. "I saw a rat!" So my mother brought her up to the bed with us and she slept there for the rest of our stay.

Another snack my mother picked up was a candy called *Sun Char Bang*. The name translates into something like Cherry Pulp, although the candy is made from haw flakes. The word "flakes" doesn't do it justice. The candy's made of berries from the Chinese Hawthorn tree and comes wrapped in a thin paper roll. Each roll contains a stack of small, flat, reddish purple discs, about the size of quarters, only thinner, and they taste sweet, like dried cherries and apples. When you put one in your mouth you can crumble it with your teeth or rest it on your tongue and then slowly savor its melting fruit taste. My mother used to eat it when she was a little girl and the candy is still available today with the same packaging and flavor. Remembering how much she enjoyed it, she absently bought a roll from a store in Hong Kong and when she let us try some we fell in love with it immediately. Every time we saw a roll in a shopping stall or at the market we begged my mother and father for more. I would bother them incessantly for it. I loved the candy so much I tried to hoard it. As I got close to finishing one roll I would wrap it back up in its paper and put it in my coat pocket, or in my little suitcase, hoping to stash away enough to take with me back to America. I had little stockpiles here and there and together I was sure they added up to at least one full roll.

One night I left the candy out on the windowsill of our hotel. I remember two partial rolls sitting there, opened, waiting for me...

And the next morning... they were gone.

I found out later that my father had woken in the middle of the night and finally spotted that rat. He saw it eating my favorite candy so he threw it all away.

There was a schoolyard outside our window, several stories below. In the morning, we'd hear the Chinese children doing the same exercises my father did when he was little. Occasionally we'd watch them perform — they stood in rows, one in front of the other, on the green grass — and Leslie and I would try to mimic their calisthenics.

Arms outstretched, hands in front.

Then arms and hands up in the air.

Then hands on hips. Lean to one side. Stretch.

Lean to the other. Stretch.

Most times we just watched. They could see us too, peripherally, I was sure of it. Sometimes I thought they even glanced in our direction and I felt embarrassed, almost guilty, knowing, just from the condition of our hotel room alone, the homes they must've come from.

I remember seeing two young girls about my age, one taller than the other, and at the age of nine I fell in love with both of them. I wanted to meet them, say something kind to them. I thought maybe they'd feel the same way about me.

I had very innocent crushes back then. On the way to China, one of our stops was Taiwan. Our tour guide there took us to a village that the Taiwanese had turned into a large, sprawling, touristy souvenir park. I couldn't have known it all those years ago, but I was getting a glimpse of what mainland China would look like in three decades once capitalism took hold. In the souvenir park we saw a bamboo dance performed by some local girls. A few of them were close to my age. They all wore shiny red and blue costumes made to look like traditional garb, and they positioned themselves around two pairs of long bamboo poles placed side by side on stage. When the music started, the younger girls raised the poles a few inches off the floor and slammed them together to a resounding drum beat as the taller, well-trained girls hopped and danced between them. Then the younger girls crossed one pair of poles over the other and the older girls skipped and danced between the perpendicular sets. They slammed the poles quickly and loudly and their timing was meticulous. A single misstep, one wrong beat, and a dancer, maybe two, could get her ankles broken. There was nothing on their girls' faces that indicated that they were enjoying this but still I watched in awe. The *clack!-clack!-clack!* of the bamboo poles made my heart pound. There was a young girl about my size near the front of the stage that I took sympathy on. I wanted to talk to her. It was one of the first times I realized how lucky I was to be an American. I wanted to show her that I was an American and thought I could quietly impress her and somehow end up marrying her. I imagined the two of us standing there backstage after the dance, smiling to each other. Those were the kind of crushes I had.

But if one of the girls from the schoolyard outside our hotel had looked up I probably would've looked away, or pretended I wasn't watching her exactly, but watching them all.

The yard wasn't full of just girls. There was this one boy that Leslie and I remember. The boy hated exercising. He went through all the motions with as little effort as possible. His classmates would raise their arms out and above themselves and he would make the barest wave. They would place their hands on their hips and stretch from side to the side. He would lean a little here and there. He looked sleepy. He looked like he was just trying to get through every tedious morning with the barest minimum effort. The boy's laziness amused Leslie and she'd surreptitiously point him out to Christine and me. Leslie would imitate him and we'd duck beneath the windowsill or step back behind the curtains, out of view.

Some mornings would start out so hot and humid that I couldn't even climb out of bed to watch the children. I'd be too weak and wilted by the time I finally got up.

One morning as my father was sitting reading a newspaper, I asked, "Can we go back to the good hotel?"

"What? Which one is that?"

"The Manhattan Hotel."

My mother was standing at the dresser making tea for breakfast and realized I was mangling the name, "Nathan Hotel" — the place we'd stayed at just a week earlier with the nice beds, air conditioning and TV that played Kung Fu soap operas.

"He wants to go back to Hong Kong," she said.

I had no comprehension of where we were exactly. I didn't understand that we were at least a two-hour train ride from what was then another country.

"Hunh? Oh no, no, no, we can't," my father said, smiling in the way that often revealed how amused and disappointed he was that his children were becoming so soft and spoiled. "We can't go there."

Then, still smiling, he returned to his paper.

We see trees coming up. They line the sides of the road. It's like entering a corridor of dark green leafy columns with sunlight speckling between them.

Behind the trees are acres of soft, willowy rice fields. Leslie points to a small mountain in the hazy distance. "That's the mountain your father used to climb when he was little."

The village of Tin Sum lies six miles southwest of Taishan. Taishan is a small city in southern Guangdong Province, and Guangdong Province is located in southern China. We've come south, south, and southwest from Beijing. The hillbilly part of China, as my father likes to call it. When we came in 1973, we traveled northwest from Hong Kong.

The name Tin Sum means "Heart of the Field". It's a small village of about forty people — half the number that used to live there when my father was a child. When he left, there were fifty-four families comprising eighty people. At the front of the village, and in front of my father's house, sits the large rectangular pond, and across the pond is another small village called Bock Jap, which means "North Gate". Together the two villages, with the pond between them, are known as "The Gate".

Just ahead is the turnoff to the two villages. There's a man-made arch in front of the turnoff. It's made of concrete, painted a soft pink and adorned with temple-like decor. It frames the farmland behind it. It's called the Gum Bien Gate, named after the village that paid for it. It's the gate to "The Gate".

We pass through the arch and drive a half mile more. The fields on both sides of the road are filled with rows and rows of tall green rice plants, all standing ready for the autumn harvest. My father tells Mr. Tong to pull over and we park on a patch of dirt underneath a tree next to a small wooden table.

In 1973 we couldn't even get this far. After a long bumpy ride we finally came to a clearing in the field and had to walk the rest of the way along an uneven farm path, but by then we were all glad to climb out of that cramped car.

My father and Yu Chung slowly step out of our van. Yu Chung knows the family living in my father's house. They could be called squatters or they could be called caretakers, depending on how my father wishes to view them. My father doesn't know when they moved in exactly; it was sometime between his second trip here, a little less than a decade ago, and today. His second trip was in 1997 and he came with my mother and little brother Mike. The house was empty and unused. Someone had written *Mao Tse-Tung* in chalk on the front door and it angered my brother. He thought someone from the government did it but my father thought it more likely the act of a young vandal.

Officially the house still belongs to my father. His father before him built it; his family lived in it; and his mother spent her final days there. Most of the villagers know the history of the house and no one else has laid claim to the property. There's been no sale of the land underneath. Even Yu Chung politely refers to it as my father's house. But that's as far as my father's claim goes. He thinks there's a deed and thinks Yu Chung knows where it might be, but even if my father got his hands on it he'd have a hard time doing anything with it. From his conversations with Yu Chung, my father thinks that the family who lives there now simply moved in one day. But they live there respectfully. They still keep his mother's photograph on the wall. And they've taken better care of the house than my father, or any of us, living on the other side of the world, could've.

When my father's father Quong finally settled in America, he not only left his house behind, he left his mother and sister behind as well. While he regularly sent money back home, it was primarily his grandfather who took care of the family. His grandfather was the one who'd taught Quong to be a butcher, and he specialized in pork. Sometimes his grandfather was hired by others; sometimes he sold meat on his own. Whatever he couldn't sell, he'd preserve with salt, or take home as leftovers for his family. So his family was never without meat for too long; and among farmers, that was considered a real treat.

Quong's sister's was named Wen Yiang. To the other girls in the village she was considered a spoiled, rotten child who'd never worked a day in her life. At first she was cared for by her father; then when her father died she was cared for by her grandfather; then when her grandfather died, her brother took care of her with the money he sent; and after she finally married, her husband supported her.

In the village it was a tradition for a teenage girl of sixteen or seventeen to move into a house with a group of other girls so they could all help each other learn the customs of becoming a woman. The oldest girl in the house usually got married first, then returned to tell the other girls what it was like and what to expect. Even back then, my father and all the other boys referred to this kind of house as a "hen house".

One day Wen Yiang came home to her hen house with several pounds of leftover pork her grandfather had given her, and there, in front of all the other girls, proceeded to cook all the meat and eat it all herself, without even offering her friends so much as a single bite. After the meal she felt so stuffed that she lay down and complained about how much her belly hurt, and the other girls saw it as fitting punishment for her selfishness. The story of her thoughtlessness followed her around for the rest of her life and when she got married almost none of her girlfriends came to her wedding.

She met her husband in school. He became a teacher, then an official in Guangdong Province, then passed an examination to enter a military school set up by Chiang Kai-Shek, and became a colonel. During the war her husband was sent to Manchuria as an assistant to a high-ranking government official and was there when the Japanese invaded in 1931. He was never heard from again. No one knew the exact circumstances of his death, but after the war the Chinese government informed Wen Yiang that they would honor her husband's army pension — but only if she had a male heir. She had had two daughters by her husband but no son, so she adopted a small boy. The boy she adopted was Yu Chung.

My father had never been close to his aunt, Wen Yiang. He barely knew her and rarely received any correspondence from her. He knew a little of the adoption but not much. But in 1970, Yu Chung, possibly prompted by his mother, sent a letter of introduction to my father, writing:

It has been nice to hear anything from you since we were children.

My father was forty-six by then. Yu Chung was in his early twenties. They'd never known each other as children; had never even met; but my father understood the words to be a polite figure of speech and appreciated the gesture.

Yu Chung wrote that his mother and sisters were living in an apartment in Guangzhou and that he was living in Tin Sum. His words gave comfort to my father. My father hadn't seen his house since he'd left China but understood that property could only be

149

passed down to the next male in the family. And he realized that Yu Chung was now taking care of his home.

Yu Chung went on to say:

> We would like to see you if you ever have a
> chance to visit us in China.

My father didn't get a chance to see him during our first visit, but in 1993, on their second visit, my father and mother met him in Guangzhou. At an apartment there, a cousin introduced him.

"This is Yu Chung."

Thirty-eight years before meeting Yu Chung, my father Yot was working on his first farm in America.

It was the summer of 1955, and Yot and his friend Chuck Fong had just started leasing a small plot of land from the Japanese farmer in Imlay, Michigan.

"I was experimenting learning how to raise vegetables," Yot recalled. "I never really had a lot of experience so I bought some vegetable seeds, borrowed some equipment from the farmer, and learned whatever I could."

The farmer's name was Frederick and, like Yot's father, he'd also owned a food store, except his imported Japanese food. During the war, Frederick's family fell on stressful times and Yot later learned that Frederick's father committed suicide during that time. After a while Frederick decided he didn't want to run the store any longer so he sold it and bought two hundred acres of farmland with his savings. From what Yot understood, he got it cheap too. He grew carrots, parsnips, lettuce and cabbage, but found he didn't like farming either, so he hired others to do the work for him. Even his own two brothers worked for him. They moved up from Tennessee and together the three men agreed to split whatever profits they made. While his brothers tended the land, Frederick ran the farm and trucked the produce to various wholesalers in the area.

That was how Yot had met him, when Frederick came to his father's store. And although he initially thought of the man as a truck farmer, he soon discovered Frederick was a businessman first and foremost. From the very start, Yot and Chuck found themselves dependent on him just to get themselves situated, and for the use of his land, Frederick charged them a little rent.

"Oh you can pay me fifty dollars for the summer," he said.

That wasn't bad, but the drive from Detroit to Imlay was sixty-five miles, so Yot asked him if there was a place they could stay.

"I got a little trailer. You can buy it from me for two hundred dollars."

"Okay," Yot said.

It was an old camper, part of it painted white, another part painted gray. It had two wheels with a hitch in front so Yot and Chuck put cinder blocks underneath to keep the vehicle level. The trailer was about five feet by ten feet and inside was a bunk bed, which Yot usually slept in, and a sleeping bag, which Chuck usually slept in.

They got water from a well on the farm and used it for washing, drinking and cooking, and had the use of an outhouse outside the barn. Frederick owned a two-bedroom house on the property but even his two brothers had to use their own outhouse. The barn had an electrical outlet and Yot and Chuck connected a small hot plate to it to cook their meals outside the trailer in the evenings. The summer was warm enough so that they never got too cold at night and during the day they spent all their hours in the fields.

Yot enjoyed farming. It was nice to rediscover that. He liked the open air and "the fun of seeing the vegetables coming up." He was nearing the end of his Five-Year Plan (although that really depended on whether or not he'd officially started it) but his main goal had always been to see if he could push himself to become healthy again. And every year, he told himself, he was going to stretch himself a little more, accomplish a little more, and find out what his limits were.

"I figured I would do it slowly. I wanted to see how soon I could get back to a normal life."

When the season was over, Yot and Chuck planned to return to the city. Yot would go back to his father's store. Chuck would resume his job as a cook. When Yot went to settle their payment, Frederick tried to change the terms. A neighbor of Frederick's had told him that the small plot of land was worth more than fifty dollars so Frederick asked for an increase. He told Yot that they'd worked past the summer season they'd talked about, but Yot wouldn't agree to the new amount.

"If you don't, I have to hold the trailer," Frederick told him.

Yot argued him on that too.

"I got a right to keep it!" Frederick said.

Even if Yot won the trailer, he realized, there was nothing he could do with it. He'd need another vehicle to tow it and he didn't even know where he'd tow it to. Finally Yot said, "Oh you can have it then!"

He knew Frederick wasn't making a lot of money off the farm. It was difficult work. Years later, he'd hear that Frederick's own brothers left to take jobs on a Chrysler assembly line. And Chuck decided it just wasn't in his blood. But Yot knew it was in his. Chuck remained a cook but the following year, Yot made plans to buy a farm of his own (perhaps his Five-Year Plan was just now beginning). Yot had gone back to the store and to living with his brother but his brother had recently bought his first house; he and his wife were living in a small suburb called Berkeley now; so during his spare time Yot borrowed his father's car and began driving around.

"I started looking around and looking around and looked in Sterling Heights and Algonac and pretty soon I was in Marine City."

He wasn't sure what he was searching for exactly but he found Marine City to be a peaceful, quiet farming community. In the distance was the city's tall, single standing water tower. He parked along the St. Clair River and saw small boats on the water, people fishing, and families enjoying the day. Across the river was Canada. Canada looked so close it almost seemed within a stone's throw.

"Pretty soon I found a farm of about five acres so I asked the farmer if I could take a look around. So I walked around and saw black soil and I thought, 'Oh, that's nice.'"

He knew how to check for fertility and richness. He would pick some soil up in his hands, play with it, rub it between his fingers, drop it; stare at the ground, give it some thought.

The farm was for sale and he wanted it but he had never negotiated for anything like this before so he asked his brother Fon for help. Together they contacted the real estate owner and found the asking price was $7,500.

"I said, 'Okay, we can agree on a price but we want the tractor and equipment for rent,' and at first they refused and I said, 'Okay, I can't farm without the equipment,' so they thought maybe that was the end of the deal, so they agreed. I think the real estate agent talked him into it."

He asked his father for a loan. His father tended to show his love through gestures rather than words and gave him the money without hesitation. They went to the bank and drew up a cashier's check for $5,500 which went directly to the farmer, but the farmer still owed $2,000 on the property, so Yot opened a checking account and made monthly installments to the bank.

By May of 1956 he was farming on his own land. It kept him busy from sunrise to sundown. He would spend at least ten to twelve hours a day in the field.

"After you work all day, you cook and have supper, you sit down and watch TV — you're so tired you just go to bed. You're working so hard you don't have an idle moment so you don't have time to think about being lonely. The only time you think about your life is when you sit down to rest."

But the work meant something to him. When he left the sanatorium seven years ago he hadn't expected to live very long. He was happy to have his health and freedom but assumed he'd never live to see the age of fifty. There were times when he thought he wouldn't even make it much past thirty. And here he was, thirty-one years old, tilling his own soil and growing his own food.

And he found company in the effort too. During his first year he mentioned to his friends that he might need some help. The farmhouse wasn't completely finished but it had two bedrooms, a kitchen, a bathroom and a laundry room. Yot could take one bedroom and a hired hand could take the other. A friend of his, Guy Yee, expressed an interest so Yot hired him for $300 a month. It was the same amount of money a cook made but Yot didn't have a lot of cash at his disposal. He paid Guy some money to start with and arranged to make further payments to him after the first crop sold. Yot knew he'd take a loss in his first few years but also had faith that, with time, the farm would become profitable.

"We knew to begin with that it was hard work. You have to go out in the hot sun and just work. But later in the fall we got to hunt birds. And I even got to buy a shotgun. You tried to hunt pheasant. There were a lot of pheasant there but I didn't shoot any. But I did kill a pheasant on the road.

"There's a lot of dirt roads up there. So you're driving along at a normal speed and sometimes when you see them they don't even care. They're not scared of cars. So you start to speed up and as you get close to them then they try to fly away, and they fly up at an angle right in front of you and you can usually hit them with your bumper or your windshield. Yeah, we got a few of those that way."

He borrowed a .22 long rifle from a friend of his and although he still couldn't manage to shoot any pheasant, he hit another one with his car and felt obliged to give it to his friend. Later, after his friend cleaned and cooked the bird, he told Yot that all the bones were broken.

He had run-ins with other animals too. Once, while shoveling in the field, Yot saw a skunk and waited patiently for it to leave. There were plenty of skunk in the area. "Not just one! I saw a few of them!" He'd often see them lying dead on the side of the road, hit by passing motorists, and they'd make a horrible stink.

But Guy had never seen a skunk before. He was from China and didn't know what a skunk was. One day he met one face to face and returned to the house to tell Yot about it.

"I threw a rock at the wildcat. Imagine! He had a white streak on his back."

"Oh, you ought to stay away from him," Yot said, and explained why.

"Too late, I already got sprayed."

And that's when Yot noticed how bad his friend smelled. They washed his clothes but still couldn't get rid of the odor. But his friend, still angry at the animal, grabbed the .22 rifle, went outside, and pumped the skunk full of rounds.

The harvest from the first year was modest. Even minor by Yot's standards. The crops had come out small and weak because of the lack of regular watering.

Anything could go wrong with farming. The plants could get too little sun or too much heat. They could receive too little water or be drowned by too many storms. Yot thought that if he could install an irrigation system he could make watering a little more predictable so he spent the next season digging irrigation trenches and installing some piping. The cost was another thousand dollars.

Later some oil speculators from Shell came to visit him. Oil had been discovered on one of the farms in Marine City so the speculators asked Yot if they could lease some of his land for a couple years. If oil was discovered, he'd get a small percentage. Even if no oil was found, the lease would help defray some of his expenses.

The following year the crops came out better, but still not what he'd hoped, and not enough to turn a profit. The irrigation system he installed wasn't working properly. It was faulty, a little undependable. So he spent the year digging up the system, laying down better pipes. He expanded the size of his field too, which meant more labor, more irrigation, and it cost him even more money: a little under a thousand dollars for the effort.

And there were times when he couldn't work. Some nights were so chilly he would just sit at home reading. During the cold season there would be nothing to do at all so he'd move back in with his brother and sister-in-law. Then one winter, Yot's father suggested he take a job as a waiter at a Chinese restaurant called Evergreen Garden. And that led to another turn in his life.

We're in my father's village.

As Yu Chung and my father approach his house, Yu Chung starts to slow his steps. He's a polite and modest man. He's told the people living in the house that he and my father will be visiting, and by slowing down he allows my father to arrive first.

The house is occupied by a family of farmers. They're former neighbors of my father's but he's not well acquainted with them. The oldest member of the family is the grandmother. She's small, frail, with white hair and kind eyes. Her back is bent, perhaps from a lifetime of work, or maybe just age itself. She wears a blue top, smokes an old fashioned pipe and has a wide, happy smile for my father. She's unable to stand straight but rises momentarily from her wood and wicker chair to say hello. Because my father is so close to her in age he refers to her as "sister". Ah Slaw. Her husband, now gone, was named Sik. So he calls her Ah Sik Slaw. Sister-in-Law Sik.

Her son-in-law, wearing a purple T-shirt and shorts, comes out to greet us. He carries a stick across his shoulders with two buckets strung on either end of it. He wears sandals, an old straw hat, and has a small beard. He and my father shake hands. His name is Fon, just like my father's brother. We meet his wife, a thin woman with short black hair. She's the most outgoing of all, smiling and making eye contact with each of us. Just like he does with the grandmother, my father also refers to the wife as Ah Slaw. Ah Fon Slaw. Sister-in-Law Fon. He considers it impolite to ask her for her name directly. As he later tells me, "You don't ask the women their names."

My father's house is older than I remember. Smaller and more run down. It's squarish in shape, two stories tall, made of charcoal gray bricks. It has a dark, speckled, mottled look. It's survived four generations so it must be sturdy, but later, after this visit, I'll have an image in my head that it's slightly slanted and a little dangerous to be in during an earthquake. I think that's because it sits next to a collapsed house and I'll tie the two together in my memory. The house to the right of my father's is just a pile of wood and old bricks.

The family owns a young water buffalo. The buffalo stands at the edge of the pond with his short rope leash tied to a small sapling. His coat is short and shiny. His eyes are wide and a little nervous. He must be a child, a teenager. He doesn't have the same tired, uncaring attitude I've seen in older water buffalo just a half size larger. He looks so innocent and cute I can't help but smile at him and Nancy is entranced too, but as we take a couple steps forward to say hello he takes a couple shy steps back.

Yu Chung's youngest son Prosper strolls about. He stops at the edge of the pond, pauses, and gives the water buffalo a slap on the ass. It's an impulsive act that makes the young animal jump a little and move away from him. Finally, after a brief pause, the buffalo climbs into the water for a swim. He can't go very far. The rope around his neck allows him to travel only a few yards; but it's hot, the water is cool, and we're making him nervous.

We see hens with their young chicks. There's a type of dog we've been seeing a lot of since arriving in southern China. It's a mutt, a mix of different breeds, but they all have the same look: short golden-orange fur, a short black snout, and a defensive, curious, halting look. Later, I'll read that they're probably Chinese Foos — a mix of Chow Chows and European hunting dogs. But they have the same look on their faces that I see on their owners: something that says This is a Hard Life and Who Are You?

A girl approaches.   She's about fifteen years old, wears wireframe glasses, white shorts and a red polka-dotted halter top. Her clothes look like hand-me-downs, possibly even third-hand, like a throwback to the American '70s.   She could pass for one of my own sisters during their awkward teenage years.   She's the youngest member of the farmer's family and as she walks up to her parents it's obvious that she's their pride and joy.   They introduce us to her with smiles.   My father refers to her with a word that means Little Girl.

My father takes out his Polaroid.   His instant friend-maker.   He asks them to pose and smile.   A flash, a whir.   A minute later he's showing them their photo.   He takes a picture of the grandmother. She smiles.

The husband returns with a long, green stalk of sugarcane over his shoulder.   Everyone in his family, and all three generations, are finally here with us.   He hands the sugarcane to his wife.   She grabs a foot-long curved blade and cuts the twigs and leaves off for the water buffalo.   He's back on shore and starts eating it right away. He chews slowly and deliberately, his mouth moving in a circular motion.   The farmer's wife cuts off a small sliver of the cane and hands it to me.   The inside is brown, fibrous, soft and chewy.   It's sweet and delicious.   Brown sugar candy.

She cuts pieces off for everyone and after a while the grandmother opens the front door and invites everyone into the house.

The inside is small, dark and musty.   Sunlight from the door illuminates the middle of the room.   There's an old, slanted bed in the right corner and lots of dirty gold urns, metal frames, and bed ends on the floor, some of it in heaps or piles.   The house has the same dank smell as an old attic.   Everything is dark red, gray brick, and tarnished gold and silver.

It's not the same house I remember seeing as a child.   I remember a cleaner, more spacious house; a house so large it looked like an old rustic mansion with stairs that led to a second floor, and a balcony that overlooked everything.

There were times, in my dreams, that I even saw a house that was spotless and new, with clean beige walls and light spilling in from a white-plastic-framed window.   The kind of house you'd find in an American suburb.   The kind of house my own mother was always trying to create.   A warm, inviting house.

I was smaller then.   The house looked more magnificent, especially when we heard that a large family was living there at the time. There was even mention of my father's former maid, and that added to its majesty. I remember my father's adoration when he stood in that house.

The stairs are still where I remember them. The window's where I remember it too. The second floor is U-shaped, not the mysterious cottage balcony that I recall. It runs along one side, then the front, then the other side, and there's an open space in the middle. We can see up into it. And on the center of the wall, in an old handmade shrine, is a picture of my father's mother.

The two women, Yu Chung's wife and Fon Slaw, the farmer's wife, begin setting up a modest sacrifice.

They move a small wooden table to the front middle of the room. On the table they place a small, round can containing several sticks of incense, and in front of the can they put some fruit and fake money. The fake money is like large play money, only the print is so big and comical that it couldn't possibly be mistaken for the real thing. The fruit is an offering to my father's ancestors and the money will be burned after the prayers are finished. If the farmers were rich, my father told me, they'd burn real money. If they were extremely rich they might even place some gold coins there. But they live a humble life, and this is one of two sacrifices they'll be setting up today. They light the incense and my father kneels before the small makeshift altar to pay respects to his mother.

The incense makes a light, sweet, gray smoke that wafts into the air. After a minute my father stands, takes a step back, and bows three times.

Then it's our turn. My sister and I kneel before the table. If there's a prayer I should be saying I don't know the words. I'm not even sure if there's a single thought running through my head except the desire to do this right: to follow my father's actions, step by step; to show reverence to my grandmother. I'm letting my sister take the lead, and I'm watching her peripherally. When she starts to rise, I start to rise. When my sister bows three times, I bow with her. If my grandmother could see us I know she'd be pleased.

Nancy, Gloria, Yu Chung and his sons look on. I know Nancy would like to kneel and show her respects too, but as a red-haired American woman she's worried about attracting any more attention than she already has, so she remains where she is, to the side, by the slanted bed. When we're finished, Fon Slaw lights the money with a match. It burns quickly, filling the room with brightness and smoke.

My grandmother's photograph hangs crookedly over a tiny, cluttered, reddish-brown shrine on the second floor. From where I'm standing I can see it through the U-shaped opening. My father has been talking about the photograph from the moment we began planning this trip. He'd like to take it back with him but isn't sure how to ask the family.

Fon Slaw sees me staring at it and gestures to me. Leslie translates. "She says you can go upstairs if you want to get a better look."

I raise my camera. Can I take a photograph of it?

She nods yes.

I head up the dark, wooden steps. The balcony of the second floor is narrow and made of wood. It feels firm enough but it's dark up here, my eyes haven't adjusted yet, and the balustrade is so low that it's more of a suggestion than a railing. One wrong step and I could easily fall over the side. I'd heard that another family used to sleep up here, but now, as an adult, I can see there's only enough room for a few people to lie down on some blankets or small pillows.

I angle for a better view of my grandmother. Her face is framed, behind glass, sitting on a dark red altar. It's hard to believe her photograph has survived all these decades here, alone like this. Something decorative rests in front of her frame: a small can of incense; some small flowers; it's hard to tell in these shadows.

My father doesn't know when the photograph was taken exactly. He thinks his mother posed for it a couple years after he left China, which would make her about thirty-seven years old, five years younger than me. He'd heard that her cousin opened a portrait studio in town but his mother never told him or his brother about the photograph, nor sent them a copy. When we first came to visit in 1973, my father looked up and saw it hanging on the wall. He said, "Oh, I haven't seen that photo before." It was a smaller picture back then; about the size of a hand; but it was a nice surprise, like a final gift from her.

Later, in between then and now, someone enlarged the photograph. There was another family who took up residence in the house for a while. The oldest son in the family, a man of about thirty, told my father he dabbled in photography. He was most likely the one who blew her image up, drew in her eyebrows, drew an outline around her eyes, and deepened the contours around her lips and teeth. In this light I can't tell that anything's been done, but my father, who's memorized the image, said he noticed the changes right away.

But this dimness makes her seem centuries away right now. It looks like the frame has rarely been touched; rarely been dusted.

I'm trying to imagine her living in this house with her two sons away in America. I imagine she must have come up here to store her clothes or stow her blankets. I imagine a woman who died over sixty years ago without her husband or children at her side, wondering perhaps if they'd ever hear what became of her.

After I come down we all step outside. It's cool and dim inside the house but hot again under this bright sun. Slowly we amble over to the van. We're going out to the fields to visit my great grandfather's grave.

Yu Chung rides in the van with us but his wife and sons take their mopeds, carrying farmer Fon and his wife Fon Slaw. We drive across a paved road, then onto a dirt road that becomes grassy brush. It's hot and cramped and bumpy. We stop outside an old, dilapidated brick house. One corner has collapsed and the house looks deserted. There are smaller houses nearby made with red, orange and gray bricks. An angry black dog is tied up in one yard and barks the moment we step out of the van, never letting up, even after we pass him by.

Farmer Fon and Yu Chung's sons lead the way, chopping through the tropical brush with machetes. We wade through weeds and stalks and leaves chest-high, some as high as our heads. It's hot and humid and our faces are hidden from the sun only momentarily by the tall plants and tree branches that we have to duck around. The terrain becomes rocky and uneven and it'd be easy to take a misstep and twist an ankle. But I'm carrying a tripod in one hand with my camera bag slung over my shoulder, and I'm more worried about damaging the camera than my own back, and somehow that keeps me focused.

The trail wraps around another large pond.

We walked another trail, not too far from this one, when I was nine years old. It was also just after we'd seen my father's house. My brother and sisters, my mother and I were standing outside the house with several villagers while my father talked with his cousins, and his cousins offered to show him where his mother was buried.

An old woman was living in my father's house at the time with her son, son's wife, and grandchildren, all grown. Several of them accompanied us into the field. One of the old woman's grandsons — a tall, thin, gaunt young man — let me sit on his bicycle. His father, the one who dabbled in photography, let Mikey sit on his bicycle. The two men steered us along. A woman carried my little sister Christine on her shoulders. Leslie, who was eleven years old, walked with my parents.

The land was green and lush. It was soft and moist and smelled like fertile, grassy farmland. There was a mountain in the distance. The man who steered my bicycle wore white. He was a kind, friendly man. He had a calmness about him. There have been times in my adulthood when I wonder how we must've looked to these people back then: four American-born children wearing clothes and shoes that probably seemed extravagant to them. Leslie, eleven years old at the time, spoke fluent Cantonese. She had metal braces and she remembered the villagers looking at her, talking openly among themselves, thinking she couldn't understand them, saying, "They must be rich. Look. She has silver on her teeth."

It seemed like a long journey. We walked up a long, grassy incline. We crossed a small, craggy gully and the two men guiding the bicycles had to be careful negotiating each bump and turn. All I was concerned with was balancing myself on the seat, listening to the *click-click-click* of the wheels and studying the rocks and grass along our way.

Finally we arrived at a large, open field. There was a high hill behind us called The Lion's Hill because it looked like a lion's head to the villagers. In front of us were tall mounds of dirt and vegetation, and beyond that was a flat field. The mounds, all piled together, looked like a long, bumpy pillow at the head of a flat, green bed. When my father was a child, he told me, they used to plant peanuts and sweet potatoes in that bed. Farther off was a rice field, some water, and even farther in the distance were two other villages, one to the right and one to the left. Sometime after my father left China, the villagers turned the peanut field into a common cemetery because the hill, field, and water made the feng shui so ideal.

The villagers pointed to one of the mounds of dirt. My father looked at it. I've talked with each member of my family about this moment but none of us have the same memory so all I can do is share my own. The villagers dug at the dirt a little. They seemed to be trying to look for something, or demonstrating something. My father talked to them. Then they stopped. My father kicked at the dirt, overturning some of it with his shoe. He looked disappointed. The villagers looked like they wanted to help soothe his feelings but didn't know what to say. My father turned and looked out at the field. I couldn't see his face but I could tell that he was crying.

My mother and the villagers let him be. Then after a while the villagers put Leslie and me on the bicycles and we all headed back to my father's house.

Along the way I started playing with the back wheel, tapping the spokes with my foot, and my foot got caught between the wheel and the metal rim. I cried out and everyone stopped. My mother asked what happened. The grandson who owned the bicycle told her, and my mother ordered me to get off the bike and walk. I told her that I wanted to keep riding, that I could do it, and the grandson agreed: it was an accident. But my mother said no. So I walked the rest of the way with everyone else.

At the house I asked my mother what happened in the field. Why was my father crying? She told me it was because he had come to see his mother's grave but no one could find it. There was a tradition, she explained. When a person was buried, he or she was buried lying down. A year later the body was exhumed and the body was placed in a sitting position inside an urn. The body was then reburied in an area with good feng shui. The bodies were seated so that they could "look ahead". The mound that formed over their urn was called a "little hill". The villagers said that they had followed the tradition but when they arrived at the gravesite, they couldn't remember where my father's mother had been reburied. They'd lost her.

That night, in our hotel, my father slept alone on the sitting room floor. Perhaps my mother just wanted to leave him to himself. Or perhaps he requested it. Later, as an adult, Leslie would tell me that in the middle of the night she could hear our father crying to himself.

Years later my uncle Fon visited the house to pay his respects too. After he returned, he informed my father that there was no body under that mound of dirt. During Mao Tse Tung's reign it was believed that bones contained a natural fertilizer and villagers across the country were told to dig up the buried bodies, grind the bones and add it to the soil. The country was attempting to increase its harvest but the policy turned out to be a catastrophic error. Something about the process — whether it was the ground-up bones or the disruption to the farming communities or perhaps, as the government claimed, a series of natural disasters — something led to a massive crop shortage and China suffered one of its longest, deepest famines.

When I ask my father why his cousins took us to the false gravesite, he thinks it's because his cousins were trying to ease his burden. When they first told him, standing outside his house, about his mother's burial site, he remembers becoming a little suspicious. They'd told him his mother was buried in the same spot as his grandmother, that they were buried together, but my father knew his mother had died fifteen years before his grandmother.

When his grandmother was buried, she had originally been buried in a corner of the village near one of the gardens and it took three years before they found a good area to rebury her. That's how her body came to be placed in the field by the Lion's Hill. But my father knew it was unlikely that his mother's body would also be exhumed after all those years and buried in the same urn as his grandmother. Yet, when his cousins told him about her grave, he wanted to see it. Later, after we left his village, he asked his aunt in Guangzhou about it, and she tried to explain... but said this, and said that, and finally admitted they didn't know where she was.

The man who let me ride his bicycle emigrated to Los Angeles. His grandmother, the old woman who lived in my father's house, died. No one remembers what became of the woman who carried Christine on her shoulders. My father may never know exactly where his mother was buried; he's lost touch with the people who knew, or they've disappeared, but he takes solace in knowing that his mother is now part of the land.

A twenty minute hike leads us to a small opening in the fields. We make our way down to a circular depression among the hills. Several trees sit in the center of this depression and provide some shade and a place to drop our bags. I can see why my great grandfather was buried here. It's a beautiful spot. A very inviting area. And the trees create a natural marker.

Farmer Fon and his wife Fon Slaw start to rake and hoe the weeds beside a little hill. Everyone else takes a moment to catch their breath. Yu Chung's wife has brought a box of bottled waters. She passes bottles out to everyone. Her oldest son Dragon kneels down and starts shaving the bark off a sugar cane. He slices pieces off for each person. My father chats with Yu Chung. This is the closest thing we've had to a picnic since we've arrived. Dragon offers me a slice of sugar cane and smiles as we both chew our pieces. It's fibrous, sweet, and cooling. Prosper occasionally teases me about something but I still don't know what he's saying.

Farmer Fon, Fon Slaw, and Yu Chung's wife have cleared the brush away and turned the little hill into a small monument. They've put fake money on the mound, poked sticks of incense into the dirt and lit the incense. It smells sweet and relaxing. They kneel before the sacrifice, clasp their hands together and pray in silence. When they finish, they welcome us over, and my father, sister and I stand before the monument. We have a moment of silence, then bow three times.

12

In the winter of 1958 my father began working as a waiter at Evergreen Garden.

I have a faint recollection of the restaurant from my childhood. It was a modest business. The inside had a green decor. It was always dim inside, always a little lonely. There was a table in the back where I would sit and draw. A small black-and-white television sat on top of a cabinet and always seemed to be on. My mother's father was the owner and he also cooked there. He was a big, tough-looking, barrel-chested man with thick dark eyebrows who always had a cigar in his mouth or in his fingers. He always smelled like smoke. He had a widow's peak and I was always a little intimidated by him. His wife, my mother's mother, was a nice woman with short, curly, permed black hair who always used to smile and address me with her sing-song voice. Sometimes she would talk to me in Chinese and, knowing only a few words, I would mostly stare back, waiting for the appropriate moment to nod my head in a vague sort of way. But usually when she saw me, she'd say, almost like a little bird, "Hello Curt-yyyy," and I'd say hello and that would be the extent of our conversation.

My parents tried to get my sisters and brother and me to speak Chinese but they never enforced it. It was more like they just occasionally remembered to nag us, so naturally we forgot whatever little we learned. My older sister was the only one who became and stayed fluent. I was always a little shy when I went to Evergreen Garden because my grandfather employed two other cooks in his kitchen and they'd try to speak to me in Chinese and I didn't know what they were saying so I'd just look down at the table or avoid eye contact.

My mother used to take Leslie and me there when she visited her family and I would occupy myself watching TV. On Saturday mornings I used to watch a show called "Sir Graves Ghastly" where a man dressed as an old vampire sat up in a casket and introduced a black-and-white monster movie. I knew he wasn't really a vampire but I didn't know he was that thing called an actor.

He had a happy Halloween-ish laugh and that was the only thing that told me he was trying to be entertaining instead of scary. I once saw an old Japanese classic on his show called *The Manster*. It was about a man who was half man, half monster. In the movie, a man screamed in agony while the monster part of him raged out of control. I became obsessed with that movie. Immediately after seeing it I started drawing pictures of a man splitting in two at the waist. On one side of the page I drew a normal person and on the other, a horrible creature of terrifying power.

I've made two visits to Evergreen Garden as an adult since that time. The restaurant is still standing, still has the same name, but the surrounding neighborhood is quite different. It's poor and depressed. It straddles Eight Mile Road, which was once the unofficial dividing line between inner city Detroit and suburban Detroit; the unspoken border between blacks and whites. Most of the residents now are African American. There was a time when African Americans couldn't find housing north of Eight Mile Road. That changed with time but only because the dividing line is no longer as obvious.

The first time Nancy and I drove there we saw a woman who was so drugged up she ambled down the middle of the street, talking to herself, and when she spotted our van she started yelling at us. She wasn't going to let us pass so I put the van in reverse and circumvented the block. On our second visit we circled the area to see the house where my mother grew up. My mother used to live in a small red brick house right around the corner from her restaurant. She and her sisters could leave the restaurant through the back door and be inside their home in less than a minute. After we spotted the house I drove slowly past it while Nancy rolled down her passenger-side window and shot some video of the exterior with her camcorder. There was a young African American woman standing on the porch next door talking on her cell phone. She wore a white T-shirt and shorts. I could tell she was offended that she'd just been caught on camera and she watched as we turned left and circled back to Evergreen Garden. We parked our van, stepped out, and I mounted a tripod to take some further footage of the restaurant. While I was shooting, the young African American woman pulled up in her own car. She had driven from her house to the front of the restaurant too, circling from less than half a block away, and parked in front of our van.

She never said a threatening word, never adopted an angry tone, and spoke only in a friendly and polite manner, but her voice had a subtle and quiet demand behind it. She wanted to know what we were shooting. I told her that we were taking a trip down memory lane. I pointed to the restaurant and told her that my parents met there. She asked us why we shot video of her on her porch. I told her it was accidental; we wanted footage of the house next to hers; my mother used to live there. She asked to see the footage. I'd noticed that just before she stepped out of her car she'd been talking to someone on her cell phone. The way she held her cell phone now, waist high, I could tell she was letting that someone listen in on our conversation. And I knew she wouldn't let us leave without seeing the footage.

She said she didn't want to be recorded in any video and stopped short of asking me to hand over the tape but, sensing things were already headed in that direction, I showed it to her. I rewound, played it back, showed her interviews with my sister Christine followed by interviews with my mother and father, then showed her the clip she was in. I told her I'd erase it. I rewound to a spot just seconds before she appeared, turned the camera toward my body, pressed the lens tight against my shirt, and shot pure black. Then I rewound again and showed her the revised footage.

"What did you do?" she asked.

"I erased your image. Will that work?"

She nodded. And smiled. "You understand, don't you?" she asked as she walked away.

"I understand completely."

Just before getting into her car she looked back.

"Your parents are very cute!"

"Thank you!" I said. "I'll tell them that!"

I've thought about that exchange every now and then. I thought about how both of us got what we wanted without a single terse word, and how even the smallest provocation could've made the situation ugly. I've thought about returning and leaving her a small thank you note, and how silly that would seem, and how sometimes it's better just to leave a moment the way it was.

The first time Nancy and I walked into Evergreen Garden we didn't stay very long. Half the restaurant had been closed up. The closed half was just an empty storefront with some old wood piled up on the floor behind the windows. The other half was still a Chinese restaurant. The outside used to have red letters on a green field. Now the facade is painted a deep red. The inside is beige. The interior doesn't even remotely resemble the innocent family restaurant from my childhood. A single table with two chairs sits alone in the storefront, and opposite that is the window where customers order their food. But the window is thick, bulletproof glass with a small slot, like a bank teller's slot, just big enough to accept money. I don't know how customers get their order after paying but Nancy said she saw a carousel built into the wall near the window that apparently spun around for delivery of the food. We saw an old Chinese couple peering at us from behind the glass. They seemed so very shy. Behind them was a small golden statue of Buddha with some incense burning in front of it. Nancy and I said hello and pretended to look at the menu, hoping to find some way of starting a conversation, but weren't sure what to say. I smiled as sympathetically as I could and said, "Thank you." Then we left.

There weren't many Chinese girls in Detroit when my mother first came over. There weren't many Chinese girls in the country at all. A large part of that was due to the Chinese Exclusion Act. For over sixty years the law had made it difficult for females from China to immigrate to America and the result was that the Chinese population had been rendered predominantly male. My mother received an immoderate amount of attention because of the imbalance. She was sixteen when she crossed the border. Few Chinese girls in Detroit were of marrying age during that time, and from early on, from the moment she first arrived, friends of her family began inquiring on her. What was she like? Did her parents have anyone in mind for her? It's a wonder she and my father ever got to know each other given all the scrutiny she fell under.

She was considered very attractive. I've seen photos of my mother from that period. She was petite with soft features, thick wavy black hair and large warm eyes. When I was growing up I thought she had a glamorous starlet quality about her. She looked like a leading lady from a 1970s Chinese movie. Male customers at our restaurant liked to tease and flirt with her. One customer, an artist, made a watercolor portrait of her and the painting still hangs on my parents' wall. It's rendered in soft reds and pinks and my mother wears a traditional high-collared cheongsam. She looks at the viewer innocently, curiously, but with a somewhat sly eye.

Even before he stepped through the front door to Evergreen Garden, my father had heard of the owner's beautiful, young daughter who worked as a hostess there. And he knew of other young men who had tried to get themselves hired at the restaurant all in the single-minded hopes of meeting her.

There was an insurance agent who was interested in her; a Ford engineer; one man came from a family that owned a laundry business but my mother didn't want to date him. She didn't want to work in the laundry business. Some of the men she met were from the American south but she didn't want to move to the American south. And she thought some of the other men were mama's boys. She didn't want those either.

One man suggested they take a tour of Detroit. They drove to city hall, took some photos, and at the end of the date the man asked her if she wanted to get married. My mother Elayne was still just sixteen. The man was twenty-nine. Far too old for her at that age. And this was just their first date — which she honestly didn't think was strange because sometimes marriages happened like that — but she didn't want to base the whole rest of her life on one date so she let him down easily. The man went to Hong Kong afterward and married another woman, then later brought his new wife to Detroit and introduced her to Elayne... and that, she thought, was strange.

She didn't know most of these men very well and didn't care to. Looks didn't matter much to her. There were only two things she wanted in a man: someone who was kind and gentle, and someone who was smarter than she was.

Then my father came along. He wasn't classically handsome, not in a Clark Gable kind of way. With his modest, unassuming demeanor and black-framed glasses he was more like a skinny Clark Kent. He was the new waiter.

"I don't want to say I was a raving beauty or anything like that," my mother recalled, "but every time I turned around the other young men would say hello, or ask if they could get me coffee, or get me this or get me that. When your father walked in, he didn't say much. He just walked right past me. And I thought to myself, 'Hm. Gotta check that out.'"

One thing Yot didn't know about Elayne, having just met her, was that she'd been on the mend from a previous romance. A year and a half earlier, she had fallen in love with another young suitor. She was nineteen at the time and the gentleman's name was David. He was a friend of the family and used to come to the restaurant to deliver supplies. They dated for a few months and one day he came to her house. As they sat in her living room, he proposed to her. It was a very casual proposal. He didn't get down on one knee; didn't bring her flowers; there was no fanfare of any kind. It came in the form of a conversation. He talked about marrying her and she agreed. She liked him. He was kind and gentle.

He ended by saying, "Next week I'm going to bring my parents to meet you."

They met, and afterward David told Elayne that his parents thought she was very intelligent. She liked hearing that. Then David told her he was going to bring a ring over.

But when he asked Elayne's parents if he could marry her, Elayne's father, knowing how beautiful and sought-after his daughter was, asked the young man for a dowry of three thousand dollars.

Soon after, David visited Elayne again and told her he couldn't afford the dowry. He explained that he'd asked his father for the money but that his father had just begun remodeling his own restaurant and that his money was tied up, so he couldn't help him. And then David asked Elayne if she would elope with him.

"I just listened to him," she recalled. "In those days I wasn't as outspoken as I am now. But I was very hurt, very disappointed that he couldn't find a better way to marry me."

She turned him down. And for weeks afterwards she cried herself to sleep every night. Her mother, seeing this, asked if she should try to make amends. Perhaps, her mother told her, she could get her father to lower the price. Perhaps they could work things out. She didn't like seeing her daughter so sad. But Elayne said no. If David didn't love her enough to try, then he wasn't worth it.

Three years later she met him at a cousin's wedding. She passed him in a hallway. She was married by then and so was he. And decades later she would hear that he'd had three children and that his oldest son had become a doctor. And she'd heard through some friends that he'd had such lasting feelings for her that he named his daughter Elayne.

When I ask my mother about him, if she ever wondered about what might've been, she likes to point at me and say, "If I married him you'd be fat, ugly and bald!"

It was a year after her heartbreak that Quong Lim found a job for his son at Evergreen Garden. Yot drove an old, green Pontiac station wagon at the time. It was his father's car, ideal for hauling vegetables. But Elayne didn't know that. She'd see him arrive in the thing and wonder why he needed a station wagon to begin with. Did he have a family? He had no wedding ring, never talked about a wife, never mentioned any children... and slowly, she found herself becoming curious about him.

Detroit had a small Chinatown at the time. It spanned several blocks but had never blossomed into the bright, busy Chinatown that other American cities enjoyed. But there was an auditorium on Abbott and Third Street, near the center of downtown Detroit, close to Quong's grocery store, and it served as a multipurpose community center. It was a large room in the basement of a three-story apartment building owned by the On Leong Merchants Association. On Leong owned the whole block. They used the auditorium for banquets, New Years' celebrations and conventions, and at the front of the auditorium was a stage where they showed movies and put on performances. One day they hosted a Chinese opera.

Yot knew the auditorium well. For about a year, from 1952 to 1953, he worked as a projectionist there. The On Leong Merchants Association ran a small theater in the auditorium and played Chinese films, a new one each week. They were 35mm films, ordered from New York, and as the projectionist it was Yot's job to receive and prepare the reels, mount them and show the movies. Each reel held approximately twenty minutes, and each film was comprised of about four reels, so the films were about an hour and a half.

His brother Fon had been the projectionist before him, and when Fon left another projectionist came in, but the audiences didn't like the second projectionist. The second man either turned the sound up too loud or turned it down too low or sometimes showed the reels out of order, so Fon taught Yot how to do it. And Yot got quite good at the job. First he would turn the light of the projection machine on, put the reel on, thread the machine, show the film on the reel, and while that reel played, he would do the same to the second machine. Then he'd wait for the little signal at the end of first reel to appear — sometimes it would be a little white circle punched into the corner of the film picture, sometimes the mark would be scratched in; whatever the editor wanted — and it would tell him to start the second reel, and he'd stop projecting the first. Then while the second reel ran, he had twenty minutes to rewind the first reel and prepare it for the next show. He rewound it by hand, mounting each reel on a wooden bench with metal spindles, turning a crank in a steady, heavy, circular motion. And he did this repeatedly, for each reel, throughout the course of the film.

To help himself with the timing of the two reels he devised a small mechanism. He attached a rope and hook to each projector so that when the time came to switch reels, he would yank the rope, turning the reel up toward the ceiling as the other reel started. It made his job easier and more efficient and the audience got to enjoy a seamless movie.

But the second projectionist still had keys to the facility and would sometimes come in and wreak havoc. A couple times the second projectionist rewound the films the wrong way so that when Yot showed the reel, the film would be upside down and start at the wrong end. When that happened Yot would have to stop the film and ask the audience to wait, and it usually took about ten minutes to fix. And the second projectionist also didn't like Yot's rope-and-hook mechanism. One day Yot arrived to find it cut.

Eventually Yot quit to start his farm, but when the opera arrived he was looking forward to going. He loved the singing; loved the drama. Elayne's parents suggested that they all go. They asked Yot to take Elayne and said they would meet them after they closed up for the night. So Yot agreed, driving Elayne there in his station wagon.

The opera was called "The River Flows to the East". It was the story of a man and a woman who get married and separated by war. The woman stays behind in her village while the man goes east with his government. He ends up in Chungking and marries another woman. One day the man and his second wife travel back to his village only to discover that his first wife is still alive and he has a son. At first the two wives fight but later reconcile and agree to raise their families together.

After the opera was over, Yot and Elayne waited but her parents never arrived. Yot offered to take Elayne home but she refused. She went to a pay phone and called her parents but they told her that it was too late for them to come. She should just let Yot take her home. But she wouldn't budge. Yot was speechless; he didn't know what to do. He couldn't just leave her here, didn't she understand that? But she was *pachu* — too shy. So he talked to her, and after a while, finally persuaded Elayne to let him drive her back home.

It became what they now consider their First Date. Only later would they realize that Elayne's parents had never intended to meet her at the opera; they wanted Yot to spend some time with her and for the two to enjoy an evening out.

They would have a couple more dates, all unplanned, none of which carried the tone of an official courtship.

Their next date came when Elayne's parents asked Yot to teach their daughter how to drive. He had previously chauffeured Elayne and her mother around but one day another young suitor arrived from Chicago to see her, and her mother asked if Yot could escort them all. "Can you imagine?" my father likes to say. "Here I am driving them around. Her, her mother, and this other man." But my mother laughs it off. "It wasn't really a date. This man was coming into town and my mother and father thought they should introduce me to him and he didn't have a car, so they asked Yot to drive. That's all it was. I never saw him again."

So Yot drove them around. And actually, he didn't really mind.

On their second date, when he did teach Elayne how to drive, they took her parents' car. They were at a gas station and had finished filling the tank when, as Yot recalled, "We were pulling out, coming out of the station when another driver comes along and BANG! Hits our fender!"

"I was so scared," Elayne says. "I didn't have a license!"

Yot told her he would take care of it. He stepped out of the car to assess the damage. The driver who hit them also stepped out of her car. She was clearly in the wrong and knew it. She should've stopped as soon as she saw Elayne's car pulling out but didn't. Yot immediately realized the woman was nervous so he decided to make a bluff. He asked her if she wanted to report the incident and the woman quickly said, "No, no," and told him her husband would take care of the damage. They exchanged their contact information and the woman quickly drove off.

"Our second date," Elayne says, "a car accident."

The account of their third date differs, depending on whom you ask. According to Yot they went out for lunch at a small countertop restaurant. According to Elayne they played chess.

Elayne can still remember how Yot spoke at the countertop restaurant. He was telling her something, giving his opinion, and every time he gestured, he pointed with his fork. She thought it was so uncouth, so backward, so hillbilly-like. Later my mother would make it her mission to teach me and my siblings the proper way to conduct ourselves at the table. I used to have an annoying habit of leaning forward in my seat just before every meal, waiting for the food to arrive like an eager dog, tapping the table impatiently with the fingers of both hands. It was such a peculiar habit that she thought I had a mental problem and considered taking me to a psychologist. And she hated the way I wrapped my whole hand around the handle of my spoon. "Only truck drivers eat that way," she'd say. Or, "Do you want something? Just ask for it. Don't just grab". And, "Don't tease your brother". She was deathly scared that one day our friends would invite us to their homes for dinner and we'd reveal ourselves to be the barbarians we truly were, so she tried desperately to groom all that ugliness out of us. And of course she taught us never, ever, to gesture with our forks, telling us about our father's behavior while he sat right there at the dinner table, in front of us, listening defenselessly.

So thank goodness when they played chess he turned out to be the winner or none of us would exist.

They played Xiangqi, a form of Chinese chess which is different than the western version. Xiangqi is also played on a square-shaped board but the game is more feudal in nature. There are borders to cross and a river that separates the middle of the board. Instead of kings and queens, there are generals, horses and cannons. The two armies are typically painted red and black, or red and green, as opposed to white and black.

As a child, my mother Elayne was very good at two things: marbles and Chinese chess. She could beat all the kids in her village at both. I've played marbles with my mother and noticed that she's able to apply a controlled trajectory to the ball as she shoots it from her fingers. The first time Leslie and I played marbles we had just set up a circle, divided some marbles between us, and my mother came out of the house with an excited smile, eager to show us her tricks. It was a strange and funny surprise to see how easily she could knock all my marbles out of the circle. But she'd never lost a game of chess until she met my father. And that's when she knew she liked him. She'd always wanted to marry a man who was smarter than she was, and my father was the first person to beat her at the game.

And while neither one of them expressed it directly, everyone else at the restaurant was starting to notice the growing friendship between Yot and Elayne... including Jim Loughlin, one of Evergreen Garden's regular customers.

Tall and lanky with glasses and gray hair, he impressed Elayne as "a very distinguished man." He was in his early seventies, usually wore a business suit, and came off as very respectable, "very refined."

He had once been an accountant but owned a nearby door-selling business. More importantly, he was a friend of Elayne's father. In those days, she remembered, there was still a lot of discrimination and it was very difficult for Chinese Americans to buy land and own businesses. When the lot for Evergreen Garden became available, her father wanted to buy it, so Mr. Loughlin said to him:

"You want to buy it? I'll buy it for you. You can pay me back a little at a time, and then it'll be yours."

Over the years her father gave Mr. Loughlin his money and — having no written agreement or contract between them — when the property was paid up, Mr. Loughlin signed the deed over to him.

She always remembered that about him. He was a very nice man and Elayne recalled that he would talk to anyone, "no matter what age you were."

He also had a good sense of humor and liked to flirt with her. His nickname for her was Lotus Blossom. When he came in he always called out, "Hello, Lotus Blossom!"

He ate at the restaurant four or five times a week and Yot also enjoyed conversing with him. Wearing his golden yellow waiter's jacket, white shirt and bow tie, Yot often attended to him and found him to be very friendly.

One day in early April, after the usual afternoon crowd had cleared out, Yot was serving him lunch and Mr. Loughlin said, "Yot, have you ever thought of getting married?"

"Oh, if I ever find the right girl I would," Yot said.

"Well I know a girl."

Yot's eyes lit up. "Oh, you *do?*"

"Sure, and she works right here."

"You mean *Elayne?*"

"Sure, and if you'd like to marry her I can arrange it for you."

"Oh, do you think you can?"

And just as quickly as the conversation had arisen, a proposal was set up. Mr. Loughlin told Elayne's mother and father, and Elayne's mother went out the back door, across the alley to their house, and told Elayne to come to the restaurant.

She brought Elayne to a table where Yot was seated. It was a table near the kitchen where the staff typically took their breaks, and everyone had gathered around to watch. Elayne couldn't understand what was going on. They sat her down across from Yot, and Yot said something to the effect of:

"All this time we've known each other and we never knew how we felt. Would you like to marry me?"

Elayne's eyes went wide with shock. She didn't know what to say. She stood up. And ran back to the house.

And Yot sat there. Stunned. In front of her parents, in front of Mr. Loughlin, in front of the whole staff, the girl he'd just proposed to had run off without a single word.

After a moment, Elayne's mother went back to her house. There she found Elayne in her bedroom, speechless and angry. No one had prepared her! No one had told her what to expect!

Her mother calmed her down, and then quietly asked, "Do you want to?"

And Elayne nodded.

Yot never heard the words from Elayne's own lips but when Elayne's mother returned to the restaurant she informed everyone that the answer was yes. The next thing Yot would have to do was tell his father Quong the news.

Then they would discuss the dowry.

13

My mother was only a year old when this happened so she doesn't remember it. She knows this only from the stories her mother and grandmother told her.

The Japanese had invaded her village and her mother and grandmother took her to a fortress to hide. There were other villagers with them and everyone was nervous and frightened. She doesn't know how many people there were but her village had at least two hundred people, maybe three hundred, perhaps more. She doesn't know if it was light or dark inside, but most likely it was dark because no one wanted to let the soldiers know they were there. The fortress was made of concrete. It was hot inside and Elayne had a rash. She started to moan and cry in discomfort — she was just a child after all; little more than an infant — and another villager, a man, said, If you don't quiet her down I'm going to choke her to death!

So her mother quickly hushed her.

She never found out who the man was. Didn't know what he looked like. Her mother never pointed him out. If her mother or grandmother ever saw him on the street they probably would've avoided him.

My mother was born August 22, 1938. She grew up in a village in southern Guangdong Province. Her village is about five times larger than my father's and sits ten miles west of his. But as close as their communities were, my father and mother would never have met in China. Four months before my mother's birth, my father was already on his way to America.

By the time my mother was born, the Japanese had begun making forays into the countryside. They raided her village several times.

My mother's village is named Wing On. It means "Forever Peace".

177

Her father was Fook Guay Yen. He was the youngest of three boys. His oldest brother emigrated to America; his second oldest became a scholar; and at the age of fifteen Fook Guay joined his oldest. Together they ran a laundry in Chicago. They washed clothes, ironed them, folded them, then packaged them up for their customers. He once told Elayne that they worked so hard, and such long hours, that his brother would often eat while going to the bathroom just so he wouldn't lose any time.

They sent money back home and were able to build a three-story house for their family. They also saved some money for themselves and just before the age of twenty-six, when he returned to China, Fook Guay got the opportunity to work as a cook in Pittsburgh. It meant splitting off from his brother, but he'd learn such invaluable skills on the job that he'd remain a cook in one form or another for the rest of his life.

On his return home, a matchmaker arranged for him to meet a girl named Mee Kam Kim. She was the youngest in her family; the second of two daughters. Her family had actually had four daughters, a girl sometime before her and a girl sometime after, but the two girls died and Mee Kam rarely talked about it; it was too sad a subject. She was eighteen when she was introduced to Fook Guay. He was eight years older. She was considered very pretty, although big-boned compared to other women. But he regarded her as attractive and a comparison of their birthdates indicated that they'd make a good match, so the two were married. By the time Mee Kam was pregnant with Elayne, her husband was on a ship back to America.

Elayne would take on her western name later, but at the time of her birth her mother reasoned that it would take too long to get a Chinese name from Fook Guay, so she asked her sister, What should I name her? Her sister then asked her own husband, so it was Elayne's uncle-in-law who named her.

She was called Wu Sloy Hen, which translates into "Rival Fragrance". When she was old enough to go to school she asked her teacher what it meant and her teacher mistakenly told her that "Rival Fragrance" implied a race or a competition. Decades later, Yot would explain that a better, more correct interpretation of her name was "More Fragrant than Fragrant".

Her father Fook Guay eventually opened his own restaurant in Pittsburgh and even after he got drafted (he went to Germany during World War II as part of the U.S. Army; never saw battle; stayed a cook) he continued sending money home. It wasn't enough to make his wife and daughter rich, but it allowed Elayne to live a better life than most children. Sometimes she visited the homes of wealthier children and admired their marble floors. The floor of Elayne's house was made of ceramic tile: terra cotta. But she knew of families that were so poor they had dirt floors, or floors of red clay. Their walls were made with red clay too and when the heavy rains came their houses were always in danger of melting away.

Elayne's house was made of brick and cement. Built to last. The only danger they faced were the floods. She'd heard of floods that carried away entire homes but she felt hers was sturdy. She and her mother lived in a small two-family dwelling; a flat with a common living area that they shared with another family. The living area had a trench — a recess dug into the floor that collected water for their household use. Above that, the roof was open and exposed so that sunlight could illuminate the room, and when it rained, the rain fell into the recess.

"If the bugs came in, they came in. Mosquitoes, moths. Those things you overlooked, no big deal." She even remembered seeing centipedes. She never knew why the house was designed that way but knew that most other homes were like that too. The mosquitoes "were a little bothersome but we had mosquito nets when we went to sleep. They didn't bother me at night."

She shared a bed with her mother. The bed was just a hard, flat, wood surface, made of pine that was sanded down and polished with carvings on the side. Bed makers cut the carvings in and the more a family spent on their bed, the better it looked. The cheaper beds didn't have any carvings. And in the summer she and her mother slept on a straw mat which helped wick away the heat.

All the furniture in their house was made of wood. A light, sand-colored white pine. It was furniture her mother had bought using her husband's dowry. And her mother was able to live as a housewife, instead of farming for a living.

But their moments of security never lasted very long. Elayne was born the year after the Japanese started bombing Taishan with their seaplanes. And long before that, her neighbors had had to defend themselves against bands of marauding thieves and any of the small feudal armies that roamed the countryside before Chiang Kai Shek and Mao Tse-Tung fought for control of China. To protect themselves, the people of her village built a small fortress; a sturdy post where they could hide during an attack. Not every village had a fortress. Only the villages that successfully pooled their money together could afford to construct one. But most of the fortresses were solidly built and still stand today. Some are cubed-shaped and have battlements atop their walls. Some are two stories tall, some three. Wing On's fortress had an observation tower and the villagers even went so far as to put a night watchman there. But the buildings weren't impregnable. It only took a well-equipped army willing to wait out its occupants to lay siege.

The Japanese raided Wing On throughout her childhood. Often, a villager on a hill would see them in the distance and "someone would climb to a higher hill and look and see the Japanese coming and say, 'Japanese coming!' Sometimes they would beat a gong to let people know it was time to go hide."

Eventually the villagers decided not to hide in the fortress any longer. Instead they would hide the young women wherever they could, fearing that the women would get kidnapped or raped. There was a crawlspace built into the attic of Elayne's house above their bed. When the Japanese came, Elayne's mother and sister-in-laws would open the door to the crawlspace, prop a wooden ladder against it, scurry up the steps and pull the ladder up after them. They'd then remain quiet inside. Once, when she was three years old, Elayne saw her mother hiding herself and after the door was shut, Elayne started calling out, "Mama, where are you? Mama, come on down!" Her grandmother said, "You're going to give away the secret where you mother is hiding!" and quietly took her away with all the other villagers.

Sometimes they would hide in a ditch or in the woods outside Wing On as the Japanese rummaged around for food that the villagers kept hidden. She was told that if the Japanese found a villager they would force the villager to lead them to the food. If the villager didn't, the Japanese would kill him. If he did, and he survived, the other villagers would beat him. They'd beat him with their fists, spit on him, anything. She was also told that the Japanese used children for sport. She heard that the soldiers would throw a child into the air and try to impale the child on their bayonets. So Elayne hid with her grandmother amidst the dirt and sticks, and while she was scared of centipedes and snakes, she was more scared of being discovered. "Worms would be crawling next to you but you had to be still, not make any noise, and lower your head, don't attract any attention. You were afraid." Sometimes she would hide in the brush, getting scratched by branches and bitten by the mosquitoes, trying not to make a sound, waiting for the soldiers to leave.

"Sometimes we would see a mass of soldiers in the distance, walking." They weren't marching, not in formation, just walking. Another time, "I heard guns going off. We heard guns, the sound of artillery."

It was about this time, when she was three, that Elayne's mother thought they should leave the village for a while. She took her daughter by boat to Macau, then another boat to Hong Kong. There they found Hong Kong already occupied by the Japanese. Mee Kam had Elayne in a *hue ai*, a small blanket tied together with strings so that she could carry Elayne on her back. Her mother was in a hurry and as they crossed the street, Elayne dropped her shoe. She cried out, "Mama! Shoe! Shoe!" She could see Japanese soldiers sitting in a small post nearby surrounded by concrete blocks placed in a semi-circle. Her mother turned quickly, bent down, picked up her shoe, and they were off again. Having nowhere left to go, they stayed in Hong Kong for a while before returning home.

When the war ended in 1945, she was seven years old. Over the next few years she had as normal a life as she could ask for. "I went to school. I played with my friends." Once, she was outside with a friend, a boy she knew from school, and they came upon a tree with white blossoms. The blossoms were finger-length, about an inch around, and they knew the blossoms were fragrant but too high for Elayne to reach, so her friend climbed the tree and picked some for her. She put one in her hair, knowing it would make her smell nice for the rest of the day. It was one of her nicer memories.

Then, about the time she turned ten, Elayne's mother informed her that she would have to leave her. Elayne's father had booked passage for her mother to sail to America but was unable to do the same for Elayne. Several months before her mother was scheduled to go, she explained to Elayne, "I have to leave you behind because your father reported you as a son. So I can't bring you along. But in a year I'll come back and take you to America."

Elayne would later learn that, ten years earlier, when her father was returning to the states, he'd known that his wife was pregnant but didn't know the baby's gender. When an immigration official asked if he had any children to declare, her father answered that he'd had a son. Perhaps he was simply taking a chance or perhaps he actually hoped it would be a boy, but the immigration official recorded his answer and that's what prevented Elayne from joining her mother.

On the day of her departure, her mother walked through the courtyard outside Elayne's school, her suitcase in hand, and headed toward the gates of Wing On, a gray brick and concrete wall her people had built to welcome visitors. On the other side was a bus that would take her to the harbor.

Just before she stepped through the gate, Elayne rushed forward, grabbed her mother's leg and cried out:

"Mama, don't go! Don't go!"

Her mother started to cry. Her grandmother started to cry.

"Mama," she begged, "don't go!"

"Don't cry," her mother said. "I'll send for you. In one year, I'll send for you."

And slowly, Elayne's grandmother pulled her away.

She took Elayne by the hand, leading her back through the village path. Wearing her dark gray shirt and pants, soft and pajama-like, her grandmother made small talk with Elayne, calming her as she guided her back to her own house. Elayne would live with her grandmother from then on.

Her last name was Seeto. Elayne didn't know much more about her grandmother than that. But with her soft, delicate skin, she thought her grandmother was the most beautiful woman in the whole village. She had an oval face and light brown eyes, almost hazel, and she'd take her long black hair that had just a touch of gray and spin it up into a bun that she'd wear in the back. The other women in the neighborhood did the same, sometimes using a soft clear paste to hold it together, and Elayne often watched as they helped each other put their hair up in place.

She shared a bed with her grandmother but soon began suffering frequent nightmares.

"They were always the same, calling out for my mother. 'MaMa! MaMa!' I would wake up in the middle of the night looking for my mother but couldn't find her. I always asked my grandmother when my mother was going to come back and take me to America and my grandmother would say, 'Soon, soon. Very soon.'"

To pacify her, Grandmother Seeto once told her, "Okay, I'm going to write her a letter just to ask her when."

So Elayne waited. Always dreaming and searching for her mother. Always calling out.

Another year went by. Elayne had an aunt named Mon Seng, her mother's sister in Guangzhou. "My aunt suggested to my mother that living in a village for a young girl wouldn't make for a very good future." Her aunt believed that living in the city would be better for Elayne and her mother agreed. She wrote to Grandmother Seeto, and Grandmother Seeto escorted Elayne to Guangzhou by boat.

She was about to have one of the most miserable years of her life. Her aunt had four sons and soon after Elayne moved in, her aunt's oldest son began beating Elayne regularly, hitting her, kicking her, spitting on her, and encouraged his brothers to do the same. She lived under those conditions for a year until Mao Tse-Tung's army took over Guangzhou. Scared of what the new revolutionary army represented, her aunt, like many of the other residents, fled the city, taking her family and Elayne back to Wing On.

Still, her troubles continued for a little longer, even after she returned to Grandmother Seeto. It was so important to have a male heir that her grandmother, who'd given birth to only girls, adopted an older boy to carry on the family name. In fact, she adopted several.

The first boy was bitten by a rabid dog and died. The second boy left her. The third boy was a full grown adult: eighteen years old when she adopted him... but he didn't die, and he didn't leave, and that's all that mattered. But then her second son returned, and Grandmother Seeto had to tell her second son that it was too late; she had a new son. She then disowned her second son, and he left once again.

But the third son had a horrible temper. His name was Gam Yin and he was a wirey man with small eyes. To Elayne he looked like a bully. She also thought Grandmother Seeto had made the mistake of spoiling him too much. He was jealous of Elayne's presence and argued with her grandmother every day. Sometimes his temper would turn violent and frightening. One day Elayne came home from school, walked through the door, and found him strangling her grandmother. Elayne screamed and fought him off her, but he grabbed a stick and chased Elayne into the yard. She was skinny and couldn't fight back, and he beat her so hard that she cried out, loudly, which brought her neighbors hurrying out their doors. Seeing them, he stopped, and slowly walked back into his house.

Afterward he apologized to her, and spent the rest of his life apologizing to her. Later in her adulthood he'd write her letters and ask Grandmother Seeto to give them to her but Elayne would refuse to accept them. She'd ask her grandmother to throw the letters out unread. Her adopted uncle would go on to marry and bear four daughters of his own, but no sons, and Elayne thought that a fitting revenge.

As she approached the age of twelve her life slowly began to change for the better. She had a great-grandmother-in-law that also lived with them and her great-grandmother-in-law adored Elayne. "She worshipped the ground I walked on." Her great-grandmother had had her feet bound when she was younger and was limited to taking small steps. While Grandmother Seeto still had to work in the fields, Elayne's great-grandmother couldn't do much manual labor and was confined to the house. But she loved to lavish Elayne with attention. In the winter, when Elayne would come home from school, her great-grandmother would warm up some water and offer to wash Elayne's feet. After a day of walking around, her feet, like most other children's, ended up darkened and dirty. Her great-grandmother knew the time that school let out and would begin heating water for her, keeping it ready in a bucket for the moment when Elayne walked through the door. Elayne wasn't used to that kind of treatment and sometimes felt shy about it; didn't know how to accept it; but her great-grandmother loved doting on her like that, so she let her. And often, too, her great-grandmother would take a handful of day-old rice, crunch it up in her hand and turn it into a little snack. She'd offer it to Elayne, saying, "Here, eat this." When food was scarce she always made sure Elayne ate first, and when Elayne asked why her great-grandmother wasn't eating, she'd urge Elayne to continue.

She learned to play marbles. She played with the boy who picked the white blossoms for her. She became the best marble player in the whole village. She played a hopscotch of sorts, and jacks too, but Chinese children didn't have jacks, not the kind American children had, so they played with stones, but they were happy with stones; stones worked just fine. She played Chinese chess too, and got quite good at it. None of the other children could beat her at chess or marbles.

She also began to look more like her grandmother with her soft skin and warm eyes.

Then one day at the age of thirteen she received a letter from her mother. Her mother had found a way to bring her to America.

The year is 2006.

Nancy, Leslie, my father and I are in the van driving to Wing On.

We're lost.

We have a map, and my mother has given us some directions, but her directions are based on recollections from over fifty years ago.

Look for a bridge, she said. Cross the bridge. Look for a long road. Look for a gate, a concrete gate. That's the gate my mother said goodbye to me at.

The map we're using isn't very helpful. It shows a road leading to Wing On, but the road has no name, no markers. It's just a short squiggly line.

We arrive at a bridge. My father knows the river under this bridge. As a child he took a ferry up this river to Guangzhou. Halfway across the bridge we stop to ask for directions and a passing motorcyclist tells us he knows where the village is.

We're on a long two-lane road now. All around us are endless acres of rice fields. Every now and then we see small buildings in the distance. Cube-shaped. Like miniature castles on a green game board. My sister asks my father what they are.

"Those are fortresses," he says. "To protect against the bandits."

The motorcyclist will eventually get us to my mother's village. There, we'll meet three of her cousins. They'll take us to the house where my mother used to live. And while her cousins show us around, Nancy will stop in a small, empty field that has a broken walkway and remnants from another house. She'll kneel down, pick up some pieces of ceramic tile and put them in a small plastic bag. She'll bring the pieces back to my mother so my mother will have something to look at and hold.

The year is 2008.

Leslie, my father, my mother and I have arrived at Wing On.

We've followed a motorcyclist here. A different motorcyclist. A big, stout man in his late fifties wearing blue jeans and a casual green shirt.

185

My mother, inspired by our first visit, has made an effort to put aside all her bad memories and angry resentments to see her village.

We made it past the bridge. We made it onto the long two-lane road. But after getting lost again, we had to pull up outside a small roadside store where the store owner and his wife stepped out to greet us. Like everyone else in this area, they're friendly and helpful and the moment we asked for directions, the owner insisted on taking us there himself. Before we could object, he was already hurrying into his store to grab his motorcycle helmet.

My mother, who doesn't like accepting anything for free, offered to pay for his time but his wife waved her hand no. My mother tried to press a few dollars into his wife's hand but she refused. So my mother hurried in after him to buy something, anything... two bottles of liquor as it turned out, so that she could reimburse him that way and still show up at her former house with a gift. It doesn't matter that she's making a surprise visit and hasn't told the occupants of her arrival. She hates showing up anywhere empty-handed.

We're at her village gate.

It was 1951 and she was thirteen years old when her parents found her a paper son.

That was the way they referred to the identity they were about to purchase, even though the identity belonged to a female. In this case it was the birth certificate of a girl who would've been Elayne's age had she not died young.

At about the same time Elayne received the news, her great-grandmother also died. The woman who had washed Elayne's feet was seventy-three years old and had always been very thin. One day she caught bronchitis and it turned into pneumonia. Elayne's guardianship now rested solely with Grandmother Seeto.

The first thing her grandmother did when she heard about the paper son was arrange an exit visa for Elayne. She took Elayne to a village elder and Elayne remembers that they had to "give him a little money under the table" to get him to approve the necessary papers. From there they took a boat to Guangzhou, then to Hong Kong. But then her mother sent another letter saying that the identity "didn't work out" and, "Wait for another chance." So

Elayne and Grandmother Seeto rented a room in a boarding house in Hong Kong. Two more years went by. Elayne took English classes and eventually her parents wrote her again, informing her that they'd found another paper son.

This one belonged to a Canadian girl who was born on August 13, 1937... exactly one year and nine days before Elayne's birth. Elayne had a distant aunt and uncle living in Vancouver and they were the ones who'd found it for her. Elayne was tall and skinny for her age and her uncle reasoned that she could pass for the girl. He negotiated a price of $1300 for the identity. The parents of the girl received $850 and Elayne's uncle got $450.

Elayne's parents bought her a plane ticket to Vancouver, sent her some money to buy some gold and jewelry to look more presentable, and arranged her passport. Her grandmother would follow later, which meant Elayne would have to fly alone.

She became nervous about adapting to the new culture. She began worrying about lots of little things and asked her grandmother, "Where I'm going, they don't use chopsticks. What am I going to do with a knife and fork?"

Her grandmother said, "Don't worry, just watch the person next to you and do what they do."

Next came a series of firsts. It was the first time Elayne had ever flown on a plane. She saw a flight attendant on board, the flight attendant was Chinese, and it was the first time she'd ever considered having a job like that. She thought it would be nice to travel and see the world like that. She arrived in Vancouver in the winter and it was the first time she'd ever seen snow. She saw it the moment she stepped off the plane. "I said, 'How beautiful!' The whole ground was white." For her, it was something magical. She stayed with her aunt and uncle while the father of the girl, the man who'd sold them her identity, filed papers to get Elayne her birth certificate. During that time her aunt and uncle took her to her first department store where she bought her first pair of snow boots.

She spent the next nine months in Vancouver and her parents paid her aunt and uncle fifty dollars a month for Elayne's room and board. She had dinner with them every night and practiced her English in her spare time. Her aunt and uncle were Christian; kind and hospitable. When the father of the girl finally gave Elayne her birth certificate, her aunt and uncle helped her apply for Canadian citizenship and her uncle thought it would be a good idea if she changed her name to "Elayne".

"It's okay with me," she thought. "I had no idea. I think it sounded nice."

But still she worried. She was always scared the plan wouldn't work. And she was lonely.

As soon as she became a Canadian citizen she contacted her parents in Detroit. They bought her a plane ticket from Vancouver to Windsor. In Windsor, a friend of her father's picked her up at the airport and she was reunited with her mother and father. It was the first time she'd ever met her father.

"*BaBa. MaMa.*" Father. Mother. She said the words like a respectful Chinese daughter.

They took the tunnel from Windsor to Detroit and on the other side her parents introduced her to her three younger sisters: Phoebe, May and Linda.

When they met, her sisters said, "*Ai-Dei*". Older sister.

They weren't a total surprise for Elayne. Her mother had informed her of her sisters by letter, and Elayne had known that her first sister Phoebe had been born almost a year after her mother emigrated to America. During her stay in Vancouver Elayne liked to knit socks and gloves for them, sending them by mail. She knit so many that her mother had to tell her to stop because her sisters tended to leave them on the floor and she'd slip on them.

She entered the United States on September 1, 1954. She was sixteen years old and almost from the moment she arrived, began working at Evergreen Garden.

Her Grandmother Seeto, in no real hurry to leave China, stayed behind in Hong Kong in a rented room paid for by Elayne's parents. She would arrive about ten years later, in time for Elayne to introduce her to her own first daughter, Leslie.

She remembers her marriage proposal a little differently than her husband Yot.

She was in her house at the time. Her mother came to get her but didn't say why. Her mother led her the short walk to the restaurant and when she entered, she saw everyone waiting for her. She wasn't sure what was happening but they sat her down at a table opposite Yot. Yot said something about the way they liked each other but was vague. She didn't understand what he was saying, and looking back, wasn't entirely sure he even spoke.

So Mr. Loughlin stepped in. Yot's American name was George. He had adopted his name just as Wu Sloy Hen had adopted the name Elayne. And Mr. Loughlin said:

"Elayne, George likes you. Do you like him? George would like to marry you. Would you like to marry him?"

She recalled, "I was so surprised. I didn't expect that. Nobody told me. I was so embarrassed that I got up and took off for the house!"

She ran to her bedroom so she could think. She felt like she had to make a decision, quickly, and on her own. "Did I really want to marry him? What were the good things and what were the bad things about him?" She knew he was a good man but she needed time to think!

After a while her mother came back into the house and asked Elayne if she wanted to marry George. She doesn't remember her exact words, but Elayne agreed, yes. She said something akin to a shy, "Okay. He's a nice guy."

She now says of that moment, "I know he's a nice guy. He knows a little bit of everything. He's got a good heart. He's very gentle. He's a gentleman. And he's very patient. I really liked him. In our case, love developed later."

When Yot told his father about the proposal, his father was overjoyed. One of the first things they discussed was how much they should offer as a dowry. Yot wasn't aware of Elayne's previous suitor or how her father's asking price had ended the couple's matrimonial plans. He only knew that, according to custom, he and his father needed to offer something.

In Chinese, the number nine is phonetically similar to the word "Long", which is synonymous with "Longevity". Nine, therefore, was a perfect number to use when offering a dowry. Yot and his father could offer nine dollars, but something that paltry would be seen as a joke, or worse yet, an insult; or they could offer ninety-nine dollars, which was still too small a gesture for a woman as beautiful as Elayne; or they could offer nine hundred ninety-nine dollars, which was a much more appropriate gift; or they could offer nine thousand nine hundred ninety-nine dollars, which Yot's father couldn't afford. Well, he could've afforded it if he had to, and he did want to see his second son get married, but $999 seemed like the right amount. Nine-nine-nine. Long-long-long.

So Yot's father, Quong Lim, sent a friend to meet with Elayne's father, Fook Guay Yen, to tell him of their offer and, if all went well, set a date for the wedding. Elayne's father knew he'd demanded too high a dowry the first time around and wasn't about to make that same mistake again. So without further discussion, he accepted. Elayne was relieved, her mother was relieved, and Yot wouldn't learn till years later how much of a discount he'd gotten on his young bride: just a smidgen over two-thirds off.

The wedding date was set for September 21st 1959; September being the ninth month, 21 being a lucky number, and the year itself ending with another nine.

Then came the practical questions. It was now Elayne's turn to talk about money. She was, after all, about to marry a skinny waiter who drove an old station wagon that didn't even belong to him. She began by asking him how much they had to start their future with.

"Do you have any money? I don't have any money. Do you?"

He told her he owned a farm.

She didn't want to live on a farm. She told him this straight out but Yot thought that maybe he could still change her mind so he took her up to Marine City to see the place. An oil company had recently discovered some oil in the area, he explained. They'd drawn up a small lease that allowed them to drill on his land. If they found oil it might make them rich one day.

No, she told him. She was *not* going to be a farmer's wife.

The lease provided a few extra dollars but not enough for them to live on so Yot put the farm up for sale. His asking price was $7,500. When his neighbor offered to buy it, Yot, generous to a fault, lowered the price to $6,000. And his father Quong, also generous to a fault, let his son keep the money he'd loaned him. It would help the young couple start their new life. And it was a good thing that Elayne was so adamant in her decision. No further oil would ever be discovered, not on Yot's farm or anywhere else in the vicinity.

Elayne asked Yot about his health and he revealed his bout with tuberculosis. The news scared her. She'd heard about tuberculosis. Was it something that could be passed down? She wanted to have children. Could their children inherit the disease? To ease her fears Yot took her to see his physician, Dr. Hogikian. The doctor told her that tuberculosis wasn't the kind of disease that could be passed on to their children and he further reassured her that, in a way, her husband was safer because he had been cured; he knew how to take care of himself and would always be on the watch for a recurrence.

She asked Yot how they'd make a living. He said he'd continue waiting on tables at Evergreen Garden. They could get an apartment in downtown Detroit. So Elayne cut her hours down at the restaurant and became more of a housewife. Yot increased his hours and supplemented it with jobs at other restaurants. Elayne tried to learn how to cook but found going to the grocery store a confusing experience. Once, at a butcher's counter, she saw a piece of meat that was so cheap she thought she was getting a good deal, so she bought it, then took it to the restaurant and asked the cook for his opinion. He said, "Yes, that's a good deal. But it's a piece of chuck. It's very tough. It's not very good meat."

And so, Yot began teaching Elayne how to cook.

The year is 2006.

After bowing at my grandfather's grave I ask my father if we'll visit his grandmother's grave. He shakes his head no and I ask him why.

"Because we can't find my grandmother. We looked for her last time and couldn't find her." He tells me that she's part of the field now, like his mother.

We make the slow, rugged trek back to the van. At a juncture in the fields where we're supposed to turn, my father stops. He takes a few steps in the opposite direction and says something to Yu Chung. He points to a small mountain in the hazy distance.

The Mountain With The Head Cut Off.

A low, squat, purplish-gray triangle. As my father stares at it fondly, Yu Chung and his son ask him if he wants to go visit it.

No, my father chuckles. He's too old for that.

We drive to Shui Bu, a sprawling town lined with tropical trees and little family-owned stores. My father used to visit this neighborhood when he was a child. The doctor who treated his ear worked here. Most of the shops in this area are small, simple, storage-like studios with rolling steel doors that the owners lift each morning to begin their day. But the shops that can afford more — like the bar across the street from where we park — have walls that are painted with a South Beach art deco style. It's as if someone visited Miami and brought back photos of what could be done with the colors mango, fuchsia and green.

One of Yu Chung's sons works here. My father steps out of the van and walks to a corner store. The owner, a tall, sinewy man with warm eyes and hair parted boyishly on the side, smiles brightly. He recognizes my father from his last trip. So does his wife.

My father chats with the tall, sinewy man, and quickly others from the neighboring stores come dropping by. An elderly man, six feet tall, burly, in a white T-shirt, brings his daughter. She's beautiful, with thick dark eyebrows and lush skin. She gives my father a welcoming smile.

Soon my father is surrounded by friends and family. They're excited to see him. They greet him, besiege him, bombard with questions, and all at the same time. He opens a pocket-sized photo book he's brought with him and shows everyone pictures of his wife, his children, their spouses and his grandchildren. Everybody smiles, laughs; they tap his arms, point to the pictures, and compliment him. He's the successful son who's come back home, and the sound of their voices becomes a loud, happy, joyous din.

Leslie tells me that the father of the beautiful woman with the dark eyebrows once tried to set his daughter up with my brother Mike. Mike was in his thirties at the time. The woman was perhaps seventeen. She's married now and has a four-year-old son. Her son has a lazy eye. He's quiet and stays close to his mother, always huddling up beside her. Her husband lives and works in Hong Kong, a couple hours away. I can't help but think that in another reality, a version of this boy is my nephew.

The father of the beautiful woman suggests a restaurant known for its seafood. The restaurant sits on the edge of a stream where old wooden houseboats sail by.

The restaurant is dim. It's lit only by the light flowing through its aging windows. My father and the beautiful woman choose the dishes. A young, doe-eyed woman enters. She's cute and petite. Her western name is Ellie. I say, *"Ni Hao,"* and as she walks past me she says, "Yes, hello." She's in college and she's had three years of English. One of my father's cousins — the tall, sinewy man — sits down with his two brothers and opens a bottle of whiskey he's brought. He pours shots for himself and his brothers. He offers some to my father but my father waves his hand as if to say, "I'm too old." But the tall, sinewy man insists and my father acquiesces, taking a shot.

We have enough cousins and guests to fill three large, round tables. There'll be no shortage of food today. With the help of the beautiful woman, my father orders chicken and duck and beef and fish for each table; steamed bass with ginger, scallions, soy sauce and oil; tripe and pork with seaweed; and the one dish my sister and I can't get enough of: scallops drowning in butter, minced garlic and white wine, still sitting in their shells.

The tall, sinewy man continues drinking, and slowly, over the course of the lunch, becomes louder and more excited, making toast after toast. He asks us questions in Cantonese. My sister understands enough to give him some basic answers but Nancy and I stay mute, smiling or nodding our heads. Finally he turns and says in Cantonese, Hey Ellie! You speak English. Make yourself useful!

Ellie, surprised, says, "Oh," and begins a polite and friendly conversation with Nancy. Nancy asks her if she'd ever like to visit America and Ellie says yes. Nancy asks her about her field of study. She's studying Communications. She looks young, about sixteen, but when Nancy asks her how old she is, she tells Nancy she's twenty-three.

After I return to San Francisco I'll take a Mandarin class and my teacher will tell my class that there's a lot of pressure on Chinese women to marry young. They mostly hear it from their parents but it comes from every direction. A woman is an old maid if she hasn't married by the age of twenty-five, my teacher will tell us, and there's even more pressure on the women in the rural areas. A year after I finish that class my family and I will visit Taishan again. We'll be sitting in this same restaurant with these same cousins and my mother will inquire about Ellie and we'll learn that Ellie's engaged to a young man from Canada. My mother will then ask all the other mothers if they know of any women they can match me up with. I'll understand just enough Chinese to know what she's talking about.

14

It's our last day in Tin Sum.

We're sitting in our van. It's not even noon yet and my shirt is already sticking to my sweaty back. I slide the door open. I step out. And within seconds the sun starts beating down on my black head of hair. In front of us is the dusty path leading to my father's village.

He wants to see his house one more time. He wants to ask the family living there for his mother's photograph. I'm sure they'd give it to him but he doesn't want to appear ungracious. He's been mulling the issue over since the moment he arrived.

The heat and stress of traveling is beginning to make us bicker. Yu Chung and the villagers are used to this climate. They smile, looking on, but my father, Leslie and I are beginning to call attention to ourselves with our increasingly biting exchanges. Finally my father walks off to explore the village on his own.

He stops at his cousin Yip's house. Yip and his family lived in a two-story, gray-bricked house, similar to my father's, just a few houses down from his. Yip was the one who'd left for America just before my father did.

About fourteen years after Yip landed in the states, Yip's father brought his younger brother over. His younger brother took on the name Bill Poy, and within a year the boys' father brought their mother over too.

When Yip's mother arrived, she stopped by the restaurant where they were working so that all their friends — including my father — could welcome her to the new country. My father's family and Yip's family had always been very close. My father's mother and Yip's mother were like sisters. My father knew she'd been there when his own mother died, so the day he greeted her, he also asked, "Can I find out about my mother?"

During a quiet moment alone, Yip's mother told him that there had been a cholera outbreak in the village. Cholera was very contagious, very deadly. An elderly woman in the village had caught it and the villagers had to put her outside her house. Yip's mother didn't explain all the details, but an infected person was sometimes put on a bed, or on straw matting, under a makeshift shed, away from everyone else.

My father's mother was also close with the elderly woman. She considered her an aunt, and when she'd heard what had befallen her, felt compelled to offer her some help. Everyone warned her not to go, but she felt she just couldn't ignore her aunt in her dying days. Her aunt had four daughters of her own, and even they wouldn't help her.

But soon after she returned home, my father's mother began feeling ill.

And in a couple days, she too died.

Sometime after that, my father's grandmother wrote him the letter telling him of her passing.

Eleven years after her death, my father's father returned to China and remarried. He chose his second wife partially because she looked like his first.

It could be said that by doing so, he had fulfilled the blind fortune teller's prediction that he would have two wives but that he wouldn't marry them at the same time.

There's a large tree near Yip's house. The villagers have built a concrete bench under it. The tree provides a wide, umbrella-like shade and it's cool and restful under its sweeping branches. I ask my father to sit and I ask him how he feels about seeing his village again.

The house brings back good memories, he tells me, but, "The only sad thing is that I can't find my mother. Every time I come back, I feel so sad about it."

He gets up to chat with his neighbors, and after a while he and Leslie stroll back to the van. They ask some farmers standing nearby if they can collect some dirt from the field across the road.

The farmers agree. My father walks over to the bumpy, green edge. Slowly, cautiously, he descends a weedy, waist-high bank. He kneels among the rice plants and, using his hands, digs up some soil, putting it in a small plastic bag he's brought with him. Then, carefully, he seals up the bag.

Like the leaf that falls from the tree and becomes part of the land, his mother is part of the soil now. She's in the field and earth all around him.

Back at the hotel, we climb out of the van and my sister turns to me.

"Did you know that Dad brought his mother's photo back with him?"

She points to a rectangular bundle of crinkled paper on the floor of the van. It was sitting at my father's feet, just behind the front passenger seat.

"He asked Yu Chung to pick it up for him. He thought it would be better if Yu Chung did it."

"When did he do it?" I ask, surprised. In the exhaustion of the day I completely forgot that that was what my father had come for.

My sister shrugs. "I guess he must've done it while we were out taking pictures. Or when we were out collecting dirt. He must've thought that Yu Chung knew the family better. Yu Chung didn't say a thing. He just put it in the van. Dad and Yu Chung didn't say a word about it."

She sees my father preparing to go into the hotel, turns and says, "Can you pick it up and take it up to the room for him?"

I nod and reach down for it.

"Careful. There's glass. And I think the frame is wobbly. Just be careful."

I lift up the bundle. It's wrapped in a loose, dark red paper to protect it but I can feel the wood frame in my hands. It's about ten inches wide by twelve inches tall.

"Dad, I have your mother's photo for you," I say as we walk up the steps.

"Mm," he nods.

I'm not sure when I became aware that my father had grown old, or when I saw myself becoming the man I once saw him as, but it happened quietly, about a decade ago, when I was in my mid-thirties.

The following morning is cool and windy.

Nancy and I knock on my father's door. He's already dressed, ready for breakfast. I ask him about his mother's photograph.

"Show him your mother's photo," my sister says. She's just stepped out of the shower and sits on her bed in her T-shirt and shorts, drying her hair. She points to a broken rosewood frame sitting in the trash can. "He took the photo out of the frame last night."

My father removes a manila envelope from inside his luggage. "Why did he take it out of the frame? Wasn't it safer there?"

"No," Leslie says. "It was cracked and dusty. And it would've broken in the suitcase. If someone threw too much weight on top of the suitcase the glass would've cracked and damaged the photo. He didn't want to take the chance."

Slowly my father pulls his mother's photograph out from the envelope, carefully unwrapping the thin cotton napkin around it. I almost feel guilty watching him do this. It's clear he's already prepared it for the trip home.

He holds up the photograph. "There. See?"

"Tell him about the smile," Leslie says. "Wait'll you hear about the smile."

My father grins. Her photograph is an old 8x10, large enough for a full-sized frame. If his mother could see him holding up her picture today she'd see a man more than twice as old as she was when it was taken and I bet she'd still recognize him from his grin. It's probably the same grin that spread across his face when she gave him his birthday drumstick or when he lit fire crackers on New Year's Day.

The woman in the photograph is just a few years younger than me but looks far more youthful. Her face is slim. She has thin, stylized bangs. She's petite, wearing a dark cheongsam over her small, frail shoulders, and she looks pleasant and modest. Her lips are parted just slightly, almost on the verge of a quiet, shy smile.

"See that?" my father asks, pointing to her teeth. One of them looks dark. "When she got married, she had her front teeth capped with gold."

"Why'd she do that?"

"Because it was the thing to do. It was supposed to make you look prettier for your wedding day."

"She wanted to make herself nice for her husband," Leslie says.

"But it always hurt her, especially when she bit into anything hard. She could never bite into apples."

I can see the touch ups now, near her eyelids, in the thinness of her eyebrows.

"After she died, someone took her picture to a photographer who did this. This isn't the original photo. He drew here, did this," my father says, his finger hovering around her eyes, "probably thinking it made her look nicer. I don't like it so much."

"Where's the original photo?"

"Who knows," he says. "Probably gone."

I ask him what he'll do with the photo once he gets back to the United States.

"Call up my brother and show it to him. I can't wait to show it to him. Make him a copy. Then get a new frame and put it up at the house."

I ask him if I can shoot some video of him holding the photograph and, seated quietly in his chair, he obliges, raising it to the level of his chest. He's wearing a wine-colored short-sleeve shirt that somehow makes him look small and vulnerable and boyish. Behind us, through the hotel window, I hear the morning exercise music starting up at the nearby school.

In 1959, within a year of meeting, my mother and father married each other at the Central United Methodist Church in Detroit.

Neither one was Christian but it hardly mattered; a church wedding was customary back then and it was the same church my uncle had gotten married in, so my father was already familiar with it. My father's father was so happy for the couple that he hired a chef from Chicago. The man was reputed to be the best Cantonese chef in the Midwest. My mother and father had so many guests that they had to host two receptions: the first at five o'clock and the second at eight o'clock.

They drove to Niagara Falls for their honeymoon, then New York City. On a crowded platform at Times Square my mother saw her first subway train. She was hesitant to board but my father said a few helpful words. He took her by the hand and entered first, but then a slew of other passengers suddenly squeezed between them, separating them, and she saw the doors shut in front of her. Quickly he pointed through the window, gesturing to the next stop, and she watched in panic as her husband sped away.

She tried to recall his instructions... the ones that, to her, he'd just barely mentioned. "'We're going to get on here, get off on Union Square, or something.'" She realized she was in a city where she knew no one, had no money and no identification. With resignation she had to tell herself that he'd been a bachelor, that he'd been single his whole life. Naturally, he wouldn't think to look out for her, his new wife. When the next car came, she took it, and at the following stop stepped off to find him waiting there for her.

When they returned home they found an apartment on Nardin Street in downtown Detroit. It was a red brick building located just behind a police station. My father's cousin Bill Poy and his wife lived next door. For my father it was like the old days, back in the village, when his cousin lived just down the path.

My parents had three children in that apartment: Leslie, their oldest daughter; me, Curtis, their oldest son; and Christine, their second daughter.

My mother was pregnant with me when she heard President Kennedy was shot. My father was taking her to the doctor for an examination when the news came over the car radio. It made her so sad she started crying. Kennedy was the first president she'd ever voted for. Later, as a child, I'd see her lying on the couch watching TV every time a commemoration for John F. Kennedy came on. She'd leave a lonely little light on in the corner of the room and I'd sit by the end of her feet. During pauses in the program she'd tell me all about that fateful day. On other days she'd tell me that I was named after General Curtis LeMay. She'd seen the name in the newspaper and said, "Curtis! That's a good name!" I don't think she knew that Curtis LeMay was the general who planned the firebombing of Japan.

Leslie arrived two years before me; Christine two years after. My mother always believed in staying friendly with her neighbors and one of them did her a kind service the night Christine came due. It was three in the morning. While my father went to get the car, my mother walked over to her friend Marie's apartment and knocked on the door. Marie, an elderly Caucasian woman with graying brown hair, answered in a bathrobe and pajamas.

"Marie, looks like I have to go to the hospital. I have no one to keep an eye on my kids. Do you mind watching them? My husband is going to take me to the hospital and I'll be right back."

"Oh sure, I'll be glad to."

Then, after Christine was born, my mother went back to Marie's apartment to thank her and tell her that she was going to name her daughter's middle name after her.

"Oh, that's wonderful!" Marie said, thrilled.

My father was still a waiter at the time. He made five hundred dollars a month working at the House of Chung.

"Things were pretty tight," he recalled. "We couldn't take a vacation."

I asked him what we did for fun.

"I don't know. We had an old TV."

Relaxing was not one of his strengths. His occupation had become his preoccupation. While he provided for the family, his wife stayed home to look after the children — and she made it her mission to give us a better life than she'd ever had.

She noticed that Leslie loved noodles. "I would give her a bowl of noodles and she would get it on her face, in her hair, on the floor, on the table — everywhere."

And I loved to run. "You ran everywhere. One time you ran under the ironing board and just after you ran under, it fell over. It frightened me. I felt so lucky. But one time you ran into a coffee table. I think you dented your head."

Once a week she took us to Palmer Park, the place my father's father used to take his brother and him to practice riding their bicycles. There, my mother would give Leslie and me bread to feed the ducks. When it was hot, my father would drive us to the Metropolitan Beach; or Novi, where we'd rent a small boat and row around the lake.

But before they found the apartment on Nardin, my mother remembers getting the runaround when looking at other apartments. They'd look at a place and when they'd express their interest, the landlord would later tell them it was a mistake; the apartment was taken. Or he'd say, "The apartment you looked at is unavailable because we decided we want to paint it."

201

"We knew it was discrimination," my mother recalled. "In those days, we knew we wouldn't win. It would take too long and cost too much money."

My father could only reply to them with, "Okay, we'll take the deposit back." As he recalls, "Back then they didn't have a law against it yet."

They stayed at Nardin for seven years before crime crept into the neighborhood. One night my father stepped out of the house to get some groceries and noticed a man siphoning gas out of his car. The man was sitting in his own car filling up his tank from my father's, and it was just a lucky coincidence that my father walked out when he did. He yelled, "Hey!" and the man drove off.

Then his cousins, the Poys, moved to San Francisco and my mother started becoming more and more worried about coming home at night. Eventually we moved to a small apartment house in Ferndale. It was a blue-collar neighborhood on the outskirts of Detroit, but the house had a small lawn for us to play on, and that was so very important to my mother. She washed our clothes by hand in the basement and hung them to dry on a long white line behind the house. She filled a small plastic pool with water for us in the summer and grew roses in a tiny garden beside our backdoor. There was a tree in the backyard that I liked to climb and my mother liked seeing me climb it. She called me *maa lau*. Crazy monkey.

In 1967, race riots started in Detroit a week before my brother Michael was born. Looters smashed storefront windows, set buildings on fire and shot at the firefighters who attempted to put them out. The riots grew so violent that the governor ordered the National Guard into the city and President Johnson sent U.S. Army troops. My father remembered the curfew that was imposed during that time. All lights had to be turned off between 9:00 p.m. and 5:00 a.m. He heard about a woman who turned on a light in the middle of the curfew and the National Guard shot at her window.

Through it all, my father remained a waiter, but kept his ambitions alive to do something more. He'd even talked with my mother shortly after their wedding about opening up their own business one day.

"We said, 'Well we can't be working all our lives. It would be more ideal to open up a restaurant.' We always figured that getting a business was better than working, because we'd still be working anyhow, but instead of working for someone else, we would be working for ourselves. So I said, 'Maybe we should look for a restaurant.'"

At first he and a cousin negotiated to buy the House of Chung; his cousin worked there too; except that the owner "was willing to sell the restaurant, but not the name, so I said, 'Forget it.'"

Then he heard about a restaurant for sale in the Northland shopping mall just outside Detroit; so he, his brother, and four friends partnered up to open the Ming Palace. My father became the General Manager and the place became a goldmine. The restaurant offered an early dinner special before five o'clock and workers in the mall would leave their shifts fifteen minutes early just to line up outside the front door. Years later, when I was in the sixth grade, a friend of mine would tell me how much his family loved going there. "We would order some fried rice and when they brought it and lifted up the cover, the rice would be this high!" he said, holding up his hand.

My father began working long hours. I hardly saw him at all during that time. He wouldn't return home until well past midnight. One evening I couldn't sleep and as I was sitting on the couch beside my mother, I saw the front door open. My father walked in wearing a long, thin blue overcoat and small gray hat. With his dark-rimmed glasses and combed black hair, he looked just like Clark Kent. In that moment I truly believed my father was a superhero of some sort and that he'd just come back after a night of performing important deeds. He was so modest, smiling as he hung up his coat.

Eventually my mother went back to work. My parents hired a series of babysitters so my mother could train to be a waitress. One of our babysitters was a nun who didn't like it when we farted and she would call us over after we committed the heinous deed to fan the wind from our behinds with a magazine. Another was a redheaded teenager named Mary Jane who lived a few houses down the block. She was skinny and perky and would smile agreeably to my mother and call her "Mrs. Lim", but the moment my parents left, Mary Jane would switch the radio to rock and roll and inspire us to all sorts of mischief. Meanwhile Mrs. Lim's big debut didn't go so well. On her first night as a waitress she walked out of the kitchen with a huge tray of dishes, tripped and — "Bang!" — all the dishes crashed to the floor.

Sometimes my mother would bring my brother and sisters and me to the Ming Palace after the last customer left and we would wait while my father closed up for the night. We'd play hide and seek under the tables, behind the bar and inside the kitchen. We also liked to follow my father around wherever he went and one night, as we tailed him straight into the men's room, he turned and said, "Hey, what are you doing?" My uncle would ask us to pick up any stray matches or cigarette butts off the floor that the vacuum cleaner didn't catch. He would hide nickels and dimes and quarters along the table legs and told us that anything we found, we could keep, and it made cleaning up a real adventure. My mother wanted to learn how to smoke and one night I saw her sitting at a table by the bar lighting a cigarette in her mouth. I didn't like seeing my mother like that. As a child I thought smoking was wrong and smelled bad. But she coughed and choked and quickly put the cigarette out in a little golden glass ashtray in front of her and I felt a quiet sense of relief.

My mother and father owned two cars by then. After my father finished locking up the restaurant doors, two of us would jump in one car with my father and two of us would jump in the other with my mother and we'd race home. If the boys were in one car and the girls were in the other, it was "Boys versus Girls." We'd cheer each parent on, screaming from the backseats. One night we approached an intersection where we made our usual right turn, but the light was red. My brother and I were in my father's car so it was the Boy's Car. As we sat there waiting anxiously for the light to change green, we could see our mother's car closing in quickly behind us. We knew she'd still have to follow us to make the turn but as she came to the light she veered into an empty gas station and used it to make the right, completely bypassing the intersection. This was clearly an illegal move and even my father yelled, "Hey!" When we got home, my mother smiled a quiet but wicked little smile as she opened the front door to the house. We told her that what she did was unfair but the girls claimed victory that night. In all our races afterward I was surprised that neither of my parents ever used that maneuver again, although I remember egging my father on, yelling, "Use the gas station, Dad! Use the gas station!"

It's 2006. We're on the way to Wing On.

To get there we've had to pass through one of the most crowded parts of China I've ever seen. At one point the road wove through an open market, and got so packed that it was like driving through a small maze. We hugged one close corner after another. On either side of the street people sold fruits, dried herbs, and toys still wrapped in their original plastic; some people selling their wares on collapsible conference tables but most just sitting on the sidewalk with blankets in front of them. I found myself noticing all the worried young mothers holding their babies and wearing faces that seemed worn with exhaustion.

My mother told me that when she was a child she used to beg her mother to buy bus tickets so they could go to the market. Money was so tight that her mother preferred not to use it that way, which meant they had to walk. My mother remembers walking miles to get to the market. It was like a special occasion and they'd buy fruit and vegetables there.

We're outside the walls of my mother's village now. The skinny motorcyclist in black has led us here. We're parked in an old, wide, concrete plaza. To our right is a large banyan tree surrounded by cement seats and behind us is a small stream. Beyond the stream are the fields where the farmers and water buffalos toil.

My father offers the motorcyclist a tip but the man politely declines. He stays to make sure we meet up with my mother's cousins but then, quietly, modestly, departs.

From Ferndale we moved to Southfield, always farther and farther out of Detroit. In Southfield we bought our first house.

My brother and I shared one room. My older sister and younger sister each got their own. Our house was so large that we had both a living room and a family room. I can't remember which was which, but one was in the front of the house and existed only for decorative purposes. It sported a gold shag carpet and the lights were always left off. It was a lonely little room. After dinner my parents always settled into the other room, the one in the back, to watch the evening news. This was the brightly lit room, the one with the red carpeting and the brown book cases. As a child I loved watching "Lost in Space" in that room. The room was noisy and warm and always full of activity. Later I grew to love "Star Trek", then old reruns of the "Twilight Zone", but when I started to gravitate toward scarier fare I had to watch it in the other room, the dim golden room, to make sure I didn't frighten anyone else.

When I was nine years old my father sold his share of the Ming Palace. My parents ordered a station wagon from Chevrolet that was supposed to be what the manufacturer called "green gold" but was more of an olive color. My mother bought us all small matching plaid suitcases; we climbed into our car, and drove to San Francisco. I became the Prince of the Backseat. My sister Leslie took the seat behind my father. It was 1973 and we were headed for China.

15

I learned basic geography in the second grade. I knew how to identify symbols like mountains, rivers and roads, and could locate the United States on a map (the cartographers made it easy; they always put the country right in the middle).

The year was 1972, and President Nixon had just visited China.

"We read about it in the paper," my father recalls. "Somehow we read about some people that already started going to China. I read in the Chinese newspaper that the government invited a group of reporters to go to China and travel and report about it. I read about the conditions back there, and what they allowed and what they didn't allow."

By the first day of the new year, 1973, my father finished selling his share of the Ming Palace and said to my mother, "Well, why don't we take a trip to China?"

But, he recalled, "At the time there was no normal diplomatic relationship between the two countries. So anyone going there had to go to Hong Kong and apply for a visa in Hong Kong; or I read in a newspaper, you could go to China by applying through a consulate office in Canada. So I sent an application to Ottawa and that's how we got the visa to get to China. So I didn't go through the United States because there was no way to apply for one here."

I made a new friend a couple days before our big trip. I found a green-and-yellow frog sitting in the rain gutter outside our kitchen window.

I put him in a tall, round jar that was way too tight for him to move around and thought about naming him "Greenie" or "Kermit" but settled on "Froggy". The night before we climbed into our station wagon, I put his jar on the wide, wooden windowsill by the front of our house so he could wake up to the early morning sun. I wanted to bring him with us and I knew it'd be dark in that car so I thought he'd appreciate the light, having grown up in the wild and all. But it wasn't until a full day on the road, when we were well past Chicago, that I remembered he was still there on the sill and I begged my parents to turn back around. They looked at each other from their places in the front seat and my father laughed, "No, we're not going back for that!" My mother asked where Froggy was and when I told her, she tried to assuage my fears by telling me that when we returned he might still be okay.

We drove from Detroit to San Francisco, stopping in St. Louis to see the Gateway Arch, then went on to see Mt. Rushmore and Yellowstone. My father had planned our trip so meticulously that he'd had to pull us out of school ten days before summer vacation officially started just to make sure we stayed on schedule. By then Nixon was under investigation for Watergate and that's all I saw on the news in every restaurant and every hotel.

When we arrived in San Francisco we visited our cousins, the Poys, then boarded a plane and flew to Tokyo. We stayed one night in Tokyo and I'll always remember it as the cleanest, most polite place I've ever visited. The hotel room was white and spotless, the elevator was silver and spotless, and the hotel key was fastened onto the end of a long, elegant, clear plastic key stick... which was also spotless. The next afternoon we went to Tokyo Tower — an Eiffel Tower-like structure that Godzilla would've loved to have knocked over — then flew to Taiwan.

We stayed five days in Taiwan. We had a tour guide named Tony. He was a friendly, charming, charismatic man. My sister Leslie noticed that he liked to flirt with the women on our bus. At night, after the tour was officially over, he would take some of the women out bowling and the next morning he always began the day looking a little tired.

We went to Sun Moon Lake, a park with small souvenir shops. One shop had a pet monkey sitting nervously on their middle counter and we all wanted to hold and play with him, but another customer, a woman in a white dress, picked him up and, out of carelessness or disgust, dropped him. He fell to the floor, cutting his lip, and immediately became frightened of all the people around him, reaching out desperately for his owner instead. My sisters and I hated that oafish woman, staring daggers at her as she walked away. We were able to put it out of our minds later when, in a theater on the shore of Sun Moon Lake, we saw some young girls perform a bamboo dance.

From there we flew to Hong Kong. We stayed at the Excelsior Hotel for one week and the Nathan Hotel for three. The Excelsior was more plush but we liked the Nathan better. The beds were bouncy, the room had air conditioning and we got a big television set. It was a comfortable home away from home. Each floor had its own clerk. Ours was a thin, kind man in his late twenties; I don't remember his name but he had glasses and a shy smile and he loved to carry my little brother in his arms. Whenever my parents wanted to go out for an evening, my mother would ask the clerk to look after us and he'd treat us like we were his own children. He'd bring us a thermos of hot water so we could have sanitized water when we got thirsty. My brother celebrated his sixth birthday in Hong Kong and he helped light the cake. I always wondered what happened to him. I was dimly aware that he didn't make as much money as my father did; that he likely had a family of his own, or hoped to; and that he was probably struggling through life.

From Hong Kong we took a train to Guangzhou. It was a two hour ride but the world changed dramatically in that space of time. On the streets of Hong Kong I'd see beggars. They'd lay a blanket out on the sidewalk and ask for money and sometimes I'd even see a child younger than me sitting beside them. Occasionally I'd ask my mother for some money to put in their cup but she didn't feel safe doing it, didn't trust them. But my father would stop to give them money. He found it hard not to. He just had to do it when my mother wasn't looking.

Mainland China was different. I don't remember seeing any beggars, but everyone just looked generally poorer. There wasn't the wide discrepancy between those who had money and those who didn't, not like we'd seen in Hong Kong. In Hong Kong, men in fancy black suits would pass children in tatters sitting outside gold-colored restaurants. In mainland China everyone wore simpler, plainer clothes. Their shirts and pants looked like workaday cotton. You could almost see the stitching and the loose threads. Their shirts were gray or beige or white. Their pants were either the same gray, like a peasant's uniform, or a dark brown. People looked gaunt. Everything seemed dustier, dirtier and old.

We stayed eight days at the Overseas Chinese Hotel in Guangzhou. We were given two adjoining rooms on the top, the sixth floor, and we knew this because our mother made us memorize *luhk lau,* "six floor," in case we ever had to say this to the elevator operator. But we never got the chance because the elevator was regularly broken down.

My father remembered that all the hotels, restaurants and businesses were owned by the government. He'd read that the Overseas Chinese Hotel had originally been built by a Burmese businessman, the owner of Tiger Balm, and that everything in the hotel was what his company had put there. When the Chinese government took over, they took over the whole business and added almost nothing new. The elevator, my father knew, didn't really break down. They just had power outages. When there were problems, he recalled, no one talked about them; no one ever admitted anything was wrong.

Every morning when we left the hotel, my mother would stop at the door and look down one end of the street, then the other, before taking our hands. She remembered that when my grandfather, her father-in-law, heard we were going to China, he got very worried. He told my parents, "Wherever you go, make sure you count heads." So my mother bought us T-shirts with our names on the back and we wore those everywhere. She recalled thinking, "If we lost you, if anyone found you, they would sell you. Every day, I got two kids and your father got two kids."

Sometimes we would go shopping or walk along the river. She wanted to make us feel as normal as possible, so one day she took us to a barber shop to get our hair washed and cut. We'd often see vendors on the street selling popsicles and we would beg our mother to buy us some. My mother was scared of uncooked food but one afternoon it got so hot that she finally bought some. We took a lick and — *yuck!* — they weren't the usual fruit juice popsicles we were used to. My mother asked the vendor what they were and he told us they were frozen tea and sweet beans.

Sometimes we would eat at a local restaurant. My father remembers the restaurants were always short one kind of food or another and always pressed for supplies. At one restaurant the owner told him, "You have to pay first." So he did. He ordered a duck and it never arrived so my father had to get a refund.

Often, though, we ate at the hotel restaurant. The restaurant was white inside. White walls, white tiles, white tablecloths. My favorite dish was a small bowl of white rice. That's all I looked forward to: a bowl of rice with a little bit of soy sauce on it. To this day that's still my favorite dish. I was so skinny back then that mother always made sure I had a bowl of rice in front of me and she would spoon a little piece of meat and sauce on top of it. She would order rice for all of us, or ask my father to, and when it arrived she would make sure her children got their bowls first.

It was always hot, crowded and busy in that restaurant and the waiters were always hurrying about. The staff was always moving tables, changing tables, putting tables together, and if we weren't waiting for a table we usually had to share one with some strangers. One time we shared a table with an elderly woman and her granddaughter. I could tell it was a special meal for them, that they couldn't afford to eat out very often. The girl was so hungry that she ate too much and had to throw up but her grandmother didn't want to leave the restaurant so she told the girl to throw up on the floor. The girl ducked under the table for a moment, and everyone, including my parents, pretended not to notice; then she sat back up into her seat.

One day we hired a driver to drive us down to Taishan. My father found him through the hotel. For a day's travel, he charged us 375 Chinese yuan, or what was then about 150 U.S. dollars. The highway to Taishan didn't exist back then. We had to cross three tributaries of the Pearl River and were ferried over by large boats with flatbeds that carried four or five cars each. From Taishan we drove to the village of Tin Sum where we saw my father's house, then walked into the fields to find his mother's grave.

My father told me a story once.

He was thirteen years old. His father had just sent a letter to his mother informing her that he would be sending for the boys soon. Fon was still at boarding school in Guangzhou. Yot was home from boarding school but now that they were planning to leave for America there was no reason for him to return, so he spent the remaining days with his mother.

One night he and his mother had just finished dinner. It was a month or so after New Year and there wasn't much to do. His mother sat in her chair, sewing, and Yot sat in a chair at her feet opposite her as he usually did during the evenings. She wore a black, heavy cotton top and bottom. It was winter, but not very cold. Yot wore a heavy cotton shirt and pants.

The light from the kerosene lamp gave the room a warm amber glow. It was quiet and Yot looked up at her.

"Mama?"

She gazed up from her sewing.

"What is it?"

He wasn't sure. "Not much," he said. "Nothing."

"Well there's something on your mind."

He didn't know what to say... didn't have the words for it... and after a moment she smiled and said, "I bet I know. I bet I know what you're thinking. You don't want to leave me, do you?"

A pause escaped his lips, "... uhh..." as he tried not to admit it.

"You don't want to leave me and to tell you the truth, I don't want you to leave me either."

And from then, till the time they got ready to part, they had several conversations like this. Sometimes they laughed it off. Sometimes the conversations ended just as quietly as they began.

But one night his mother said, "You want to know what it will be like without me. Is that it?"

And he nodded.

"Well then now we know. And at least we can talk about it."

Then, after a while, she asked, "Will you remember me?"

And he nodded yes again.

At the village we met my father's cousin. In Chinese, there's a designation for every relative, every member of the family, and his was Biew Bok. Cousin Uncle. That's what my father had us call him. Biew Bok was a strong, sturdy, outgoing man; a true villager. He was the son of the aunt my father stayed with when he ran away to see the opera; the son who carried his mother on his back when she was dying.

We didn't know it at the time but China was nearing the end of the Cultural Revolution. It was the movement started by Mao Tse-Tung the same year that Christine was born, and it would lead to bouts of famine, neighbor denouncing neighbor, and the separation of family members. It would affect the lives of just about every Chinese citizen, including many in the village. Including Biew Bok, although he wouldn't speak much of it.

Decades later, we'd meet Biew Bok again. He'd be married to another woman by then. And the next time my father returned to

212

his house, he'd find Mao Tse Tung's name written very clearly, one stroke at a time, in white chalk, on the dark brown wooden surface of his front door.

After the village we drove to Taishan for lunch. We ate at the Lakeside Hotel, the same hotel we'd stay at thirty-three years later, except that after being torn down and rebuilt they'd call it the New Lakeside Hotel. From there we drove back to Guangzhou.

We invited our cousins to visit us. We were still staying in the Luxury Suite, and to them we truly were living in luxury.

My father's aunt, Wen Yiang — the one who ate all the pork her grandfather had given her (and which resulted in her legendary belly ache) — was among our relatives there and, as my mother recalls:

"She was at our suitcase. The suitcase was open and she just grabbed different clothes and said, 'Why don't you give me this one? Why don't you let me have this one?'"

My mother thought of her as very rude. She remembered Wen Yiang saying, "You can buy more clothes. You're wealthy. You can get more." She held up a pair of pale green pants that belonged to Leslie and said she wanted to give it to her oldest grandson so my mother acquiesced, letting her have them.

But my mother had different feelings for Biew Bok and his two daughters. She felt more warmth and sympathy for them. She noticed that the girls liked Leslie's harmonica, especially the youngest daughter.

"She kept admiring it. She had it in her hand. She didn't want to let it go, so I said, 'Oh would you like to have it?' and she said, 'Yes,' so I gave it to her. Leslie was okay with it. But Biew Bok said, 'No, no, no, that doesn't belong to you. You cannot just have anything.' So he made her give it back."

Still, my mother wanted his daughters to have something. It was a hot day, so she asked them if they wanted to take a shower before going home and they said, "Yes, yes, yes!" The shower was just a tub with a handheld spray hose but they were overjoyed.

Sometime after that, I woke up one morning to another hot, humid day. I walked into the sitting room and saw my father relaxing in a chair, reading a newspaper. I said, *"Dousin, BaBa."* Good morning, Father. He looked up and smiled and I noticed something odd about his face but couldn't quite place it. My mother said, "Do you see anything different on your father?" I stared but couldn't figure out what it was.

"Your father has a mustache!" my mother said.

And sure enough he did. He looked like someone else, someone a little more dashing.

One day, after finishing lunch at the Overseas China Hotel, my father left a tip on the table, and as we walked out of the restaurant our waiter came out after us. He caught up with us in the dim, gray light of the lobby and handed my father's money back to him. He told my father that they were a "proud people" and didn't need a handout. The words took my father by surprise but he later got the sense that the people of Guangzhou saw us as snobs.

Three and a half decades later we encountered a similar situation... but with a slightly different outcome.

On our last visit to Beijing, my father, mother, Leslie and I were left by our tour guide to find dinner on our own one night. We chose a small hotpot restaurant in the basement of a shopping mall, but the main dialect in Beijing is Mandarin, and at that point I was the only one who spoke Mandarin, and only a few phrases at best. We were tired and hungry and our waitress, who didn't speak any Cantonese or English, did a great job of bridging the gap. She gestured to items on the menu that she thought we'd like, deciphered what we wanted, and indicated which dishes they no longer had. She made sure we got our orders on time, then led me to the table where they kept bowls of sauce so I could show my family. I was so grateful that I tried to give her a twenty-five percent tip, but she waved her hand no. No, she seemed to be saying, that's nice of you, but I can't accept it.

"Nin shi hen hao," I said, attempting in a very basic way to say, "You are very good." I'm sure I sounded like an idiot but she still wouldn't accept my money.

I lowered it to twenty percent and still she gestured emphatically no. She pointed to her boss standing at the back of the room and drew her thumb and forefinger in a quick cutting motion across her throat. "Ynrrrr!" she uttered, making the universal sign for "I'll lose my head." It reminded me of a gesture Lucille Ball might make.

I smiled, nodded, indicated that I understood, then took away several more bills until the tip was just five dollars. I'd reduced it to a twelve percent tip but it was an amount she could finally accept. She thanked me, I thanked her, and as we left I saw her quickly and prudently splitting the money up with her co-workers.

From my point of view, our waitress didn't need to stay too cautious, at least not for too much longer. As I understood it, restaurants in the big cities preferred hiring young women; but if she also happened to be single, her country's economy gave her another advantage. China had gotten caught up in the same real estate frenzy my own country did. With the gender imbalance there, this now allows marriageable women to be more financially demanding with their suitors. Just three years later, Chinese women would be able to require that single men own their own houses and cars before proposing to them, before even going as far as a second date; with the men at risk of becoming the "bare branches" of their family trees.

The boom in construction also gave rise to the first billionaire in the occupied region of Tibet. And China is so competitive with the United States that it not only has a Walmart sitting in its capital, it has its own version called Wumart.

I remember asking my friend Brian, the business instructor, what he thought of all this.

"If I'm not wrong, China was once a socialist country," I said. "But now that you're experimenting with capitalism, your country is getting so good at it that you're outpacing us. My country calls it 'capitalism on steroids'. What do you think of that?"

He turned and, almost with a wink, said, "We like to call it a market economy."

1973.

We arrived home by the middle of summer.

The moment our station wagon pulled into the garage I hurried into the house and went straight to the windowsill — but it was too late. Froggy was dead. He had become a stiff, dried, skin-on-skeletal remnant of his former self, and just stood there, leaning against his tubular glass prison as if making one last futile attempt to hop out. My mother told me to throw him out so I picked up the jar, took it outside, and with a single swing of my arm, tossed him onto the front yard.

By the end of summer I entered the fourth grade. My father didn't have a restaurant to manage any more so I got to see him every day when I came home from school.

Every night my little brother and sister's chore was to set the table for dinner. My oldest sister would help my father cook and my mother clean. My mother was always enlisting Leslie's aid so she was forced to grow up a little faster than the rest of us. My father would cook us dinners that, even as children, we knew were special. He'd make steamed bass with ginger and green onions; beef kabobs roasted with tomatoes, onions and green peppers; a minced pork pie with egg and noodles; and for himself, from Hong Kong, he'd purchased some thin slices of dried deer antler. It was a prescription; enough for one small meal; something he remembered from childhood that would help build up his body. The slices were tough, and he had to steam them in an urn for six hours, continually adding water. To make the dish more palatable, he added pieces of chicken and ginger.

For us, every other Sunday for lunch, he'd spend all morning boiling a whole chicken in a vat of sweetened soy sauce. *Si-yau Gai.* Soy Sauce Chicken. And we always had interesting conversations over these meals. Sometimes he would tell us a Chinese story or some tidbit of American history or explain a scientific principle that one of us had learned in school. He loved talking about science and history.

After dinner my mother would leave the leftovers in the pots or bowls and wrap plastic over them. I would clear the table. She'd lay several sheets of newspaper on the kitchen floor and we would scrape the remaining food onto the paper. Then, starting from one corner, she would fold the newspaper over the food and roll it into the size of a small football and I would drop it in the trash. In the adjoining room, my father would read the newspaper while sitting on one end of the couch, the end closest to the big, round, gaudy, gold lamp, and Walter Cronkite would report the evening news. My mother would nap on the other end of the couch with her feet against my father's thighs and my little brother and I would steal the cushions from behind her to make a fort around my father's legs.

Although I didn't realize it at the time, seeing my parents together every night was warm and reassuring.

After a while I noticed that my father would take us for long drives farther and farther outside of Detroit. Some of the places we passed were still farmland and I could see urban life slowly inching its way outward under the guise of shopping plazas and newly paved roads. One day we drove so far out that the road grew bumpy and hilly. We were surrounded by fields of tall grass and small churches and after we rode under the long arm of a giant, stout tree, my father said, "This is where we're thinking of opening our new restaurant. What do you kids think?" And I suddenly became apprehensive. We'd have to move. I wouldn't see my father reading the newspaper after dinner anymore and I tried to imagine what it would be like living in farm country, away from all my friends.

There was a restaurant he could get a good deal on but his lawyer talked him out of it, telling him that he might get a good price but he wouldn't get much business out there. My father started eyeing another restaurant closer to home. It was a modest white-bricked restaurant called The Golden Dome. I don't know why it was called The Golden Dome except that it had a small golden dome on top of it. My father wanted to make a bid. His lawyer told him to wait. The owner was going out of business, losing more and more money every day, and if my father waited a little longer he could get a better deal. But my father was eager to get back into the restaurant business. Troy, where the Golden Dome was located, was a rapidly growing city. Bloomfield Hills, one of the richest neighborhoods outside of Detroit, was only a few miles away. He didn't want to miss out on the opportunity so he bought the place. He and my mother would be the owners and my uncle Fon would be a co-owner. They'd name it the New China Restaurant.

After it opened, my father and mother worked there six days a week, rarely taking the same day off. My father wore a bow tie that never matched his jacket, and his jacket never matched his slacks. Our most reliable customers were the loud, jolly car salesmen from the row of auto dealerships just down the street. A week never passed when one of them wouldn't fail to ask, "Hey George, whatever happened to the Old China?"

16

My parents faced great difficulty for the first seven years that they ran the New China Restaurant.

"You never knew, did you?" Leslie later told me. "They really struggled. Dad was always calling the butcher shop to delay the bills. He would ask them if he could skip paying the meat bill for a couple months so he could pay the laundry bill. Then he would ask if he could skip paying the laundry bill so he could pay the utilities. Then he'd pay the butcher and it would start all over again. We were always right on the edge of going under."

No, I didn't know. Although I should have. I worked at the restaurant. We all did. By the age of twelve my parents had me washing dishes. My little sister started doing the same thing at ten and my brother at nine. We went to school during the weekday, came home, did our homework, and a couple of nights a week put on aprons, peeled shrimp and washed pots and pans. On Saturday night, while our friends went to parties and arcades, we cleaned the kitchen filters mounted over the woks. Leslie seated people, I moved up to bussing tables, Christine became a waitress, and my brother helped pack carryouts.

Leslie learned the family business. Late at night, after the last customer left, Christine, Mike and I would sit at the bar sipping Shirley Temples that we were allowed to mix for ourselves and we'd watch something dreary on TV. Leslie, meanwhile, would help my father add up the day's receipts and we'd often see her step out of the office from behind the bar and yell something like, "We're short seventeen dollars!"

Occasionally I'd see the worry on my father's face. If the night was slow, he'd ask several waitresses to leave early and then turn the lights off in the back. On rainy days I'd hear him say, "This is no good."

"Why?"

"Because when it rains everyone just stays home."

Sometimes, while stripping pea pods at the corner table with my mother, I'd see the worry on her face too as she watched my father moving about, trying to keep himself busy.

I suppose I was preoccupied with my own problems. A few years after opening the New China we moved again, this time to a neighborhood that was predominantly white. We'd had friends of several ethnicities in our last neighborhood — we were even close to a Korean family — but now, for the first time, we started encountering racism. It was 1980 and Japan had risen as an economic power in the east while the auto industry in Detroit tumbled into layoffs. The recession dragged down my parent's business while my brother and sisters and I got picked on at school, got harassed on the street. People called us chink and jap, pulled on their eyelids to make slanted eyes, but mostly they made mocking oriental sounds. They yelled slurs from their cars and from their front porches as we walked by. I got into fistfights in school and got knocked out once. One afternoon a couple boys walked up to my brother in a field and punched him, scarring his face under his eye.

My parents didn't know what to say or do. After years of trying to give us the opportunities they never had, they didn't know to handle these new troubles in our lives.

While I wasn't exactly thankful for it, the bullying did give me ambition. I had always been an awkward, sensitive child but the racism made me resentful, which steeled my resolve, and in the process I picked up my father's stubborn determination to constantly improve my standing in life.

It even turned Christine into a more pronounced version of my parents. She not only opened up her own restaurant, which became wildly successful, she turned into a super mother. She recently told me that, realizing her three children were about to enter high school, she took them for a drive, stopped, parked, and, while they were held captive in the backseat of her car, told them about all the immaturity they were about to face.

"You have to toe the line in middle school because there's a lot of peer pressure. In high school you have to fit in as best you can or else it can get even worse. But in college, life is a lot more open and you get to be more independent and have more fun."

Fifteen years after my parents sold the New China Restaurant, my father, mother, Nancy and I went back to Michigan to see the place again. The restaurant still has the same modest appearance: a white facade with a reddish-orange sign out front; and on the sign is a large gold Chinese coin, a drawing my father made himself.

"Times were tough," my father said as he watched cars pulling into the parking lot. "We never told you, but we robbed Peter to pay Paul. When we needed money, your uncle went around to all his friends asking to borrow money. We borrowed money from everyone."

"For ten years your father didn't get paid," my mother added. "We lived off of my pay. We brought home food from the restaurant and we lived off of my salary. He didn't get paid a dime."

"It wasn't until after seven or eight years that we started to make money. And then finally after ten years, business was good. But it was a struggle."

Just as things were turning around, I went to college. I enrolled in a small technical institute to study architecture but wasn't happy so I dropped out. My mother, who'd always worried that I was so skinny, now worried that I wouldn't go back to school. But I showed artistic talent at an early age and wanted to do something more creative; architecture had just been a way to please my parents; so I transferred to the University of Michigan to study art instead. Then my mother started worrying that the only thing I'd ever graduate to was serving fast food. But at least I was back in school and I'd get a degree, and the only thing my parents ever wanted was that their children got college degrees.

Christine studied communications and Mike studied psychology at Michigan State University. After graduation, I moved to San Francisco, and Christine and Mike followed me.

Leslie went to Pace University in New York, dabbled as a stock broker, but occasionally returned to the restaurant to help my father. When she got married, she was the last child to move out of the house.

A year later my father invited Biew Bok to come visit. It was 1991. Biew Bok had gotten divorced five years earlier and my father thought it'd be nice if his cousin stayed for a while, maybe even worked and earned some money, so he sent him a letter.

"I wrote, if I can get him a visa to visit us in Michigan, would he like to do that? And of course I knew he would jump at that chance."

My father knew that his cousin would want to do nothing else except work and save up money so he submitted paperwork allowing him to work at the New China.

"I took him to the restaurant every day. He didn't have enough time in the United States to learn to be a cook. The only thing he had time to do was be a dishwasher and mop the floor."

But still my father tried to show his cousin around.

"At first I took him to some restaurants to let him try some American food but he wasn't used to it. I ordered a steak but he couldn't eat the whole thing because he's not used to that much meat. So I ordered a hamburger because it's small and it's ground, which makes it easier to eat, but he wasn't used to eating meat on a bun, so I just let him be.

"He stayed in the basement where Leslie used to live. He's an old fashioned guy. I told him that life in the United States is different from China but he couldn't get used to it. He just stayed down there. In a way he's a very stubborn person. So I let him stay there instead of making him do things with us." To help him stay occupied, "I bought him his own TV so he could watch TV downstairs. And when he went home a year later, he took the TV with him!

"I said, 'How can you take a TV home with you?' But it's only 13 inches so he put in his traveling bag with him.

But the power supply in China is DC. "The TV we bought for him was set up for AC, so when he got home, he plugged it in it but it didn't work, so he had to take it to an electrical shop to have it converted."

He had stayed a year. With the money he made he opened a small sewing business, employing several seamstresses. Eventually he met another woman and married again.

The year is 2006.

We're in Guangzhou, walking with Biew Bok. He's eighty-two years old, the same age as my father. He's lost some weight over the years but still has the frame of a stocky, sturdy man.

We're on Number Nine Road, a bustling part of the city that's like one long, glitzy plaza. Girls with short black skirts and boys with spiky, gelled hair dot the crowd. The older Chinese don't frequent this street as much as their children and grandchildren do. They inhabit the shops just a few blocks over, the ones selling medicinal herbs and bags of dried shark fins. This street is dominated by kids eating candied meat kabobs and perusing leather goods.

Biew Bok wears a cap and denim shirt that reminds me of the film clips I've seen of state-owned factory workers. When I hold up a camera to take his photo he strikes a statue-like pose for me, a hand on one hip and a friendly smile on his face. I can only imagine all the changes he's seen. He lived through years of children confessing political crimes against their parents and now he's wading through a sea of teenagers blabbing away on their cell phones.

We step into a two-story restaurant that my father wants to try out. It's decorated like an imperial palace. The waiters and waitresses are dressed like royal servants. My father and Biew Bok sit together and chat as a waitress brings a set of teacups and a small, shallow bowl. She's going to sanitize the cups in front of us as a form of entertainment. Using a pair of chopsticks, she picks up each cup, places it in the bowl, and pours hot water over it from a teapot, turning each cup in its place. Throughout our trip we've been wiping down our own cups to prevent the threat of dysentery. It's a habit we picked up from my mother. Whenever we went to a Chinese restaurant, even in the United States, my mother would take each of our cups and chopsticks and wipe them down with a napkin. Here, our waitress uses only chopsticks, touching not a single cup with her fingers, and when she's done, places each cup on the lazy susan in the center of the table. Then she pours us tea from another, separate teapot.

Another waitress comes to take our order. She wears a long, theatrical, white robe. My father and Biew Bok converse with her for a moment. On a small pad of paper my father has written down a few dishes he'd like to try, and as our waitress recommends several more, he adds them to the list. He tears off the piece of paper and shows it to her but doesn't give it to her. Instead he folds it up and puts it in his pocket. I ask him why.

"Oh, I like to keep this as a souvenir."

"You've been doing this at every restaurant?"

"Yeah," he nods, smiling. "I like to remember what I ate on every trip and where I ate it."

He and Biew Bok return to their conversation and Leslie gestures for me to lean toward her.

223

"Look at Dad and Biew Bok. Don't they look like two little boys talking?" I nod and she adds, "That's why I like watching them. You can tell they're two really good friends."

"What are they talking about?"

"Oh, about people they know. They're catching up."

It's our last day in China.

After breakfast we drive to Lotus Mountain, home to a 134-foot-tall gold statue of Quan Yin, the Goddess of Mercy. It's the largest statue of Quan Yin in the world.

Behind the statue is a tree filled with red ribbons. Each ribbon has a small wire loop attached to one end, and for one yuan you can write your wish on a ribbon and toss it into the tree. If the ribbon catches onto a twig or a leaf and stays up there, your wish will come true.

My father and Leslie each buy a ribbon. Leslie tries tossing her ribbon into the tree first with no success. My father goes next and his ribbon catches on his first try. Leslie makes a loud competitive groan. She tries again, and again. We cheer her on and after several attempts, her ribbon finally sticks. The tree is so full of ribbons that it looks like a giant red bouquet.

After Lotus Mountain our tour guide Gloria takes us back to Guangzhou to visit the Wah Lam Jade Market. The market is just a few blocks from Number Nine Road. My father wants to buy a piece of jade for my mother. Leslie wants to buy a piece carved like a peach for her daughter Jillian. And Gloria, we'll discover, is quite the haggler.

The market is named after the Wah Lam temple beside it. Part of the market is inside a shopping mall but most of action is outside, along the open alley where the dealers sit behind makeshift stalls packed tightly together. Some stalls have umbrellas mounted for shade but most of the dealers display their wares on simple tables, or in boxes, or, if they're in the back, on blankets on the street.

My father looks for his piece of jade first. The bargaining process works the same as it did when we were at the Great Wall; the same as it does everywhere. My father will express interest in a piece and ask the dealer what the price is. The dealer will bring out a small plastic calculator, the universal translator for talking numbers. Sometimes the dealer will start by typing in a price, but some of the slyer ones will ask my father to type in the price he believes the piece is worth. That's an old trick. The one who throws out the first number loses. If my father offers too high a price, he's just made the dealer's job that much easier, and the dealer might still try to talk him even higher. If my father suggests too low a price, the seller will express surprise, maybe even shock, and counter with a much larger number. But my father has bought jade before. He knows the prices in America and knows he should get a substantial discount here.

At one stall the dealer types in a price so high my father says, "Is that Chinese or U.S.?"

"RMB," the man says. Renminbi, the Chinese currency.

He hands the calculator to my father and gestures for him to counter the offer. My father types in a low number. Not too low, a modest amount, but the dealer shakes his head no. Back to the dealer. He drops his price a little, but not by much. They go back and forth a couple times but the negotiation is about to fall apart. My father can't get the price he wants and is becoming exasperated. And the dealer is standing firm.

Perhaps these are the real prices. None of the dealers want to budge. But I can see something on Gloria's face. She's been standing nearby, politely making herself available, but now she's leaning in. She won't impose herself. She's modest that way, and after a week in her company I've come to appreciate her approach. She asks my father a question to make her presence known and as the deal crumbles she gently steps in.

"Mr. Lim, do you mind?"

And that's when I get to see this young, soft-spoken, seemingly innocent girl turn into a smart, sure tiger.

She takes over where my father left off. But she's confident. She's done this before. She knows the price she can get. The dealer puts on a good show but when he finally reaches his lowest price and won't go one cent lower, Gloria turns to my father and says in English, "We must go now."

"Go?" my father says.

"Yes, turn and go."

Sure. He's game. He smiles, thanks the dealer, and Gloria leads him away by the arm. They get a couple paces and the dealer suddenly yells out, "Okay! Okay!!"

My father is pleasantly surprised and Gloria instructs the dealer to wrap the piece up.

We let her do this for each of us. I want to buy a small wooden monkey for $2.50 U.S., and Gloria believes that's too high. She wants me to walk away, telling me she can get the dealer to go down further, but in my mind I see this man carving this wooden monkey the size of my thumb late into the evening hours and I don't have the heart to continue. Gloria says, "If that's okay with you, Curty." In other words, if you don't want to get a good deal, fine, it's not my money. But it isn't until after I pay that I walk past another vendor, see the same monkey and realize it's a mass-produced product. That's when Gloria says, "I could've gotten you that monkey for lower."

Her bite, apparently, cuts both ways.

Later I see a small wooden chess set and I let Gloria use her talents to purchase it for me.

We all thank Gloria and when we return to the hotel we sit down in a small lounge to wait for Biew Bok, who's coming to visit us one last time. We order coffee and tea and Gloria pulls some paper out of her book bag.

"Curty, can you draw a picture of me?"

The day she picked us up at the airport, as we drove to Taishan, I told her I studied art in college and she'd asked me if I could make a portrait of her. I told her yes, if we could find some paper, so she stopped by an art store, picked up a large sheet, and also grabbed some small hotel stationary.

I'm happy to oblige, so I draw her two pictures: a "serious" one that takes an hour to draw and a quick little cartoon.

Biew Bok arrives with his daughter and second wife. Leslie recognizes his daughter. She's his youngest, the one who admired Leslie's harmonica when we came in 1973. She's a programmer now, living in Australia, and her English has a slight Australian roundness to it. She tells us that she originally studied medicine but when the tech boom took off she changed her field to computer programming. Biew Bok's second wife, a thin woman with short black hair and wearing a modest short sleeve shirt, doesn't say much, perhaps out of shyness. She mostly sits there, smiling quietly.

When I'm done with my drawings I hand them to Gloria. She looks at the serious portrait first, is impressed, then after a few minutes asks, "Is it good?"

"'Is it good?'"

"Is this a good drawing?"

I'm not sure how to answer but my sister gives it high marks. "It looks like you," she says, and Biew Bok's daughter compliments it as well.

"I think it's nice," I tell Gloria, "but I like this one more," holding up the cartoon. The cartoon took less than two minutes to draw but seems to capture her bright, youthful personality more.

We say goodbye to Gloria, Biew Bok, his daughter and wife, then go out for one last dinner. There's a restaurant across the street my father wants to try.

It's 5:30 a.m. and I go out for one final run.

We have a two hour flight from Guangzhou to Beijing followed by an eleven hour flight to San Francisco. If I don't get some exercise now I'll be restless on the plane, then too jet lagged by the time I get home to do anything. But if I can wear myself down maybe I'll sleep for most of the flight. And there's something else on my mind. For the two weeks I've been here I haven't tasted any street food. I didn't want to try anything in Beijing because that was the beginning of our trip and I didn't want to ruin our plans by getting sick, but we got so busy during the second half that I never got the chance.

I know exactly where I want to buy food from. I saw a vendor selling green onion pancakes my first morning here, when I went for a run in Yuexiu Park, across from the Dong Feng Hotel where we're staying. There's a high wall surrounding it but inside are three man-made ponds, small pagodas, and a variety of bridges. Near the north entrance sits a large sculpture of the Five Rams. The local legend says that over two thousand years ago, five immortal gods arrived on rams to bless the people and when they left, their rams turned to stone.

Residents play ping pong and the elderly do t'ai chi here. On my second morning here I was watching a group of three dozen women doing t'ai chi to some recorded music when a group of Japanese fan dancers arrived, took a place on the opposite side of the walkway, turned their music on, and a loud warbly war of exercise ensued.

After the park I ran into one of the nearby neighborhoods where I got disoriented and discovered a tiny alleyway street market. A butcher was cutting meat on a chopping block and a woman was scaling fish on a blanket. But it was on my way back to the hotel that I noticed the pancake vendor, and from then on I noticed him every day, outside the park walls, standing in a white apron and green shirt next to his glass pushcart.

But it's 5:30 in the morning and he's not out now. It's dark and the park isn't open yet. Nothing is open. There's a full moon out and the only ones awake are the cabbies, gambling in a small corner by the side of the hotel. I do a one mile loop around the block and head back to my room to finish packing.

Two years later I'll come back to China and make it my mission to eat street food every day and in every city. Outside a hotel in Guilin I'll see a man selling rice mixed with peanuts, green onions, sausage and hot sauce in a woven basket. He'll scoop it up with his bare hands and cup it into a small ball in front of me. I'll order a horsemeat hotpot in an alleyway restaurant and the owner's daughter will show me how to cook it properly. One night in the shopping district I'll see a girl behind a window making crispy sandwich rolls. She'll take rolls made with sesame seed oil and chopped onions, cut them in half, and ladle juicy pork meat over it to make a crunchy, messy sandwich. In Beijing I'll go for a run along the hutongs, those centuries-old corridors, and buy salty, chewy buns made with sesame seed oil, then I'll buy sweet, fried bread from a girl in a dusty alley. In Taishan I'll visit a street stall with my father and sister to eat small, orange, tentacled, fishlike creatures off wooden skewers. My father will notice that the meat is too salty and he'll suspect it isn't as fresh as it should be. And in Yangshuo I'll buy a cornmeal bun with bits of chicken and green onions held together with an egg batter that an old lady cooks on a charcoal grill outside Silver Cave. I'll be so amazed at the taste that I'll try to duplicate it for months after I return home.

It's seven o'clock now. Gloria and Mr. Tong drive us to the Guangzhou airport. Gloria's been good to us and we give her a tip of 1400 yuan — the equivalent of 200 U.S. dollars — folded into a lucky red envelope.

From Beijing we stop in Narita, Japan, for a two-hour layover. There we walk around to stretch our legs and find a small noodle shop next to a Starbucks. We order several bowls of udon, sliced fish, rice and eggs. For all we know this could be the McDonalds of Japan, but everything tastes good when you're traveling and it's one of the most delicious meals we've had.

It's so good that in 2008, on our second layover in Narita, my sister Leslie and I will hunt down this little shop again and order another meal of sliced fish, rice and eggs.

17

I experienced a certain wistfulness after returning home.

During the day I kept to myself. I didn't call any of my friends to tell them I was back.

I had trouble sleeping but it was more than just the usual jet lag.

For days afterward I'd wake in the middle of the night believing I was still in China. I'd think I was in my hotel room, and one time I even thought I was in my father's house, in a room there, and that somehow I'd been left alone. I'd call out to Nancy or my sister and quickly stand up, taking a couple steps toward the door, thinking my father was just outside waiting to go to dinner, and it would take a few seconds before I'd recognize my own table, my chair, my hardwood floor.

There was this one memory, this feeling that I couldn't let go of. In Guangzhou our hotel room faced west, overlooking Yuexiu Park. The day we arrived, Nancy and I were given one room and my father and sister were given another room several doors down. We'd just driven up from my mother's village and it was late in the afternoon, close to evening. We were all tired from the long ride and I needed a nap. My father told me he would stop by in a couple hours to take us out to dinner so sometime in the middle of my sleep I forced myself awake and began unpacking my suitcase and cleaning my camera equipment. It was something I'd learned to do in college: jolt myself awake if necessary; and as a filmmaker I learned the habit of always prepping my cameras before the next shoot. I was still in a daze when I looked out the window and saw the setting sun. It was hazy outside. Foggy almost. Perhaps it was the air pollution but the sky was a bluish gray and the sun had dimmed just enough so that I could look at it for a little longer than normal. I tried to memorize it, and even wondered how I could meter my camera for it, but I was still cleaning my gear and before I had a chance to capture that beautiful blue sun it began to disappear behind the clouds. Later over dinner Leslie mentioned seeing the same sun and we talked about how breathtaking it was.

"Did you get a picture?" she asked. "I got a picture!" she laughed, gloating as only an older sister could.

Several days later in San Francisco there would be a couple afternoons when I would wake to see the sun filtering through my blinds and believe it to be that beautiful sunset in Guangzhou. I'd sit up, look for my camera, and it would take me a moment to realize I was back in my own apartment, on my own bed. Sometimes I'd just lie there. It would be morning, or evening, and it would be half dark outside, and I'd stare at my window, not wanting to give up that quiet feeling.

Leslie's daughter Jill was happy to see her again and my parents stayed at Leslie's house in Walnut Creek for a week before flying back to Las Vegas. On their last night there I drove over to visit them. Sitting on the couch with my father, I asked him if he'd ever want to go back to live in China. I broached the idea of the two of us living in Taishan for a few months. Or maybe, I suggested, I should just go live in Beijing for a year. There wasn't much holding me to San Francisco. I wasn't in love with my job and didn't have a family of my own.

He mused over the notion for a moment, and didn't dismiss it outright, but said the most he might consider was a month in his old township. He wouldn't mind a month. But when he started asking me where we would live and what I would do, I could tell he was quietly trying to wake me from my dream.

Still, over the next half year, I'd be so taken with the idea that I'd sign up for a Mandarin class and begin researching how to live in China as an expatriate. My father had spent his whole life making a home for himself in this country and here I was, his oldest son, fantasizing about moving back to his.

We talked a little more and my father told me he was anxious to get home, call his brother, and tell him he'd brought their mother's photograph back with him. He asked if I wanted to visit my uncle with him soon. My uncle Fon was retired and living in Texas now, and we'd planned to see him a year ago but then his health took a sudden downturn. His feet and lower legs had swollen up and he'd become forgetful; my father noticed his fogginess even as they spoke over the phone; so we postponed our visit.

Then my father told me he wanted to make a copy of the photograph for his brother. I asked him if I could see it again. He retrieved it from his suitcase and carefully unfolded the red wrapping paper around it.

231

"Isn't she beautiful?" he said, holding the photo in his hands.

I asked if I could scan the image. "That way you'll have a digital copy. We can all have a copy. It'll be another way to preserve it."

He agreed and we drove to a shop, rented some computer time and made a scan. The computer was slow and it took several tries to get the correct exposure. My father sat behind me the whole time, watching as his mother's face gradually appeared on the monitor.

"Can you reverse that?" he asked, pointing to the embellishment around her lips and eyes.

"I can't reverse it," I said, "but I think I can make it look more natural. But since someone drew that in to begin with, all I'd be doing is drawing on top of that. I'd have to blur it a little and soften it. Do you want me to do that?"

He thought for a moment.

"In other words, I can do my best to take it back to what you think it should be, but I'd still be affecting it."

I was getting too technical and confusing him in the process. It's an old habit of mine.

"Let's do this," I said. "You have the original, and I'm about to make another copy of it. Why don't I try it out on another copy and then you tell me what you think."

"Okay."

The next day my parents flew back to Las Vegas. My father thought it was too late to call his brother when they arrived home so he decided to wait till the next day.

The day after that I came home to a message on my answering machine. It was from Leslie. The recording was brief and her tone was downcast:

"Hey Curty. This is me. When you get home, give me a call, okay?"

I'll always remember that as the point when I began to fear any message that was too short or too inconclusive. From that moment on, if anyone called and left a message that sounded as if they needed to speak to me in person, I'd suspect the worst.

When I called my sister back she told me that our Uncle Fon was gone. Before my father had a chance to talk to his brother, he'd died in his sleep.

Two weeks later we flew to Houston for my uncle's funeral.

It was while buying a black suit for the memorial that I remembered the last time I'd seen him. He'd come to visit my parents in Las Vegas and I hadn't seen him in twenty years. My life had become so needlessly busy. My college years had been filled with too much studying and after I moved to San Francisco it got filled with too much work. Twenty years had gone by and I thought my uncle would feel awkward around me, but when we met at a restaurant for dim sum his face turned into a big, warm smile. He opened his arms wide and exclaimed, "*A Men Doy! Curty! How are you?!*"

At the funeral, my uncle's son Alex spoke, then asked if anyone wanted to say a few words. My father stood and approached the podium. I'd heard him make speeches in the past, usually at weddings or family reunions, but his words seemed unrehearsed that day. He spoke about how much his brother had been a part of his life and how much he had depended on him. He said his brother was like his right arm, and he felt as if he'd just lost that arm.

Six months went by. I left my job, used the same black suit to interview with another company, and after getting hired, used the time in between jobs to visit London and Paris with Nancy.

A month after returning, my mother's health improved and she expressed regrets about not going to China with us, so we discussed the idea of taking a second trip.

By the following year we started saving up our money and talking about all the places we wanted to go. Then, in the middle of the year, my father's cousin Biew Bok died. Leslie was the first to hear about it when Biew Bok's daughter emailed her. He had broken his hip, she told Leslie, and during the slow recovery he died after a bad cold.

I called my father to express my condolences.

"Yeah," he said, "we're all just getting older."

While planning our second trip I contemplated taking my own excursion to Guilin. I'd always wanted to see the mountains there. We could all fly to Beijing together, I suggested, and then I could fly to Guilin. After a few days I could take a train and meet them at the Guangzhou station. The train passes through the mountains and it's supposed to be quite beautiful.

"Remember the last time we rode a train in China?" Leslie asked me.

I didn't. She told me it was when we first visited China, when we were children, and we took a train from Hong Kong to Guangzhou. And suddenly I remembered my mother holding my hand tightly, leading us through the crowded train station. It was a hot, bright day and we were rushing along, surrounded by poor people, and my mother was worried.

I asked my brother Mike if he remembered this but he didn't. He was too young. But he did go back to China later as an adult with my mother and father and remembered the train ride they took from Guangzhou to Hong Kong.

And he told me a story about the trip...

My father wanted to visit his village. He wanted to see his house again. No one was living in the house at the time but when my father and my brother arrived, they saw Mao Tse Tung's name written on the front door. It incensed my brother but my father was willing to overlook it. His house was still standing after all.

My father's father Quong Lim had been the last official owner of the house but he'd once told his two sons Yot and Fon that whichever one of them "returns to China and reaches the house first, gets it." My father was the first to reach the house in 1973, and then he said the same thing to us, his four children. Whichever one of his children "returns to China and reaches the house first, gets it."

The year was 1997 and Mike was the first.

To get there they flew to Hong Kong and took a train to Guangzhou. The weather was hot when they arrived. The stress of traveling made my parents bicker constantly. One day, in the hotel, my brother, in his adjoining room, heard my parents arguing, and he started to cry. When my father walked in and saw him, he asked, "What's wrong?"

"You keep fighting," my brother said.

"Oh, we don't mean it," my father said to his little buddy. "Don't cry. We won't do that anymore."

So they traveled from Guangzhou to my father's village, Tin Sum, went to see his house, and, true to his word, my father and mother didn't argue for the rest of the trip.

The next day they took the train from Guangzhou back to Hong Kong. It was late in the evening. They were all worn out. My father and mother sat on a bench seat together. Across from them, in a small open area, my brother lay down on another bench and fell asleep.

After a while he slowly awakened to the sound of my father talking quietly to my mother. My father was talking about his own mother. He was wondering if he had done everything he could have done. He was crying. My brother was half awake and he could hear my father wondering if he should ever have left his mother behind. My brother had never seen his father like this before. For a moment my brother saw him as a young boy again.

My father rested his head on my mother's shoulder and she held him, soothing him, and said, quietly, "You're a good man. Your mother would be proud of you. You're a good man."

18

Until I started writing this book, I'd never known that my father was once a projectionist. He's always been a modest man, but in his old age has become even more modest. Twelve years ago, after I'd finished shooting a documentary on my parents, I invited them into the editing room to see the footage. I was shooting on 16mm film back then, an arduous medium that requires lots of heavy lifting. I think I was trying to impress them a little with all the labor I had to perform. After the screening, as I was winding up the film on a noisy, green, metal spindle, my father never said a word. He'd expressed a pleasant surprise upon seeing the film, and even complimented my work, but never once told me that he used to play with the same equipment; never once mentioned that he'd mounted reels four times heavier for audiences in his neighborhood theater. The only thing I knew about his film-related background was that he used to show 8mm home movies to my brother and sisters and me when we were little.

Years later, after I found out, I asked him why he didn't tell me this when we were in the editing room.

"Oh, I don't know. It never came up."

Lots of things had never come up. He'd never told me about the Japanese seaplanes until I asked him why he left China. He only recently revealed to me how much he cherished his last conversations with his mother during their evenings alone together before his departure. And I didn't know until just a few years ago that his father used to tell him that he was a happy child: always smiling... smiling when he went to bed, and smiling when he woke up.

"Just like you," my father added.

These days his biggest joy is seeing his children and grandchildren. Every time we visit him in Las Vegas, he gets excited about making dinner. "Whatever you kids want." Our pictures sit on his mantel: me finishing my first marathon; Leslie, Christine and Michael at their weddings; his grandchildren Kyle, Jillian, Elise and Ian in their baby clothes... and in the center of it

236

all sits the photograph of his mother in a light brown wooden frame.

He never thought he'd live this long, and every day after the age of fifty has come as a gift to him. He and my Uncle Fon believed they'd only lived as long as they did, and enjoyed such great health, because of their mother; that somehow she was watching out for them.

In a small way, this book has been my father's gift to me. When I was growing up, he didn't get much of a chance to impart many lessons from his own life onto me. He was always too busy or perhaps didn't have the right words. But writing this book allowed me to see my own life more objectively through the prism of his. The mistakes I thought I'd made were very similar to his own, and I can only hope I'm as gracious about my successes as he is about his. With everything he's been through, he still sees himself as a very fortunate man.

My father has told us that after he passes away, he'd like his ashes scattered over the Pacific Ocean. He doesn't believe in an afterlife but still hopes that somehow his mother and he will meet up between here and China. When Leslie asked our own mother what her wishes were, she said she wanted to be with my father. He cooks for her all the time, she said, and she'd miss that. Then she wondered, "How's he going to cook for me?" And after a little more thought, added, "Oh, it doesn't matter."

As I write this, my father and mother are a day away from flying to China for their fifth trip there together. The following year, they hope to take Jillian to show her the house where he was born. There's nothing that gives my father greater joy than planning his next big trip, and his next big adventure, with his family.

Yot Lim's
Soy Sauce Chicken

(preface by his son Curtis Lim)

My father used to make this once a month for our Sunday family lunch. You can make it using a whole chicken or chicken parts. After my brother and sisters and I grew up and left the house, my father tended to cook only for my mother and himself, so he'd use chicken parts. After rediscovering this recipe as an adult, I'd often make different versions of this for my friends, and sometimes just for myself, altering it to fit my liking (sorry, Dad), and I'd typically cook whole thighs. But when we were children, and there were six of us around the table, my father would cook a whole chicken. When it was done, he'd pull it out of the pot, let it sit, cool down, then slice the meat into small, slender pieces about the size of a child's palm. He'd hum an old Chinese song as he carved it, and the chicken would end up so succulent, and so tasty, that this recipe came to represent everything about family to me. I loved this dish.

You'll have to experiment a few times to get this the way you want it, but the sauce should have a taste that's a balance between salty and sweet, and tempered by either garlic or the sesame seed oil.

What you need:

- 1 whole chicken or chicken parts.
- 2 large bottles of soy sauce (40 oz.) for a whole chicken.
  or
- 1 medium-sized bottle of soy sauce (10 oz.) for chicken parts.
- 1/2 lb. brown sugar for a whole chicken.
  or
- 1/4 lb. brown sugar for chicken parts.
  or
- 6 oz. honey.
- 1 pt. water

Optional:

- garlic cloves or crushed garlic.
- ginger, about the size of your thumb, sliced thinly.
- 1 tsp of sesame seed oil.
- 1/2 tsp cinnamon.
- 1/4 cup of white wine.

Yot Lim says:

"You buy a whole bottle of soy sauce. What we used was sweet soy sauce made by Lee Kum Kee. Because that's not entirely too salty but it's just a little sweet. You use two bottles.

Then you get half a pound of brown sugar, and boil a pint of water, then add the brown sugar and dissolve it in the water. (This becomes a sugar water solution.)

Then in another pot, add the soy sauce. Then add the sugar water solution to the soy sauce a little at a time. Don't pour it all in. Pour it in a little at a time, keep tasting it, don't let it become too salty, and pour in enough so that you become satisfied with it. The important thing is to taste it until you're satisfied with how it tastes. If it's too salty, you add more of the sugar solution in it. Then add a couple cloves of garlic and sliced ginger. Put the chicken in. You can either buy chicken parts or a whole chicken. Whatever you buy, you have to submerge the whole thing into the soy sauce.

It's optional, but you can add half a teaspoon of cinnamon to the soy sauce solution. Also optional is a teaspoon of sesame seed oil. And white wine is optional. But your mother never liked that because it would make her hot and turn her face red. But the main ingredient is the soy sauce and the brown sugar solution. Personally I like adding sesame seed oil because it adds a great flavor. But keep tasting it. Make sure it's not too salty and not too sweet as you're making it.

You heat up the soy sauce solution in a pan or a pot, depending on whether you have chicken parts or a whole chicken. You heat it until it comes to a light boil, then you add the chicken to it. If the whole chicken submerges, you don't have to turn it over. But if it doesn't submerge, you have to keep turning it over every five minutes. After fifteen minutes, it's cooked, but you can check by using a knife or fork to cut a little into the chicken. If it's not bloody, then it's done."

Acknowledgments

This book would not be possible without my father's razor-sharp memory, joy for storytelling, and generosity of time.

It also wouldn't be possible without my mother. Thank you for not running too far (or staying away for too long) from my father's proposal of marriage. And thank you, Mom and Dad, for giving birth to me. On that note, thank you to your families and ancestors for giving birth to both of you and for living such wonderfully rich, entertaining lives.

I also want to thank my sisters Leslie and Christine, and my brother Michael. All of your memories, and everything you shared, helped fill in the missing pieces and gave me a fuller, more detailed picture. Thank you for your continual love and support.

My friend Nancy Phelps also played an important role, not only in our journeys together, but also in her insight and inspiration. She has been, and always will be, my friend. She's my guardian angel.

I'd also like to express my appreciation to Mei Li Ooi, Jen Yuen, Jane Phan and Ann Wemeier for their advice and feedback; especially Mei Li Ooi, who was instrumental in drawing out the imagery of the story. Kathie Middlemiss, of Kat's Eye Editing, was my wise and watchful editor.

I also received some very valuable guidance and direction from two writing groups and their respective hosts: the San Francisco Writers Community, hosted by W. Ross Ayers, and the monthly writing critique of Shut Up & Write! hosted by Cindy Powers.

Finally, I'd like to thank Tish O'Dowd Ezekiel, my writing instructor at the University of Michigan, Ann Arbor, for helping me find my voice.

www.ingramcontent.com/pod-product-compliance
Lightning Source LLC
Chambersburg PA
CBHW030415100426
42812CB00028B/2969/J